TOWARD INTERNATIONALISM

Readings in Cross-Cultural Communication

Elise C. Smith
Overseas Education Fund
of the League of Women Voters
Washington, D.C.

Louise Fiber Luce
Miami University
Oxford, Ohio

EDITORS

Newbury House Publishers, Inc. / Rowley / Ma. / 01969

Library of Congress Cataloging in Publication Data

Main entry under title:

Toward internationalism.

CONTENTS: Stewart, E. C. American assumptions and
values: orientation to action.--Fieg, J. P. Concept
of oneself.--Oberg, K. Culture shock and the problem
of adjustment to new cultural environments.--Hanvey, R. G.
Cross-cultural awareness.--Szalay, L. B. and Fisher, G. H.
Communication overseas. [etc.]
    1. Intercultural communication--Addresses, essays,
lectures.   2. Cultural relativism--Addresses, essays,
lectures.   I. Smith, Elise C., 1932-   II. Luce,
Louise Fiber, 1935-
GN496.T68   301.2   78-17153
ISBN 0-88377-123-3

NEWBURY HOUSE PUBLISHERS, INC.

Language Science
Language Teaching
Language Learning

ROWLEY, MASSACHUSETTS 01969

Cover design by KATHE HARVEY.

First printing: April 1979

Printed in the U.S.A.   5   4   3

ABOUT THE CONTRIBUTORS

Dean C. Barnlund is an expert in the field of interpersonal and intercultural communication. Currently, he teaches in the Speech Communication Department, San Francisco State University. He has published widely in the field of communication and is at present continuing an extensive study of human interactions in a variety of cultures.

John C. Condon is a professor of intercultural communication at the International Christian University of Tokyo, Japan. He has spent ten years studying and teaching abroad, particularly in Mexico, Brazil, Tanzania, and Japan. He received his Ph.D. in Communications from Northwestern University.

John P. Fieg is an attorney for the Zuni Legal Services in New Mexico. From 1974 to 1977 he was Program Coordinator for the Washington International Center. He is also a coauthor of *There Is a Difference—12 Intercultural Perspectives.* He has a special interest in Thailand as a result of service as a Peace Corps Volunteer in that country.

Glen H. Fisher, Adjunct Professor, School of Foreign Service at Georgetown University, is an anthropologist who has specialized in international communication. He formerly was a career foreign service officer and Dean of the Center for Area and Country Studies of the Foreign Service Institute. He is the author of *Diplomacy and the Behavioral Sciences.*

Raymond L. Gorden is Professor of Sociology at Antioch College. One of his prime areas of study has been nonlinguistic behavior as a barrier to communication, particularly among Colombians and young Americans living with Colombian families in Bogotá. He is the author of *Living in Latin America.*

Edward T. Hall is a noted anthropologist whose research on man's use of space was seminal to the development of proxemics. He has written *The Silent Language, The Hidden Dimension,* and *Beyond Culture.* Among his previous teaching affiliations are Northwestern University, Illinois Institute of Technology, and Harvard University.

Robert G. Hanvey is Professor of Education at Indiana University. He is especially interested in the development of school curricula which promote international awareness. He is the author of *An Attainable Global Perspective.*

Daniel Lerner is Professor of Sociology at the Center of International Studies at the Massachusetts Institute of Technology. Among the many books he has written are *The Passing of Traditional Society, Modernizing the Middle East,* and *The Human Meaning of the Social Sciences.*

Horace M. Miner, Professor of Sociology and Anthropology at University of Michigan, is the author of several monographs and books. He both edited and contributed to *The City in Modern Africa.* In addition, he has done research on the ecology of change among the Hausa of the Anchau Corridor, Nigeria, on a National Science Foundation Grant in 1970-1971.

Kalvero Oberg (deceased) was an anthropologist who served with the Health, Welfare and Housing Division, U.S. AID/Brazil. It was during this time that the author developed a well-known model of culture shock.

Melvin Schnapper is a specialist in multinational intercultural training. At present, he is a systems development consultant for G. D. Searle, a multinational health care organization. He has also worked as a trainer for the Peace Corps in Nigeria. He received his Ph.D. in Communications from University of Pittsburgh.

Lawrence Stessin is Professor Emeritus at Hofstra University. His specialization is in the field of management. He has published several books, including *The Practice of Personnel and Industrial Relations.* He has been a regular contributor on management to *The New York Times* Business and Finance Section.

Edward C. Stewart is Adjunct Associate Professor at the University of Southern California, Washington Education Center. He received his Ph.D. in Psychology from the University of Texas. His research and interest have been in the area of culture, especially American culture, and the development of simulation as a method of education and training for intercultural communication. He has worked with the Peace Corps and the Business Council for International Understanding, and has taught at several universities.

Lorand B. Szalay is Director of the Institute of Comparative Social and Cultural Studies, Inc. He received his Ph.D. in Psychology from the University of Vienna. His professional interests include social psychology, communication, analysis of subjective culture, and psycholinguistics. He has taught at George Washington University, American University, and the University of Maryland, and is the author of many publications.

Fathi Yousef is Associate Professor of Communication Studies in the Department of Speech Communication, California State University, Long Beach. Dr. Yousef has an extensive background in education and industry. His areas of specialization are intercultural communication, verbal and nonverbal behavior, and organizational communication.

The Asian Society's study on Asian stereotypes in U.S. textbooks reflects its purpose as an organization. Its goal is to deepen American understanding of Asia and to stimulate trans-Pacific intellectual exchange. It also offers services to educators to help strengthen school resources on Asian peoples and cultures.

CONTENTS

INTRODUCTION

In *Toward Internationalism: Readings in Cross-Cultural Communication,* we have brought together fourteen articles by leading authorities in cross-cultural communication. The material was selected with the view to help the nonspecialist reader gain an understanding of culturally conditioned behavior as it relates to intercultural relations between people of different nations. The book does not presume to cover all aspects of cross-cultural communication. The book can, however, provide a general introduction to the major components. Specifically, the articles illustrate the influence which a society's value orientations, role expectations, perception, nonverbal patterns, and language behavior bring to bear on the international cross-cultural encounter. In other words, the material selected for this volume deals with the substance, rather than the theory, of cross-cultural interaction between Americans and nationals from Europe, Asia, the Middle East, Latin America, and Africa. We believe the articles will bring readers not only a greater awareness of their own cultural identity, but fresh insight into the causes of communication interference, if not outright communication failure, across cultures.

The Larger Context The time has come when we can no longer ignore cultural pluralism and its influence on contemporary life. Among the problems facing our country today, the random examples of foreign import restrictions, fishing rights, oil reserves, grain embargos, and international waterway boundaries are all too familiar by now. They touch not only the public official, but the auto maker in Detroit, the textile worker in Massachusetts, and the housewife in Memphis. Even those events which appear to be limited to distant nations' internal affairs increasingly have repercussions on a larger political and economic environment. The immediate impact of these problems on American society has led to a new public awareness, from the federal to the local level, of the growing imperatives of internationalism and global cooperation. Indeed, to continue to treat issues from a single, national perspective would be as unrealistic as diagnosing a disease on the basis of a single symptom and ignoring all others.

There is a fundamental question at the heart of this reality. Simply stated, how can a nation and its institutions better assist its citizens to comprehend global perspectives? Put another way, how can we help the individual citizen understand the international implications of problems which directly or indirectly touch his life?

It is significant that one area of agreement between Russia and the United States in the Helsinki SALT negotiations is that each nation recognizes the need to promote among its citizens a greater understanding of other cultures and their language. This would suggest that the degree of success for international cooperation depends not only on the formal terms of treaties. It depends as well on the public's comprehensive awareness of, and empathy for, the variables of national cultures. In the Helsinki example, we see that governments are beginning to recognize the mutual understanding necessary for modern man to function beneficially in an international world. We are already past the stage where our former concern for successful cross-cultural empathy was localized in the Peace Corps training program, the State Department's Foreign Service Institute, or the foreign student adviser's office. Both here and abroad concern is growing, sparked by the new global consciousness, that nonspecialists, the ordinary men, will need guidance if they are to understand at a significant level not only other cultures, but their own as well. Our book is part of a larger effort to respond to this need.

Once we have a general understanding of how culture influences our perceptions and actions, the comparative study of several cultures becomes a meaningful enterprise. At this point, it is increasingly difficult to disregard the reality of cultural pluralism. So too is it increasingly difficult to continue to accept former stereotypes and cultural clichés about other nations. What has shaped an American way of life may or may not have shaped the attitudes and beliefs of other cultures. Another set of assumptions may be at play which accounts for dissimilar cultural patterns. Thus an American culture takes its place beside other national cultures. It is one more construct, neither better nor worse, within the cultural spectrum of human diversity.

In the past decade an impressive specificity and seriousness of purpose have replaced our former, more generalized interest in cross-cultural communication. In this country, specialists in speech communication, psychologists, sociologists, linguists, anthropologists, and the business sector are now sharing in ever-growing and more aggressive efforts to elaborate the dynamics of cross-cultural communication. The diversity of our contributors' backgrounds is indicative of the pervasive interest in both the private and public sectors given to cross-cultural communication theory and practice. It is an interdisciplinary venture which challenges the psychologist as well as the sociologist, the humanist as well as the anthropologist. Undoubtedly it was difficult to limit our choice of articles for this reader. In the end, however, we decided to direct our selection toward a collection of readings which were international in focus.

Appropriately, *Toward Internationalism: Readings in Cross-Cultural Communication* opens with Edward C. Stewart's perceptive analysis of *American* cultural patterns from a cross-cultural perspective. He addresses the issue of American cultural identity and some of its underlying assumptions and values (among them, action, the achievement motive, and individual responsibility). When he sets concrete descriptions of American behavior beside contrasting cultural patterns from several parts of the world, the reader begins to focus on cross-cultural relations with a keener sense of who he is culturally and how this identity can affect cross-cultural communication. John P. Fieg's discussion of the concept of self in Thai culture is, like Stewart's, comparative. Fieg relates the concept of self to various aspects of Thai value orientations and then compares them with value orientations of other cultures, including our own. Moreover, he suggests that by isolating cultural values, by having a conscious awareness of them, we have a means of understanding another society. Only then can we begin to shape the framework for true intercultural communication.

Two articles in our collection pertain to adjustment to new cultural environments. Kalvero Oberg's analysis of culture shock is well known in the cross-cultural communication field. After first describing the symptoms of stranger anxiety, the author then discusses the stages through which the foreigner passes (i.e., rejection, regression, hostility, aggression) before integration into the new culture is accomplished. Robert G. Hanvey addresses yet another dimension of adjustment to new cultures. He discriminates between degrees of cross-cultural awareness and the means by which they are achieved. He further posits a correlation between the personality type of traditional, modern, and postmodern peoples and the quality of empathy each is able to bring to the cross-cultural situation.

We selected readings by Raymond L. Gorden and Lawrence Stessin to demonstrate through actual case studies and incidents the concepts of culture shock and cross-cultural empathy. Or more accurately, we selected them because they demonstrate moments of *interference* in the adjustment process and empathy for new cultures. Gorden examines the attitudes of Colombian hosts and Peace Corps volunteer guests who lived with the families during their assignments in Latin America. He shows how misunderstandings arose when behavior patterns and culture cues were misread—by both Colombian nationals and American visitors. He goes to the sources of communication interference which, in this instance, came from conflicting role expectations ("guest" and "member of the family") and different uses of formal customs of courtesy.

Lawrence Stessin, in turn, looks at cases of culture shock experienced by the American businessman overseas. We see communication interference occurring in employee relations, in management styles, and in conflicts between the impatient, time-conscious American businessman and his less harried counterpart in Latin America, the Middle East, or Asia. Even status symbols of upper-level management, including the location and dimensions of office space, can be another source of communication interference. Stessin's many examples cannot fail to impress the reader that frequently the causes of communication failure lead back to a conflict in values.

"Communication Overseas," by Lorand Szalay and Glen H. Fisher and "Verbal Self-Disclosure: Topics, Targets, Depth," by Dean C. Barnlund explore different facets of the relationship between culture and communication. Szalay and Fisher, in investigating the effect of culture on the meanings of words, have used a Korean/American comparison. They selected words from the two languages which have accepted, direct equivalents in translation. Yet, by asking native speakers to use free associations with each word, the authors show that the connotative meanings of seemingly similar words in the two languages are quite different. Through the use of semantographs, the authors demonstrate that the cultural frame of reference gives subjective meanings to words. As for Dean Barnlund, he examines the results of a comparative study dealing with verbal interaction patterns of the Japanese and Americans. On the one hand, Americans and Japanese seem to have similar attitudes with regard to the people with whom they can communicate and the topics they can communicate about. However, it is the great difference in the amount of verbal self-disclosure which distinguishes the two peoples. According to Barnlund, this difference in style of communication is a consequence of a difference in values.

Of the articles in our book which deal with contrasting patterns of nonverbal communication, John C. Condon and Fathi Yousef explore the use of home space and home styles. Through examples drawn from the eastern and western worlds, they show how houses both reflect and shape communication patterns in different cultures. We discover, for example, a correlation between such values as privacy or community and the type of spatial differentiation within the home. In this sense, the house is more than an extension of personal space. Condon and Yousef state that, because of the cultural assumptions the home discloses, the home could well be considered a microcosm of society as a whole.

In Edward T. Hall's article on proxemics, we move from home styles to a more general usage of space. The contrasts between American spatial patterns and those of the English, French, and Germans are seen in definitions of "private sphere," in eye behavior, in order in space, and in what constitutes an intrusion into personal space. Hall's article helps us to understand that when the unwritten rules of spatial patterns are ignored, we are at best accused of being obtuse. If, however, we acquire the ability to perceive these distinctions, we have opened one more avenue for successful communication.

Other aspects of nonverbal behavior are found in Melvin Schnapper's article, "Your Actions Speak Louder . . ." He cites several incidents where Peace Corps volunteers in Africa failed to use the tools of nonverbal communication. He accounts for this by suggesting that just as language proficiency is essential for volunteer success overseas, a systematic knowledge of nonverbal modes of communication also must be learned. He then describes simulation exercises where trainees experience nonverbal signs firsthand. According to Schnapper, such exercises are one part of a process whereby a new nonverbal language can be acquired and in turn become part of the trainee's communication tools.

The concepts of perception and stereotyping are demonstrated in two quite different formats in our book, first in an article by Horace M. Miner, then in a report from the Asia Society. Miner's description of body ritual among the Nacerima is an explicit (and entertaining) exercise of how, through perception, we classify and give meaning to the multiple impressions we have of reality. Miner's imaginary anthropologist helps us to see how our attitudes and actions might be interpreted through an alternate frame of reference. As for the report produced by the Asia

Society, it offers the results of a comprehensive study of how Asia is depicted in American school textbooks. The Society discovered that despite expert knowledge of the subject matter, Western biases and stereotyping of Asian people were frequent. In fact with few exceptions, American ethnocentrism left little margin for alternative value systems. It is difficult not to heed the Society's conclusions that major rewriting of the textbooks is necessary.

Finally, patterns of cognition, which can vary strikingly from culture to culture, are the point of departure for Daniel Lerner's article describing a project which involved interviewing Frenchmen. He examines how thinking patterns of the French affected the way interviewers formulated questions and how they presented them to the interviewees. Lerner shows how French reserve, disengagement, and the predilection for codes and rules of behavior come from the prevailing conventions of cognition. It was only by trial and error that Lerner's interviewers learned how to integrate these cognition patterns into the interview process. Had they not done so, it is highly unlikely that the interview teams could have successfully completed their project.

In closing, we would like to stress that in our descriptions of the articles selected for the reader, we have attempted to focus on the *primary* thrust of the material. Needless to say, within each article there is considerable overlap and interaction of several of the components of cross-cultural communication. Given the complexity of communication itself, this is understandable. As for the reader itself, we see the entire collection as evidence of the progress being made to respond to the needs of modern life.

Acknowledgment   Both editors wish to thank Dr. Glen Fisher for the advice and support he offered during the completion of this book. Dr. Luce would like to express her appreciation to Miami University for an instructional development grant which allowed her the time to pursue her interest in this topic and to begin the current volume.

Elise C. Smith   *Louise Fiber Luce*
Overseas Education   Miami University
Fund of the   Oxford, Ohio
League of Women Voters
(Formerly with American University)
Washington, D.C.

AMERICAN ASSUMPTIONS AND VALUES:
ORIENTATION TO ACTION

Edward C. Stewart

From *American Cultural Patterns: A Cross-Cultural Perspective,* by Edward C. Stewart. Copyright © 1972 by Edward C. Stewart. Reprinted by permission of author.

Action in the real world requires a source, since for the American, it does not simply occur. An agent or, in the more abstract sense, a cause is required. More often than not the American does not stop with the identification of the agent of action but continues to search for the background reasons which led the agent to decide to act. Furthermore, the agent exists for the purpose of getting things done. The orientation to action, or the phase preceding behavior, is frequently conceived as decision-making or problem-solving. Both of these concepts are vague in meaning and they are employed indiscriminately by Americans to refer to cultural norms of the society. Decision-making includes a loose constellation of both assumptions and values in American culture and hence provides a convenient entry into the subject.

In face-to-face situations the locus of both the action and the decision to act lies with the individual. Its foundation is established early in life. From the earliest age, the American child is encouraged to decide for himself—to make up his own mind; he is encouraged to believe he himself is the best judge of what he wants and what he should do. Even in those instances where the American cannot decide for himself, he still prizes the illusion that he is the locus of decision-making. Thus, when he needs to consult a banker, teacher, counselor, or expert of any kind, he perceives it as seeking information and advice that helps him to make up his own mind. The expert is treated as a resource person and not as a decision-maker. The American believes, ideally, that he should be his own source of information and opinions and, also, solve his own problems. Aesthetic judgments are frequently equated with personal preferences, since the American often resents accepting canons for judging the worth of a work of art. He prefers that value reside in the self; if the individual likes it, it is good. The result is an intense self-centeredness of the individual—so striking that an American psychologist has suggested this as a universal value (Rogers, 1964, 166).

Although American culture provides examples of situations in which another person decides for the individual who is chiefly affected by the decision, more striking instances of this kind of displacement of decision-making usually occur in non-Western countries. In many parts of the world parents choose a wife for their son. In this and in many other situations, the decision-maker is not the person most affected by the decision but the occupant of a traditional role in the social group—in the example above, the parents.

Another variety of decision-making prevalent both in the United States and in the non-Western world is that in which decision-making is localized in a group. More kinds of decisions are likely to be made by the group in a non-Western society than in the United States. Many matters that require action by family or community in the non-Western world will be settled by a private decision among Americans. Furthermore, the manner in which the individual participates in the group may differ considerably among societies. The American usually expects to be able to express his opinion and to exert a fair influence in the final decision. To fulfill his expectations, an American can be quite concerned with "matters of procedure," with "agenda" and voting procedures. These concerns are not ritualistic or ceremonial as they may be in some cultures, but are for the purpose of ensuring fairness to all and facilitating action. Even when bypassing formal procedures, the American is persuaded by the appeal to give everybody a chance to speak and an equal voice in the decision. When interacting with members of different cultures who do not hold the value of fairness and equality for all members of a group, or who do not discriminate between means and substantive questions, the American may be accused of subterfuge or evasiveness when he raises matters of procedure or agenda (see Glenn, 1954, 176).

The American value of majority rule is not universal. The Japanese reject the majority voice in decision-making, which becomes binding upon both the majority and minority alike. Rafael Steinberg writes:

One Western concept that has never really functioned in Japan, although written into constitution and law, is the idea of majority rule. The Confucian ethic, which still governs Japan, demands unanimity, and in order to respect the "rights of the minority" the majority will compromise on almost every issue until a consensus of some kind is reached.

This principle applies not only to government, but to business board rooms, union halls, association meetings and family councils. No one must ever be completely defeated, because if he is, he cannot "hold up his face."[1]

In American society the participation of many members of a group in a decision ideally is based on the assumption that all those, insofar as possible, who will be affected by a decision are capable of helping to make it. Overseas, the group's function in decision-making may be quite different from American expectations. A group meeting, ostensibly held to reach a decision, may represent only public confirmation of a decision previously made in privacy by critical members of the group. In addition, the deliberations of the group may be neither substantive nor rational according to American concepts.

In certain areas of American life, decisions are reached by a process significantly different from those described above. The first point of difference is the locus of decision-making: in the examples mentioned the individual took part in the decision as a person, as a vote, or as the occupant of a role. The American doctor, however, reaches a decision about his patient's symptoms in a different manner. The patient's report and the doctor's observations are matched against categories of diseases. The doctor's diagnosis and prescription follow automatically from the particular category in which the constellation of symptoms fall. When the fit is not close between symptoms and categories defining disease, the doctor may call certain symptoms "benign," a label indicating the lack of correspondence between symptoms and disease categories. The process by which the doctor makes his diagnosis and prescription is pertinent because it conforms with the manner in which people in the non-Western world habitually reach decisions. The individual merely applies preestablished principles to classify an issue; his actions follow from the result of the classification. Normally, Americans reach decisions on the basis of anticipated consequences for the individual.

These points can be illustrated in the following example taken from an interview with an AID technician in Cambodia charged with training the police:

When we first tried to get a program of first aid for accident victims going, we did have some trouble because people said if somebody was struck by a car, it was fate, and man had no business in interfering because the victim was being properly punished for past sins. We tried to explain to them that auto accidents are different. They were not due to supernatural intervention, but rather to causes, to violations of laws. Now we do get policemen to give first aid.

It will be noticed that the technician did not attempt to change the ways of the Cambodians along American lines by emphasizing the personal consequences of suffering and the danger to the auto victims or by appealing to the personal humanitarianism and sense of duty of the Cambodian policeman. Instead, he modified the scheme of classification by which the Cambodians evaluated an automobile accident and decided that a victim was not their concern. The accident was reclassified into the human sphere, where its effects could be ameliorated by human efforts.

The American locus of decision-making in the individual is paralleled by the insistence that motivation should also arise with him. Responsibility for decision and action devolve on the individual. The idea of individual responsibility is reflected in the typical questions of "Who did this?" and "Who is responsible?" Overseas, where the locus of decision-making is not the individual, the question of responsibility is relatively meaningless. Responsibility is likely to be delocalized in cultures where the people have strong ties to their immediate family or community and reach decisions by consensus.

In Japan, the typical formal or semiformal group decision is reached by a system that provides for a feeling around—a groping for a voice, preferably the chairman, who will express the group's consensus.

> The code calls for the group to reach decisions together—almost by a sort of empathy. The function of a chairman is, therefore, not to help people express themselves freely but to divine the will of the group, to express its will and state the decision reached—presumably on the basis of divine will. This ability of the chairman is called *haragei* (belly art) (Kerlinger, 1951, 38).

The Japanese consider it brash for an individual to make definite decisions regarding himself or others. It is offensive for an individual to urge the acceptance of his opinion as a course of action. He must use circumlocution and maintain a rather strict reserve (Kerlinger, 1951, 38). These features of Japanese decision-making contrast sharply with the American pattern where responsibility for the decision is normally attached to the individual decision-maker. Among Americans, the individual is ideally the locus both of decision-making and of responsibility for it. The relationship is usually symmetrical, although instances occur in which one individual makes a decision while another shoulders responsibility. In government circles, for instance, it is not unusual for an administrator to call in an individual who is asked to make a decision on a given issue. Once the decision is reached, the decision-maker departs, leaving the issue and decision in the hands of the administrator.

Among the Japanese, the relationship between loci of decision-making and responsibility is asymmetrical. The individual Japanese is subjugated to the group, and when faced with a decision leading to action, he

> shrinks and may go to what seem fantastic lengths to avoid making a decision. Even if he should commit himself verbally to a course of action, he will frequently end by doing nothing. He lacks a sense of personal responsibility; he feels only a sense of group responsibility. If at all possible, he will try to throw the onus of decision responsibility on a group or, at least, on some other person (Kerlinger, 1951, 37-38).

The Japanese pattern of decision-making is to some degree characteristic of all peoples whose self-reference is the group or for whom decisions should be unanimous—the Samoans, for example (Goodenough, 1963, 511-515).

The American's concept of the world is rational in the sense that he believes the events of the world can be explained and the reasons for particular occurrences can be determined. It follows, then, that certain kinds of training and education can prepare the individual for working in the real world. Experience itself is not the only source of effective performance. Training and education and the kind of knowledge the American values must be practical and applicable. Overseas, the American adviser is prone to act on his rationalism and knowledge, believing that in dealing with non-Westerners it is sufficient to tell them what they should do and how to do it. The assumptions and values of the non-Westerner are often ignored.

The stuff of rationalism turns out to have a typical American flavor, eventually derived from the assumption that the world is mechanistic and the things worthy of effort are material. It is saturated with facts, figures, and techniques, since the American's tendency is to be means-oriented toward the world. He is not a philosopher or logician. He is impatient with theory; instead, he conceives of the technological goal of the material world in terms of problems which a rational problem-solver can solve.[2]

Since it is a popular and pervasive cultural norm, the conceptualization of the world in terms of problems is difficult to evaluate. Perhaps only the foreigner who has failed to exploit its terms can effectively analyze it and then oppose it. His resentment would stem from the realization that his country, himself, and his work, all differently, may be problems for his American counterpart. It is this focus that arouses resentment in the counterpart when he recognizes he is a problem—an obstacle in the American's smooth path. This conceptualization of the world in terms ripe for action is likely to give rise to a feeling of depersonalization and a lack of proper regard for others and their ascriptions. The distinguishing aspect of a "problem" is that it includes anything and everything which impinges upon it.

In decision-making the individual focuses on the preliminary step to action, whereas conceptualizing the world in terms of "problems" shifts the focus to the action itself.

Usually, the American does not conceive of only one possible course of action for a given problem. Instead, he tends to conceive of alternative courses of action and chooses one. His attitude is comparative; a particular course of action is best for a given purpose rather than the only one. The notion of absolute rightness is repugnant to Americans in the world of action; a purpose for judging the action is present if only implicitly (see Glen, 1954).

The concept of a plan for action leads us to the idea that action (and, indeed, the world itself) is conceived of as a chain of events. The term "course of action" already suggests this. In the ideal form, the world is seen as a unilateral connection of causes and effects projecting into the future. Since the American focuses on the future rather than the present or the past, the isolation of the critical cause becomes paramount. If events in the world are conceived in terms of a multiplicity of causes or even, more radically, in terms of multiple contingencies, as with the Chinese, planning and the control of events and actions become more difficult. The action orientation of the American, therefore, is conducive to a concept of a simple cause for events conceived as a lineal chain of cause and effect.

The final aspect of the American's orientation toward action is his emphasis on choice. After anticipating the future and, specifically, the consequences or effects of his actions, he then chooses that course which will produce the preferred consequences. His conception of desirable consequences is arrived at through a practical empiricism. The effects desired are preferably visible, measurable, and materialistic. While the material or empirical effects are more or less objective, what is practical is not. What is practical for one person may not be practical for another. Practicality refers to the adjustment to immediate situations without consideration for long-term effects or theoretical matters. The means-orientation of operationism of the American from the point of view of the non-Westerner often appears to sacrifice the end for the means.

VARIATIONS OF FORM OF ACTIVITY

The foreign visitor in the United States quickly gains an impression of life lived at a fast pace and of people incessantly active. This image reflects that *doing* is the dominant activity for Americans. The implicit assumption that "getting things done" is worthwhile is seldom questioned (Kluckhohn and Strodtbeck, 1960, 17).[3] The ramifications of the *doing* assumption impinge upon other values and assumptions of the culture and pervade the language of Americans, as in the colloquial exchanges of greeting: "How're you doing?" "I'm doing fine—how are you coming along?" All aspects of American life are affected by the predominance of *doing*.

> Its most distinctive feature is a demand for the kind of *activity* which results in accomplishments that are measurable by standards conceived to be external to the acting individual. That aspect of self-judgment or judgment of others, which relates to the nature of *activity,* is based mainly upon a measurable accomplishment achieved by acting upon persons, things or situations. What does the individual do? What can he or will he accomplish? These are almost always the primary questions in the American's scale of appraisal of persons (F. Kluckhohn, 1963, 17).

Kluckhohn's definition of *doing* is compatible with other characteristics of Americans such as the importance of achievement, emphasis on visible accomplishments, and the stress on measurement. *Doing,* however, is not to be interpreted as a member of an active-passive dichotomy, since people who are not distinguished by this form of activity can be very active (F. Kluckhohn and Strodtbeck, 1961, 16). The converse can also hold—some persons who are oriented toward *doing* can be relatively inactive. In American culture, however, along with the assumption of doing, there is a dominant value of "keeping busy." "Idle hands are the devil's workshop." Approximate synonyms to "keeping busy" approach the status of accolades, as when someone is described as "active" or "energetic." Being active may also refer to career-related activity. When a man is characterized as no longer "active" what is frequently meant is that he has retired. Both the assumption of *doing* and the value of being active are dominant patterns in American life.

In the non-Western world, the two remaining forms of activity, *being* and *being in becoming,* are dominant (Kluckhohn and Strodtbeck, 1961, 15-17). Quite often it is the contemplative man, the intellectual, who is prized, rather than the cultural hero of the American—the man who performs visible deeds. Differences in values and assumptions regarding what are the qualities of a leader sometimes confuse Americans overseas who expect the influential persons in a community to be men distinguished by doing. Quite often, however, it turns out to be the intellectual or the man who contemplates and meditates who is respected, honored, and listened to.

> In the being form of activity, there is a preference ... for the kind of *activity* which is a spontaneous expression of what is conceived to be "given" in the human personality. As compared with either the *being in*

becoming or the *doing* orientation, it is a nondevelopmental conception of *activity*. It might even be phrased as a spontaneous expression in *activity* of impulses and desires; yet care must be taken not to make this interpretation a too literal one (Kluckhohn and Strodtbeck, 1961, 16).

Concrete behavior usually reflects several assumptions and values simultaneously. Pure impulse gratification of the *being* form of activity is restrained by the demands of other assumptions and values (Kluckhohn and Strodtbeck, 1961, 16).

The notion of being is very similar to, if not identical with, self-actualization—"the motivational and cognitive life of fully evolved people" (Maslow, 1968, 72). Maslow's description of the experiences of self-actualizing people—or the rare, peak experiences of most people—can be interpreted as the ideal manifestations of the *being* variation of activity. Maslow cites several features of the peak experience which are frequently described as characteristics of non-American cultures. During peak experiences objects tend to be seen as intrinsic wholes, without comparisons; perception can be relatively ego-transcending, appearing unmotivated; the peak experience is intrinsically valued and does not need to be validated by the reaching of goals or the reduction of needs; during the peak experience the person is fused with the experience which occurs outside the usual coordinates of time and space (Maslow, 1968, 74-76). These characteristics of experience are similar to descriptions given by persons who come from societies where *being* is assumed to be the proper form of activity.

A focus on the person is found with the *being in becoming* form of activity. This is in contrast with *doing,* as we have seen, which emphasizes visible and measurable actions. *Being in becoming* introduces the idea of development of the person, which is absent in the other two forms. It emphasizes:

> that kind of activity which has as its goal the development of all aspects of the self as an integrated whole (Kluckhohn and Strodtbeck, 1961).

All aspects of the personality receive due attention. The intellect, emotions, and motives are seen as synthesized into a developing self.

WORK AND PLAY

One of the most important distinctions in the forms of activity in American life is the separation of work from play; application of this twofold judgment yields an unbalanced dichotomy. Work is pursued for a living. It is what a man must do and he is not necessarily supposed to enjoy it. Play, on the other hand, is relief from the drudgery and regularity of work and is enjoyable in its own right, although many

Americans engage in recreation with the same *seriousness* of purpose expended on work. The American overseas often finds this distinction between work and play absent in the men with whom he associates. His counterpart may appear to take work very casually. Non-Westerners do not usually allow work to interfere with the amenities of living and are also likely to expect the foreign adviser to integrate his own personal life and work. In Latin America the American who calls upon a businessman encounters difficulties in expeditiously concluding his agenda. The Latin makes the meeting into a social event and hence does not feel compelled to be brief and businesslike in his conversation (Hall and Whyte, 1960). Essentially, the Latin does not make the American discrimination between work and play (or business and play). In each case, the view regarding activity matches the definition of the person provided by Latin and by North American cultures.

TEMPORAL ORIENTATION

The American's concepts of work and action are attached to his orientation toward the future. The unpleasantness which may be connected with work and the stress of doing result in the cultural values of change and progress. These values, however, are not part of societies which look either to the present (as in Latin America) or the past (China, for example) and hence tend to focus on immediate conditions or on traditions rather than the intermediate steps required for change and progress toward the future. These differences in temporal orientation are distinguishing marks of cultures and are very important since time is a major component in any constellation of values. For Americans, as an illustration, the orientation toward the future and the high value placed on action yield the principle that one can improve upon the present. Action and hard work will bring about what the individual wants; hence Americans are described as having the attribute of effort-optimism (C. Kluckhohn and F. Kluckhohn, 1947). Through one's effort or hard work one will achieve one's ambitions. No goal is too remote, no obstacle is too difficult, for the individual who has the will and the determination and who expends the effort. Hard work is rewarded by success. The converse also holds—failure means the individual did not try hard enough, is lazy, or is worthless. These harsh evaluations may be moderated, since one can have bad luck. Nevertheless, they remain as vital American values which shed light on the frustrations of many American advisers in trying to initiate action and attain achievements with a people who are oriented to the past or present, who assume a fatalistic outlook toward the future, and whose individualism is upset by the American drive and energy.

Effort-optimism, with its underlying orientation toward the future, gives rise to one of the most frequent and pervasive problems for overseas advisers who often complain about the delays and dilatoriness involved in trying to accomplish anything. The American finds it difficult to adapt to the frustrations that accompany giving advice to people of different cultural backgrounds, with the consequence that the morale of the adviser is impaired and his optimism is dampened. His failure to achieve strikes at the heart of his value system. Think, too, of the foreign student adviser who fails to get results. The foreign student may be placing greater importance on his relationship with the adviser or others with whom he is associated than on *doing* what is suggested.

Some advisers interpret their experiences overseas in terms of the long-range effects their work will have. Others point out that their mere presence and personal example were beneficial. A third way of avoiding the consequences of failure is to interpret the mission overseas as a learning situation. The next mission will be more successful, since the adviser has profited from the frustrations and experiences of the last one. This reaction makes use of the American values of training and education as well as the orientation toward the future—in this case, the next mission.

MOTIVATION

Doing describes what a person does to express himself in action of some kind. As we have seen, however, Americans insist on identifying an agent who can take purposeful and sequential action. The concepts of *motive* and *motivation* provide the link between action on the one hand and the agent (and his purposes) on the other. Motives are attributes of the individual which arouse him to action. The concept of motivation reveals the connection and direction in a sequence of actions and, in everyday life, provides a convenient explanation for performance. It is appropriate to say someone succeeds or excels because he is well motivated. The observation is usually a tautology, since the inference about motivation is commonly derived from the performance and not independent knowledge of the individual. As commonly used, however, it is not questioned.

The importance of motivation in American society may well be associated with the phenomenon that the self-images of Americans tend to be general and vague. Motivation helps to fill this void, since it is a dynamic concept that associates the self with action and leads to the belief that the self is what the self does. The fulfillment of the individual, isolated in a mechanistic world, is attained in achievement—the motivation that propels the American and gives the culture its quality of "driveness" (Henry, 1963, 25-26). Restless and uncertain, he has recurrent need to prove himself and thereby attain an identity and success through his achievements. Hence his accomplishments must be personal, visible, and measurable, since the culture does not provide a means of evaluating the knowing the self except through externals of performance and attainment. It is this kind of motive which has been called *achievement*.

The achievement motive has been intensively studied in the United States and other societies. The results of the research reported by David McClelland (McClelland, 1961) portray the individual with high achievement motive as a person who enjoys taking the initiative in making decisions. He prefers to participate in activities that challenge his skills and abilities. He is usually confident of success, but tends to be too optimistic when the conditions for a successful performance are unknown. When he possesses information which permits an objective appraisal of success, he is inclined to use it for a rational assessment of the situation, his abilities and skills, and for guiding his performance. Persons with high achievement, often identified with the business or economic entrepreneur, have been described as risk-takers. This attribute emerges from the research studies as a complex quality subject to many contingencies. McClelland concludes that those who have high achievement motivation appear to prefer situations involving risk "only when they have some chance of influencing the outcome through their own skills and abilities" (McClelland, 1961, 214). In this conclusion, the focus returns to the individual.

Although achievement is the dominant motive for Americans, ascription exists as a variation. It is marked by an emphasis on *being*; the individual may be defined as the member of a family, for instance, as is sometimes found in New England and the more traditional-oriented parts of the South, or the individual is defined according to his status or profession, as in the military. It is this kind of motivation, rather than achievement, which is shared by many cultures throughout the world as the dominant motivation. Many of the actions of people in non-Western cultures can be understood as directed toward preserving and enhancing their particular position within the social structure, whereas considerations about tangible progress and improvement are secondary in importance, if present at all.

Individuals with an ascriptive motivation are usually enmeshed in reciprocal relations with members of their family, community, or trade and profession. These social links are much more binding than in the case of Americans. In Vietnam, for instance, an operator of a printing shop reports supporting his employees to the limits of his ability for six months after he was put out of business by government action. An American would probably not expect the same responsibility from his employer. When an American joins an organization or a business he does so as a free agent and usually preserves the right to move out whenever his purposes are no longer served by being a member. On the other hand, he usually accepts the fortunes of the organization, and if it fails, then it is up to the individual to find another position. The organization is not expected to maintain its employees on the payroll.

The patron system prevalent in much of Latin America also presents an intricate set of social relations between the individual and the patron. The latter may be the godfather of members of his estate and may extend, as a matter of obligation, personal services and considerations which would be foreign to the American overseer. As with the Vietnamese businessman, the obligations incurred are expected to transcend adventitious events of failure, poverty, or change of plans.

Ascriptive motivation introduces assumptions about the sources of action and purposes of behavior which differ from the view implied in the achievement motive. The individual is perceived to belong to a social group and to behave according to the obligations, duties, and privileges inherent in his social and professional position. To understand and manage behavior, the American must contend with the psychological predisposition of the person, since motivation is a quality of the individual. In ascriptive societies, however, the sources of motivation are more likely to be in the group or society. In the words of a Ghanaian, an employee of the government, "We do not concern ourselves with motivation, as Americans do. We know what our job is and we do it."

American assumptions regarding the dynamics of behavior are so thoroughly dependent on some motivational concept that it is nearly inconceivable that other people in the world find it more natural to refer behavior to role or social order. Yet, in one work enterprise with Dutch medical missionaries in Africa it was necessary to analyze their work and the problems of their hospital from the perspective of their duties, responsibilities, and privileges as doctors, nurses, technicians, and administrators of the hospital. An analysis of human relations problems based on conflicting motives of hospital personnel and the consequences for the work and management of the hospital was unconvincing to the Dutch personnel. In American language, it did not communicate. American members of the same medical society, operating a hospital in East Pakistan, perceived their hospital problems in terms of conflicting motives of individuals. Issues of human relations within the hospital were readily perceived as conflict among personal, religious, professional, and social motives of the medical personnel. The Americans then naturally accepted a description of human relations according to a loose analysis of motives. The Dutch rejected the same terms of analysis, since motivation in the American sense was not a significant concept in their thinking.

MEASURABLE ACHIEVEMENT

In American culture, achievement is given a material meaning or, at least, a visible and measurable interpretation. This attitude leads to the American emphasis on technology and, secondly, on publicity—rendering visible unrecognized accomplishments. Acting on these assumptions, technicians and advisers in the field define progress in terms of technological change, more often than not reported in statistical data. Social progress too often comes to mean the number of schools erected, while there is no mention of the training of teachers. The concern with visible achievement often leads the American to lose sight of main issues; he may settle for a sensation, a personal triumph over a counterpart of a specific accomplishment which has visibility and therefore can be reported as an achievement. One military adviser is described as becoming personally involved in the choice of headgear for a particular unit, which he finally succeeded in changing. This was his achievement and he was described as determined to have it before his tour of duty was over. Another frequent visible achievement in the military is the building of latrines. This cannot be dismissed as lightly as the incident of the new caps. The persistence of Americans all over the world, however, in building latrines for people who refuse to use them suggests that their appeal as projects may reside in part in their concrete visibility rather than in their potential role in controlling disease.

Since achievement has to be visible and measurable, Americans become very sensitive to praise or blame—more so than perhaps any other people except the Japanese. They do not develop the Englishman's self-assurance and confidence in his own judgment or the self-sufficiency of the French. They depend on feedback from associates and particularly on the visibility of their achievements. Both of these factors are missing in the overseas situation: achievements are usually few and the reactions of one's associates are likely to be both delayed and diffuse (the same is true in many situations for a foreign student adviser). The American adviser is quite often uncertain about the effects, if any, of his advising. His work is incompatible with an achievement orientation, since he should only be a catalyst to his counterpart with the primary function of providing information, skills, and judgment rather than concrete achievements. The counterpart is likely to have an ascriptive orientation and hence to be somewhat unconcerned with achievements. Deprived of his own visible success and frequently not seeing it in his counterpart, the adviser considers himself a failure; Americans find this kind of situation very difficult to handle. They tend to shift their sights to another future achievement or disregard the present situation as the fault of another person. Finally, Americans may face failure with the "let's get the hell out of here" attitude (see C. Kluckhohn, 1954, 120), which may be interpreted as a disguised admission that their actions have been on the wrong track. This suggests one way of removing the stain of failure—that is, by considering it as part of the learning process.

COMPETITION AND AFFILIATION

Competition is the primary method among Americans of motivating members of a group, and some have seen it as a basic emphasis in American culture (Potter, 1954, 59-60). Americans, with their individualism and ideas on achieving, respond well to this technique but, where the same approach is applied to members of another culture who do not hold the same values, the effort is ineffective at best and may produce undesirable consequences. People for whom saving face is important or for whom dependency on others is desirable will not accept competition among members of the group with the same enthusiasm as Americans. Thus attempts to instill a competitive spirit in social, economic, or military activities in many non-Western countries, such as Laos and Vietnam, have not been very successful, as the American advisers should have been able to foresee from observing the intense attachment of the people to their family and village. The communal feeling toward each other excludes the incentive to excel over others either as a member of a group or individually. An adviser shows his bewilderment at the Lao's lack of competition in the following words:

> Watching them play a game—volleyball. To us, it's a game. I know when our teams compete, whether it's baseball or basketball—anything, we'd be serious, playing it because we like to win. With them, they wouldn't be; they would team up and have teams going, but they just didn't give a hoot whether they won or not.

The non-Westerner, with an aversion to competition, is likely to show more strongly developed *affiliation*,[4] as we have seen, for his own family and community. He knows, and knows of, fewer people than the typical American. Both his direct interaction with others through travel, work, and social life and his indirect contact through the mass media are likely to be much more circumscribed than for an American. He will be less self-conscious (see Bell, 1965, 209-212) and less analytical of himself as an individual than the American. Beyond the confines of his immediate world and interest lies a world largely unknown to him. It is often endowed with danger to the unwary who travels beyond the limits of his own territory. An American adviser in Laos, training the Meo tribesmen for military service, points out that they were effective soldiers only within their own environment. Their knowledge of the outside world was meager and overridden with superstitions which made the soldiers fearful and ineffective in operations outside their own geographical area. Within their own domain, however, their willing acceptance of military discipline and complete dedication to training made them excellent trainees.

The example of the Meo tribesmen is perhaps extreme, but the lack of feeling for being a member of a political entity, a nation, is generally prevalent. This fact is often obscured by the reports in the mass media of instances of intense nationalism on the part of individuals and groups in the non-West. These certainly exist but are not typical of the great majority of the people throughout the world. It is misleading to consider peoples such as the Lao and the Vietnamese to be self-conscious members of their respective countries in the sense that most Americans consider themselves to be citizens of the United States.

Although Americans have been described as primarily motivated by achievement, it does not mean that they do not show some affiliative tendencies. These tendencies, however, are diluted in contrast to the strong social and territorial adhesion found in affiliations in the non-Western world. Margaret Mead describes the American's nostalgia for his home town as symbolic of the question: "Are you the same kind of person I am? Good—how about a coke?" (Mead, 1965, 29). But the preoccupation with the home town is not an establishment of the influence of family and community with defined status and prescribed norms of behavior, as in ascriptive societies. It is instead a way of establishing an affiliation among people who have little in the way of "common origins and common expectations" (Mead, 1965, 30).

It has been mentioned that the values of American culture are changing, that Americans are becoming more group-oriented and less autonomous in their behavior. It is well to point out that in the case of the American military we find a well-documented thesis that the primary motivational force for the American soldier during World War II was affiliation. It was not achievement, since military service usually represented an interruption in the typical American's career and life. Nor was it ascription, since the military usually did not provide a needed or desired identity to be preserved and nurtured. The force to fight for the typical American soldier was derived from a sense of loyalty to the other men in the immediate group (Stouffer et al., 1949). The spread of loyalty was primarily horizontal and based on equality rather than vertical and based on authority. There can be no doubt that affiliation is a motive in other areas of American life, and it may be ascendant as American individualism becomes subservient to organization and the goals of groups and institutions.

THE LIMITS OF ACHIEVEMENT: THE INDIVIDUAL

Externalized achievement is the dominant motivation for the typical American. The pursuit thereof has produced in the United States an unparalleled economic abundance (Potter, 1954, 78-90). It has been argued that the achievement motive provides a key psychological factor in economic development (McClelland, 1961; 61, 105, 157). But hand-in-hand with this motivation there has been in the United States a willingness to exploit and control the physical environment (Potter, 1954, 164-165). These two characteristics of Americans, found as both individual and collective qualities, have been key factors in producing economic abundance.

During their history, Americans have exploited their physical environment as if it were unlimited. The vastness of the land and the opulence of its resources no doubt strengthened the preexisting belief that the limits to achievement are measured within the individual. The limitations on success are not ascribed to resources, to the actions of others, to the agency of government, or to fate. For, as the Protestant ethic prescribed, if one has the desire and works hard enough, his labors will be rewarded with success. "Where there's a will, there's a way."

Furthermore, the achievements of the individual are not gained at the expense of others since there are enough rewards—material wealth, prestige, popularity—for everyone who aspires and tries. Doctrines such as Marxism which promulgate inevitable conflict among classes because the limited goods of the world are acquired by a few who exploit the masses have rarely achieved great favor among Americans. Traditionally, Americans have seen failure as a lack of will and of effort on the part of the individual. Successful accumulation of worldly wealth was a sign that the individual belonged to the select group who enjoyed the grace of God. The same idea is still present in a newer version: a rich man cannot be completely bad—or else he would not be rich.

This expansive view of achievement and of a world of economic abundance contrasts sharply with the perception of limited wealth prevalent throughout much of the rest of the world. This latter outlook is more than just a view appropriate to an economy of scarcity in which the individual's aspirations and potential achievements are necessarily limited. It is central to an ascriptive view of society which tends to maintain the status quo in relationships among people. To explain the norms of behavior of such societies, especially those which are traditional and peasant, we turn to George Foster's idea of the Image of the Limited Good. The individual or family that acquires more than its share of a "good," and particularly an economic "good," is viewed with suspicion (Foster, 1965, 302). Likewise, the individual who accepts a role of leadership will find his motives suspected and

> he will be subject to the criticism of his neighbors. By seeking or even accepting an authority position, the ideal man ceases to be ideal. A "good" man therefore usually shuns community responsibilities (other than of a ritual nature); by so doing he protects his reputation (Foster, 1965, 303).

People do not compete for authority by seeking leadership roles, nor do they compete in material symbols such as dress, housing, or food which might make the individual stand out from the rest of the members of the village. The people in peasant villages show a strong desire to look and act like everyone else. By means of uniformity they attempt to be inconspicuous in position and behavior (Foster, 1965, 303).

Despite the stress on conformity in traditional peasant villages, there is a place for individuality. Once a person fulfills the obligation of family, community, and tradition, he may be allowed considerable freedom to express his own individuality. Both conformity and individuality can be found in non-Western societies where the individual is perceived in terms of ascriptive qualities. It is necessary, however, to ascertain for each society those areas in which individuality or uniformity holds.

The motive of achievement, along with its stress on effort, work, and the taking of rational risks is not widely evident outside the West. The individual works to survive, but not to amass wealth, which, like land, is perceived as inherent in nature (see Foster, 1965, 298).

> It can be divided up and passed around in various ways, but, within the framework of the villagers' traditional world, it does not grow. Time and tradition have determined the shares each family and individual hold; these shares are not static, since obviously they do shift. But the reason for the relative position of each villager is known at any given time, and any significant change calls for explanation (Foster, 1965, 298).

It follows from the above discussion that innovation or new techniques of working are also not perceived as related to wealth or, in our terms, to achievement. Instead, achievement is a matter of fate, an intervention by an outside agent that does not disrupt the relationships among the members of a community. One such agent is the lottery. By winning, the individual can improve his position without endangering the community (see Foster, 1965, 308-309).

People who have a "lottery" motivation, or a belief in an outside and adventitious intervention in their behalf, are difficult to convince of the virtues of hard work, effort, frugality, and initiative. Even if this attitude does not exist, or if it has been penetrated, the individual may still not accept the necessity of improving his position, for it will extend his obligations. Thus a young Peruvian fisherman refused aid to modernize his fishing technique for the reason that if he had more money he would have more relatives to take care of. He doubted that he would be better off because of his increased responsibilities (Foster, 1962, 92).

An absence of achievement motivation is not necessarily connected to the social and economic conditions of the peasant society. Apparently a belief in "fate" or "luck" can be found in parts of the non-Western world where density of population and limited land holdings are not a problem. In the interior of Brazil there exists a frontier environment. Land holdings are not limited, population is not dense, and to the west there is new land offering economic opportunities. Yet the people still subscribe to the "luck" motivation, being more concerned with buying tickets for the local game of "bicho" than with developing their local resources or moving west.[5] It might be argued that the psychological horizon is limited and that they do not recognize that land and economic opportunities are available. Nevertheless, in the same area there is the precedent for squatters' rights. Individuals and families take possession of land, work it, and eventually acquire a right to it. This tradition does not indicate that the possession of land is seen as traditionally limited; there are ways of acquiring it even if the individual is not aware of new land to the west.[6] This particular case of Brazil suggests that the absence of achievement motivation is not necessarily associated with closed communities of dense population and limited land holdings. Indifference to personal achievement, associated with a belief in "luck," can also be found among people for whom the attitude has little relation to the economic conditions in which they live. It reflects their perception of the self and of the world as well as their concepts of motivation and of fate.

THE LIMITS OF ASCRIPTION: TOTAL POWER

In a society in which motivation rests on an ascriptive base rather than on achievement, cultural norms will be different. Status and inequality will characterize the value system. Each person will have his own fixed position in a vertical, hierarchical tier. In some cases, though not all, as we have seen, ascriptive motivation is associated with an image of a world of restricted resources—in contrast to the American perception of a world of abundance. Some of the permissiveness and competitiveness of American society can no doubt be traced to the belief that there are enough material goods for everyone. David Potter argues that the majority of the world, even Europe, assumes an economy of scarcity, so that the volume of wealth is assumed to be fixed (Potter, 1954, 118). If there is not enough for everyone, if a generous volume of the goods of the society are restricted to only the select few, it is unlikely that the society will countenance perpetual (and probably internecine) competition for the economic and social spoils. It is more sound to assign arbitrarily to each person a status which is transmitted by heredity and rigidly maintained by authority, with both the favored few and the unfavored bulk of the people maintained in their respective statuses from generation to generation.

> The status-bound individual often gained a sense of contentment with his lot and even of dignity within his narrow sphere, and all that he sacrificed for his new psychological advantage was a statistically negligible chance for advancement (Potter, 1954, 115).

Within its limits the ascriptive way of life, flourishing in an economy of scarcity, will most often develop a relatively rigid culture pattern with authority providing a primary focus. Authority rather than the self or the individual will become a center for motivation. In contrast, authority in American culture is seen as a social rather than as a motivational question, since the dominant pattern in American culture limits the role of authority to providing services, protecting the rights of the individual, inducing cooperation, and adjudicating differences. Although many variations on the dominant value exist in American society—the military for example—or in individuals who prefer strong, clear authority, these deviant patterns provide little help in understanding the complete display of authority traditionally found in governments in many of the countries of Asia, the Middle East, and elsewhere. In these states total power may be vested in the members of the government. The centralized organization of political and social power permeates the society, profoundly affecting the way of life of individuals. Considerations of status, loyalty, and ascription replace the American stress on individual competition and achievement.

Delineating a few of the characteristics of a society organized according to what Karl Wittfogel calls "total power" should be helpful in putting into perspective American attitudes toward authority as they are contrasted with those of many non-Westerners. Rather than pick a country which has these characteristics and contrast it with American patterns, we shall follow Wittfogel's analysis of total power in its political, social, and psychological characteristics. Wittfogel draws his materials from historical and contemporary examples and develops a theme regarding total power which, while not fitting any one society precisely, characterizes in a general way many societies around the world.

In societies with more or less absolutist governments, political power is not checked by nongovernmental forces found in most Western countries. Historically the power of the central governments in the West has been limited by constitutions, large individual landholdings, and political, cultural, and organizational subdivisions. In absolute governments, these checks are generally not present or not effective. Religious and military power are normally both identified with the state and do not place a check on the government (Wittfogel, 1957, 49-100). There is no nongovernmental center of power (Wittfogel, 1957, 101-103). Intragovernmental balances such as those found in the American system also do not exist (Wittfogel, 1957, 101-103). Therefore, "there develops what may be called a *cumulative tendency of unchecked power*" (Wittfogel, 1957, 106). The exercise of unchecked authority easily becomes arbitrary and results in intimidation, secrecy, unpredictability—and in the extreme, terror and brutality (Wittfogel, 1957, 137, 141). The psychological climate thus created engenders mutual mistrust and suspicion among officials of the government. The key factor for the official is his relation to the authority figures (Wittfogel, 1957, 345). Promotions may relate to aptitude but more often depend on the loyalty and subservience of the individual. The prized quality for promotion is "total and ingenious servility" (Wittfogel, 1957, 364).

Parts of the society may lie outside the power system of the absolute state. To varying degrees families and villages, for example, may enjoy autonomy to run their own affairs. There are official requests, impositions from the central government, constables, and often a tax collector, but beyond this, outside control usually ends (Wittfogel, 1957, 122-124). The central government does not intrude into those areas where its authority and revenue are not jeopardized.

The people usually have little love for the government and its representatives. The society is clearly demarcated into the ruled versus the rulers, with the people demonstrating a fear of involvement with the government (Wittfogel, 1957, 156). The aloofness of the people from the government and from others with whom specific social relations are not established may approach pathological proportions from the point of view of the American. Thus assistance to the victim of an accident or a drowning may be withheld for fear that the rescuer will be saddled with the responsibility for the occurrence. The reason for this fear of involvement is certainly not entirely traceable to the nature of authority and of the government, but these are contributing factors. This very brief and simplified description of a state of "total power" is not intended to describe any particular country at any particular point in time. It nevertheless shows us some of the characteristics of states with highly centralized governmental structures and helps us understand certain aspects of the value systems which develop therein. In such countries motivation is rooted in efforts to maintain status and in the personalized ways in which both official and social relations are conducted. There is little incentive for achievement or change. Significant relations are vertical; hence the impetus for successful action, or for change, usually comes from above. There is little precedent for initiative, information, or opinion to originate spontaneously with the people and move upward to the leaders. There are no serious competing interests to the government officials who see the people tied to them by obligations. They do not assume responsibility toward the people in the manner characteristic in more decentralized governments. Government traditionally, as in Burma, for instance, is not concerned with problem-solving or with improving society, but in maintaining loyalty and status (Pye, 1962, 78). Thus authority becomes a source of both social control and motivation.

It is clear from the above examples that the nature of motivation may be quite different in the non-Western countries with centralized governments from what it usually is in the United States. Especially significant is the fact that the definite acceptance of a personal bond between subordinate and superior makes the authority figure an acceptable source of motivation. Direct orders, explicit instructions, and demands for personal conformity may be much more acceptable, and even desired, in the non-Western world than in the United States. American preference for persuasion may be seen as weakness, and self-determination may become egotism and a threat to others.

NOTES

1. In the *Washington Post,* June 7, 1964.

2. A means orientation, like the concept of *problem,* carries a meaning similar to that of the term *operationism.*

3. The component of form of activity is a rewording of Kluckhohn's value-orientation—activity. The three variations also come from her as well as the important distinction between *doing* and *action.*

4. *Affiliation* refers to the social need for the company of others, for companionship; whereas ascription refers to the qualities of being a person, a member of a family, a profession, etc.

5. Foster, 1965, pp. 308-310, argues that the "brakes on change are less psychological than social." Foster might disagree with the example above. On the other hand, the case of Brazil might be considered outside the scope of peasant societies. Foster stresses limited land holdings and density of population.

6. Communication from Charles T. Stewart, Jr.

REFERENCES

Bell, Daniel, "The Disjunction of Culture and Social Structure: Some Notes on the Meaning of Social Reality," *Daedalus,* 94, 1 (Winter, 1965), 208-222.

Foster, George M., *Traditional Cultures and the Impact of Technological Change,* Harper & Row, New York, 1962.

Foster, George M., "Peasant Society and the Image of Limited Good," *American Anthropologist,* 62, 2 (April, 1965), 293-315.

Glenn, Edmund S., "Semantic Difficulties in International Communication," *ETC.,* 11, 3 (1954), 163-180.

Goodenough, Ward H., *Cooperation in Change,* Russell Sage Foundation, New York, 1963.

Hall, Edward T. and William F. Whyte, "Intercultural Communication: A Guide to Men of Action," *Human Organization,* 19, 1 (Spring, 1960), 5-12.

Henry, Jules, *Culture Against Man,* Random House, New York, 1963.

Kerlinger, Fred N., "Decision-Making in Japan," *Social Forces,* 30 (October, 1951), 36-41.

Kluckhohn, Clyde, "Some Aspects of American National Character," in *Human Factors in Military Operations,* Richard H. Williams (ed.), Technical Memorandum ORO-T-259, Operations Research Office, The Johns Hopkins University, Maryland, 1954, pp. 118-121.

Kluckhohn, Clyde and Florence Kluckhohn, "American Culture: Generalized Orientations and Class Patterns," in *Conflicts of Power in Modern Culture: Seventh Symposium,* Lyman Bryson (ed.), Harper and Bros., New York, 1947.

Kluckhohn, Florence R., "Some Reflections on the Nature of Cultural Integration and Change," in *Sociological Theory, Values and Sociocultural Change: Essays in Honor of P. A. Sorokin,* E. A. Tiryakian (ed.), Free Press, New York, 1963, pp. 217-247.

Kluckhohn, Florence R. and Fred L. Strodtbeck, *Variations in Value Orientations,* Row, Peterson, New York, 1961.

McClelland, David C., *The Achieving Society,* D. Van Nostrand, Princeton, 1961.

Maslow, Abraham, H., *Toward a Psychology of Being,* D. Van Nostrand, Princeton, 1968.

Mead, Margaret, *And Keep Your Powder Dry,* William Morrow, New York, 1965.

Potter, David M., *People of Plenty: Economic Abundance and the American Character,* The University of Chicago Press, Chicago, 1954.

Pye, Lucian W., *Politics, Personality, and Nation Building: Burma's Search for Identity,* Yale University Press, New Haven, 1962.

Rogers, Carl H., "Toward a Modern Approach to Values," *Journal of Abnormal and Social Psychology,* 68, 2 (1964), 160-167.

Stouffer, Samuel A., *et al., The American Soldier,* Princeton University Press, Princeton, 1949.

Wittfogel, Karl A., *Oriental Despotism: A Comparative Study of Total Power,* Yale University Press, New Haven, 1957.

CONCEPT OF ONESELF

John P. Fieg

From *The Thai Way: A Study in Cultural Values,* by John P. Fieg, © 1976 by Meridian House International. Reprinted by permission of Meridian House International, Washington, D.C.

Does the Thai conceive of himself essentially as an individual unit or basically as a member of a group? Is "individualism" as it has been applied to Americans characteristic of the Thai mentality? Numerous studies have noted a decidedly individualistic bent in the Thai character as evidenced by the self-centered nature of Theravada Buddhism, the general preference for noninvolvement over strong affiliation, the resistance to regimentation, and the absence of a strong sense of familial duties and obligations.

On the other hand, there are aspects of Thai social relations that make one wary of applying to Thais the concept of "individualism" as it was coined by de Tocqueville to refer to Americans. In the first place, there has traditionally been no satisfactory translation for "individualism" in Thai. The recently coined *"pàccèkníyom"* seems to be an attempt to put into Thai the concept embodied by the English, "individualism." But it is doubtful if someone who did not understand "individualism" in English would clearly comprehend the concept underlying the Thai expression. Use of the word *"pàccèkníyom"* seems also to be limited to scholarly circles; it is certainly not a part of the working vocabulary of the vast mass of people. Significantly, it comes from a Pali word which refers to those who are themselves "enlightened" in the Buddhist sense but who have not taught others. This is important in that it ties the concept of individualism to Buddhism, clearly one of the chief sources of any individualistic tendencies among the Thai.

The idiomatic expression *"tua khraj tua man"* is also related to "individualism," but it has the negative implication of "everyone acting for himself" in a somewhat selfish, chaotic way. The importance of group harmony is illustrated in the concept of *"kreng caj,"* which translates freely as "taking the other person's feelings into account" at all times. A sense of "groupness" also manifests itself in the way that Thais refer to older men as *"lung"* (uncle), older women as *"pâa"* (aunt), and slightly older acquaintances as *"phîi"* (older brother or sister). A certain sense of conformity to the group norm is illustrated in the phrase *"phìd pòkati"* (unusual). Whereas the word "unusual" does not necessarily have a negative connotation in English, and indeed can often be construed as a compliment, in Thai such a description carries with it a negative meaning. One who is *"phìd pòkati"* is somehow beyond the pale of normal behavior.

We must somehow reconcile the dual strains of individualism and group-centeredness which are together present in the Thai national character. For while sharing in the overall Asian framework of smooth interpersonal relations and group harmony, the Thais are certainly more individualistic than, for example, the Chinese or Japanese. But this individualism is of a different emotional hue from that which characterizes the American personality.

A convenient starting point for sorting out the ingredients of Thai individualism is John Embree's seminal article entitled "Thailand—A Loosely Structured Social System."[1] Embree saw Thai culture as having a loosely as opposed to a closely woven social structure, loosely integrated signifying "a culture in which considerable variation of individual behavior is sanctioned." He compared Thailand with Vietnam and Japan, both of which he viewed as having more tightly woven cultures—"cultures whose patterns are clearly marked and which emphasize the importance of observing reciprocal rights and duties in various situations to a greater degree than is to be found among the Thai." The first characteristic of Thai culture to strike an observer from the West, according to Embree, was the individualistic behavior of the people. "The longer one resides in Thailand the more one is struck by the almost determined lack of regularity, discipline, and regimentation in Thai life."

While noting that the father was the putative head of the Thai family and that the children were supposed to obey their parents, Embree found none of the strong sense of duty and obligation to parents which he maintained was characteristic, in diverse ways, of Vietnam, China, and Japan. "Even the family precepts in this regard are milder, since the Thai follow the Buddhist rather than the Confucian rules. . . . (W)hile obligations are recognized, they are not allowed to burden one unduly."

Mulder has cautioned against an uncritical acceptance of the "loose structure" concept, maintaining that such an acceptance has led to the creation of a kind of social science myth about Thai society that has little relation to Thai social reality. "In all social interaction, in Thailand as in any place else, people meet as occupants of social positions, or roles, that can be clearly defined in structural-functional terms; there is nothing 'loose' about that," Mulder said.[2]

The Swiss psychologist Boesch goes Mulder one step further and stands Embree's "loosely-structured social system" on its head. Rather than viewing the Thais as a nation of individualists, Boesch is impressed by what he considers the rigid hierarchic structure of Thai society. "The hierarchic order of relationships diminishes the impulses for individual initiative; the social emphasis on conformity lessens the impulses for creativity, discussion and experiment," according to Boesch.[3]

The conflicting views of Embree and Boesch force us to face anew the enigmatic individualistic pattern that somehow emerges from a rigid hierarchical structure that clearly breeds a measure of conformity. Kirsch points out that if loosely structured and tightly structured systems are seen as polar extremes of some hypothetical continuum, the words "loosely" and "tightly" are meaningless until they are put in some comparative context. "Thailand might be classed as *relatively* loosely structured when contrasted with Japan but classed as *relatively* tightly structured when compared to some other society such as the United States," Kirsch said.[4]

Phillips attempts to resolve the dilemma by pointing out that use of the terms "loosely structured" and "tightly structured" contains the implicit premise that all areas of sociocultural life are necessarily structured to the same degree. This, he feels, is simply not the case. He contrasts the "tight" structure embodied in the Thai ranking structure with the "loose" structure evident in the Thai friendship system.

> (T)here is little doubt that the Thai ranking system represents one of the most clearly and tightly structured phenomena of Thai life. This is evidenced by, among other things, Thai speech patterns (pronouns, titles, honorifics), wearing apparel (including uniforms), decision-making processes and the fact that almost the first thing that any Thai learns about any other Thai is the latter's status. However, I defy any analyst . . . to come up with an equally clear, certain, and internally consistent set of data on the structure of the Thai friendship system.[5]

Phillips maintains that "most Thai peasants do not want to think about the nature of friendship; do not have clear, consistent, or rigorous conceptions of friendship; are unsure or indifferent about the stability of friendship relationships; and are uncertain about what they give to or derive from such relationships." He adds parenthetically that the Thai approach to friendship is in some ways akin to the American approach, both systems characterized by considerable "looseness of structure."

Thais distinguish between "play friends" (literally "eating friends") and "die friends," those who will be your friend until death. " 'Play friends feast with you when you can feast them, betray you if it is to their profit to do so, and certainly disappear if you become a nonentity."[6] Die friends, on the other hand, are rare indeed, and Thai stories emphasize that they are probably never to be found.

In discussing the widely noted Thai individualism, Piker concludes that "the villager approaches interpersonal involvement with considerable caution and suspicion, and interpersonal relations are characterized by a relative absence of binding, mutual commitment."[7] Hanks and Phillips add, "Thai resist strong affiliation as do rejected lovers who fear suffering again. . . . On the level of action and conscious decision, the moral for a Thai runs: invest not thy love in a shadow."[8]

Several authors have noted a certain sense of aloofness or noninvolvement engendered by Thai individualistic behavior, particularly evidenced by minding one's own business when it comes to matters of action. This sense of noninvolvement is reflected in several Thai expressions, particularly "*mâi pen rai*" ("It doesn't matter" or "Never mind"), "which signifies the Thai desire to keep relationships peaceful and on an even keel, to shrug off the little frustrations and disagreements of life, to prevent anger or passion from coming to the surface."[9]

A feeling persists that, within wide limits, a person is responsible only to himself and that his actions are no one else's concern. Thus Thais are not amenable to sustained regimentation. "Not only is the military tradition weak, but Thai peasants, when drafted into military service, show little aptitude for the life of a soldier. They do not care for its discipline, and they show a marked reluctance to go into battle."[10] Even the dance girls in Bangkok cabarets exhibited more individualistic behavior than their Chinese counterparts in Singapore, according to Embree. "Each girl comes or does not come on a given night as she pleases; she may or may not require a guest to buy a dance ticket; and if she goes home with him afterward she may or may not be mercenary about it, depending on how she feels."

Former Thai Prime Minister Kukrit Pramoj, in a book he wrote about Hollywood, said that Thais could easily identify with Marlon Brando. "He is like Thai people in that he is a person who loves independence above all else and believes most strongly in being his own man (acting for himself)."[11] The word "Thai" means "free," and one writer maintains that probably no other word describes Thais more accurately. "It refers to national independence, never lost from the beginning of the nation's history. But most of all it is a characteristic of the individual."[12]

This desire for freedom from outside control—be it on the national or individual level—is perhaps reflected in the use of the passive voice in Thai, which communicates a definite meaning of unpleasantness or distasteful association. Better to be active, to control the situation, than to be trapped into an uncomfortable position. For example, one can say in Thai, "The boy was hit by the car," "The building was burned down," or "The old capital was destroyed." But one cannot say, "The woman was praised," or "The girl was kissed" (unless it was against her will). The passive construction is tied necessarily to the negative.

In terms of family patterns, one study concluded that two-thirds of rural Thai families are nuclear, but this is not identical to the nuclear family as it exists in the United States. For the Thai family is flexible enough to include occasionally a widowed parent, other blood relatives, and even unrelated persons. One social scientist, moreover, was not entirely satisfied with the characterization of the rural Thai family as nuclear. "Is it appropriate to say that the nuclear family predominates in rural Thailand in view of indications that the vast majority of newly married couples spend at least a few years as part of a limited extended family?"[13] In many cases the traditional extended family persists. The married sons or daughters have residences adjacent to that of their parents and siblings, yet consider themselves part of a single household. When additional residences are needed, they are built in the same or an adjacent compound.

There certainly exists none of the sense of lineage or the feeling of ancestry that is characteristic of the Chinese, Japanese, and Vietnamese. Family members are primarily oriented toward agemates and cousins, rather than toward ancestors or descendants. Family names, established by royal decree in 1916, do not meet any felt desire for a formal link between generations: "Indeed, children may be quite unaware of their family name; nor is the name often used among neighbors for either address or identification."[14]

As mentioned earlier, the reference to nonrelated persons by family names, the emphasis on group harmony, and the desire not to be "unusual" are indicative of a certain sense of "groupness." This is further illustrated by the absence in Thai of a satisfactory translation for "privacy." In fact urban Thais who know English well will often say something like this: "*Yaak ja yai bâan phráw mâi mii privacy thîi nîi*" "I want to move because I don't have any privacy here." The point is that they have to borrow the word from English and insert it into an otherwise all-Thai sentence. Tied to this absence of "privacy" is a tendency to ask what Americans would consider "personal" questions, even of casual acquaintances. Questions include such items as salary, age, and the cost of articles the person is wearing. "But these interrogations are not undertaken to indulge a taste for gossip or to find ways of embarrassing others. They are authentic expressions of friendly interest. While respecting the Westerner's reticence to divulge personal information, the Thai asks how can friendships develop unless persons know each other's affairs. . . . When a Thai fails to ask personal questions, it usually means he either distrusts or has no interest in the other person."[15] It should be noted, however, that Westernized Thais may approximate the American pattern of reluctance to divulge such information and may consider such questions improper. They may thus resist the notion that in Thai society generally such questions are the conversational norm.

How then ultimately to reconcile the group-centeredness and the individualism which are both somehow bound up in the Thai national character? Part of the answer may be a confusion between "individualism" and "individuality"; for as Stewart points out, "The value of *individualism* as found among Americans is quite different from a stress on individuality."[16] This is not a case of a distinction without a difference. For individual*ism* relates to self-concept, the idea that the self is an individual unit whose behavior is aimed at individual goals as opposed to a member of a group whose behavior is aimed at smooth interpersonal relations. Individual*ity,* on the other hand, refers to the cultivation of differences within the personality, the freedom to exhibit a variety of behavior patterns in different social contexts.

Americans, according to Stewart, possess individualism but tend not to assert their individuality. The interface between the individual and his culture in American society tends to cover all areas of behavior; it operates whether the person is within the family unit or out in society. The constant presence of the culture in all social contexts serves to inhibit idiosyncratic, nonconformist behavior. This is not to say that American culture requires complete conformity at all times; there is obviously some room for differences. The point here is that although the contact between culture and individual in the United States is not as strong as in some traditional societies, it is more pervasive. Certain other societies—because of the strong contact between individual and culture— display more conformist behavior within the family or tribal unit; but since the culture does not follow the individual outside this basic group, he is allowed considerable latitude in his behavior outside the tribe or family.

Stewart notes that Americans overseas are often surprised to find persons who evince strong personality, personal convictions, and idiosyncratic behavior in cultures where authority (usually family) or tradition exercise considerable control over the person. "The contradiction is only apparent. In some cultures where the individual is subject to the norms of his family or tradition he is allowed considerable room to cultivate individuality, as long as these (actions) do not interfere with his obligations to family or tradition," according to Stewart. In the Thai context, persons could assert their individuality without having the same self-centered individualism which has been attributed to Americans.

Yet this seems at best a partial answer with respect to the Thai, for there does seem to be a certain individual*ism* at work as well. But is it identical to American individualism, and if not, how does it differ? One could argue that both societies are highly individualistic and at the same time conformist but that the individualism is manifested in completely opposite ways and that the conformity is exercised in different behavioral settings. The American pattern might be termed "assertive" individualism, in which the self is thrust out into society in order to achieve, to do, to carve out one's own place. Thai individualism, on the other hand, could be termed "nonassertive" or inner-directed. While the American thrusts the self out, the Thai draws the self in in order to control it. The epitome of this inner-directed movement would be the attainment of the "nonself" and Nirvana in Buddhist terminology.

These opposite notions of individualism spring from the divergent metaphysical underpinnings of the two societies. The American pattern is based on Greek dualism, which views the nature of man as an immaterial soul imprisoned in the body until death; the Thai pattern is rooted in Buddhism, which argues that there is no soul, no identifiable self or personality that persists after death. American individualism is, in a sense, a manifestation of the teachings of Calvin, who maintained that man had to achieve in the temporal world in order to ultimately "save his soul" for future life in the supernatural realm. According to Buddhist philosophy, there is no soul to be saved and what is termed the "self" is only a temporary, momentarily changing compound of five psychological factors (form, feeling, perception, impulse, and consciousness)—called "*khandha.*" The learner seeking enlightened knowledge, because of his ignorance of the true nature of the universe, mistakes the "Khandha" for his real essence. "It is, therefore, one task of the educative process to bring about true knowledge of the learner's nature as a non-self."[17]

Overt manifestations of the difference between American assertive and Thai nonassertive individualism are clothing styles, bodily movements, and emotional expressiveness. All will be treated in more depth later. Suffice it to say here that the American's more ostentatious apparel; informal, assertive bodily movements, and forceful, direct emotional expression stand out in sharp contrast to the more subdued Thai dress, physical mannerisms, and modes of expression.

Because the American is constantly thrusting himself forward while the Thai is continually drawing back, there is a more outward or action-oriented approach to American life as opposed to a more inward or passive-oriented approach in Thailand. The more assertive American individualism seems ideally suited to the realm of action or work yet appears abrasive from the Thai perspective in the area of interpersonal relations. Conversely, the nonassertive Thai individualism leads to more harmony in social relations, but appears to Americans to impede efficiency in the work environment.

To clarify this last point we must introduce the nature of conformity in the two societies. Perhaps because American individualism is more outward and direct, American "selves" can more readily interact when there is a problem to solve or a task to perform. They are more comfortable in expressing themselves openly in this world of action than are the Thais and thus find it easier to cooperate, coordinate, and organize in the work setting. Americans tend to display considerable conformity and group cohesion in this problem/task environment; and their assertiveness here is a virtue, for it leads to efficient, decisive action. Once outside the work situation, however, this sense of conformity breaks down. No longer is it essential that each individual self channel his individualism into a positive result for the group. Each person is, in short, free "to do his own thing." The same assertiveness that was a positive factor in performing a task can now become what Thais would view as a hurdle to smooth social relations. No longer is there a common goal to channel the assertiveness in a constructive manner, and the direct forceful approach—which worked so well in the realm of work—can lead to what Thais might consider unnecessary friction among family members, friends, and acquaintances.

Thai society presents a mirror-image reversal. Whereas American conformity manifests itself in the area of action, Thai conformity is seen most clearly in the realm of passivity—in interpersonal relationships. Here is where a sense of harmony and group-spiritedness leads to an exquisite empathy in which nonassertiveness is definitely a postive factor. For each person *"kreng chai"* (takes the other person's feelings into account) at all times and takes every measure necessary to ensure that the individual one is relating to is physically and psychologically comfortable. Differences of opinion are muted, and one's individuality is constantly subordinated to the desires of the group. Each "self" is conscious of the fact that he must somehow merge into the group identity and thus do nothing in the way of nonconformist dress, assertive physical movements, or overt emotional expression that would call undue attention to himself. Such a system obviously diminishes abrasiveness and contributes to a pleasant, emotionally secure approach to interpersonal relations.

But just as the assertive American individualism appears to Thais to create friction apart from the task/problem setting, so also does the nonassertive Thai individualism seem from the American perspective to cause difficulties outside the area of social relationships. For the empathy and reserve that serve the Thai so well in the social sphere tend to inhibit action in the problem/task environment. The sixth sense that enables Thais to read one another's thoughts and feelings (and consequently make the appropriate response) in the social setting is not readily transferable into the work situation, where new problems and tasks present themselves for solution and action. For in social relations there is always a background, a context, which provides the cues to appropriate behavior for someone who has been culturally conditioned to look for them. But when a fresh problem or task presents itself, there is no cultural cue to appropriate response, no context to draw on to dictate behavior. Unaccustomed to expressing opinions directly and forcefully, individual Thais will not assert themselves in order to come to grips with the question at hand. Rather than risking an unpopular opinion, the Thai will hold back. Harmony will be preserved, but the problem will be left unresolved.

Thais thus tend to be more group-oriented in the area of interpersonal relations and more individualistic in the task/problem context. Mosel notes the "very low emphasis upon formal groups as a means of goal achievement. In getting things done, the Thai naturally thinks in terms of his own self-reliance or in terms of assistance from one or two other well-placed persons, and although he is gregarious, formal, enduring organizations, with carefully defined roles, objectives, and rules seem unnatural to him."[18]

It is in fact difficult to get a satisfactory translation of "to organize" in some situations; several Thai expressions translate as "to organize," but none connotes the clear concept of bringing resources or people together for purposeful achievement that is immediately brought to mind when the American hears this term. Americans, as was pointed out earlier, tend to be more group-oriented in the task area and more individualistic when it comes to interpersonal relations. An added dimension to the differences between the two societies is the general "business" cast that pervades American society as opposed to the "social" cast predominant in Thai life. Americans tend to have job-related talk spill over into the social area; Thais tend to have social talk spill over into the work environment.

Neither the typical Thai nor the average American is aware, of course, of certain advantages and disadvantages inherent in both patterns of behavior. For each accepts his own way—both in the social and the business sphere—as the norm; he sees no real alternative to the pattern which has evolved in his own society. It is only when the two societies are compared that the more efficient American approach to tasks and problems and the more empathic Thai approach to interpersonal relations come into sharper focus. This certainly does not mean that there are no efficient Thais or empathic Americans. It simply highlights a different cultural tendency in the two countries and shows how such terms as "individualistic" and "group-oriented" can be misleading unless they are related to specific areas of behavior within a particular society.

HOW ONE SHOULD ACT

Just as strains of individualism and group-centeredness were noted in the Thai self-concept, so also are there dual tendencies toward self-reliance and dependence when it comes to matters of action. Many studies note a measure of self-reliance among the Thai. Ruth Benedict, for example, sees this self-reliance as first inculcated in the child's learning of motor skills, in which he is thrown on his own responsibility. This attitude is reinforced in later life through the accent on self-responsibility as one of the major tenets of Buddhism.

"The self-reliance inculcated by carrying-habits, by learning to swim and walk under his own steam, as it were, and reinforced in later childhood remains permanently with the Thai, and their selection among Buddhist teachings is that what a person is depends on himself alone. A person's first duty is to meet a situation adequately; to bemoan the existence of the situation itself is weak and foolish, as is also to seek for recognition of one's adequacy from others," according to Benedict.[19]

Another observer concludes that with the exception of his own immediate family, where specific age and sex roles are assigned, and his own village, where traditional patterns are in effect, "the individual Thai travels a relatively uncharted course and is required to find his own way."[20]

Piker maintains that the Thai villager considers the intentions of others essentially unknowable and therefore deliberately refrains from developing specific expectations whenever possible. "Hence he is seldom confounded. As regards patterns of individual behavior, this conviction of relative unpredictability seems to be associated with proclivities for self-reliance and ... with the highly developed ability to cultivate alternatives and shift to them with facility."[21]

Noting that Thais generally join relatively few organizations or associations, relying instead on individual strength and fortitude, Blanchard adds that "among the first things a Thai child learns is that he can depend only on himself and that his duty is to meet every situation adequately."[22]

Ayal sees a parallel between Thai personal values, which he contends require very little in terms of obligation or commitment to other individuals or institutions, and Buddhist teachings regarding the individual's responsibility in working out his own "*karma*" (rebirth according to one's merits). "Thus self-reliance and the avoidance of attachment or involvement of emotional commitment are at the same time an essential part of the Thai value system and of Buddhist ethical teachings."[23]

The Buddhist precept states: "By oneself is evil done. By oneself one suffers. By oneself evil is left undone. By oneself one is purified."[23] One's own thoughts and deeds determine reward or punishment; it is a private affair. In everyday speech this idea is phrased, "Do good, receive good; do evil, receive evil."

Despite these strong undercurrents of self-reliance in the Thai personality, there are countervailing forces at work as well. For the point about the unpredictability of others' behavior mentioned earlier cuts two ways. On the one hand, it can lead to a flexible self-reliance and an ability to shift alternatives quickly. On the other hand, it can lead to a somewhat fatalistic attitude; for if so many aspects of life are elusive, why strain to prepare oneself to meet a will-o'-the-wisp? "Thai peasants seem to show little anxiety about what fate holds for them. . . . (T)hey are quite prepared to tolerate ambiguous fate in a generally uncertain life."[24] Phillips adds that "human volition represents only one of several indeterminate and uncontrollable factors giving rise to events," that if things do not work out as one expects, it is most likely due to the inauspiciousness of the time, place, and persons involved.[25]

An added factor which would tend to diminish self-reliance is the traditional notion of having a patron to turn to for help. Under King Trailok in the 15th Century, there was a shift in the feudal system from a territorial to a personal basis. "Peasants and freemen were no longer attached to the land of their chief; instead, they became clients to their chief, who, now as a government official, acted as the client's patron. Every freeman had to have a patron on whom he could '*phûeng*' (depend) and who received his taxes, produce, and services in the name of the king," according to Mosel.[26]

"While the patron-client system no longer has any legal foundation, it frequently appears in the form of seeking influential persons to '*phûeng*' and it is still expected that one may shift patrons opportunistically when it is profitable to do so," Mosel adds.

Rural development programs based on the concept of "self-help" have had to contend with this entrenched dependency dimension. "To succeed in promoting self-help (Thai Government programs) must reduce the effects of the traditional Thai dependency culture," is the opinion of Herbert and Irene Rubin.[27] Another commentator speaks of the "Thai fondness for dependence on others. While displaying great independence and self-reliance in his dealings with the world at large, he is eager in his personal life to enjoy the protection and generosity of a 'patron,' some distinguished or powerful person to whom he can attach himself."[28]

How then, does one reconcile the strong undercurrents of independence and dependence which seem to pull the Thai personality in two opposing directions? Piker believes that the ambivalence toward dependency postures is rooted in the Thai child's upbringing, in which the first two or three years of life are marked by an almost complete indulgence, especially by the mother. This indulgence of dependency ends suddenly at the age of two or three because of a new pregnancy or economic reasons. Though harsh physical punishment is rare, the child's often aggressive attempts to reassert his lost primacy are to no avail. "The second youngest sibling, then, is plunged into limbo: dependency is effectively ruled out, but no viable or attractive alternative to dependency is made available to the child."[29]

This sudden loss of indulgence does provide ample grounds for concluding that dependency—though immensely satisfying—is also highly unreliable. The strong desire for dependency—virtually complete reliance on a particularistic relationship with an influential patron—must coexist with the realization that such a relationship can be suddenly and unexpectedly uprooted. "These considerations may clear up . . . an apparent paradox with respect to Thai behavior: on the one hand, proclivities for patron-client relationships are conspicuously present, while on the other hand the Thai peasant enjoys a reputation for tenacious individualism and self-reliance."[29]

Piker concludes that neither dependency nor independence strivings enjoy clear-cut priority but that one or the other tendency will assert itself depending on the social situation. "(M)any if not all actors in the Thai social system must be capable of sustaining such diverse social postures as loyalty to superiors and thoroughgoing, self-seeking, dependence upon influential others in critical situations together with independence in formulation and pursuit of goals, moderate religious ascetism . . . as well as pursuit of often hedonistic, mundane purposes."[30]

Pointing out that the personality traits characteristic of any individual Thai need not—and in all likelihood will not—be consistent in terms of content, Piker maintains that the social system makes possible a good deal of shifting from dependent to independent postures. Husbands, for example, may take refuge ("*phûeng*") in their families more or less when they please but can also remove themselves from entangling family obligations (especially economic) with little difficulty.

Stewart looks at the dependent/independent paradox in a slightly different way. The Thai, he believes, may be more dependent within the family unit than the American but more independent once outside that unit. He draws a parallel between the manifestation of dependent and independent behavior on the one hand and the distinction made earlier between conformity and individuality on the other. Just as the Thai might exhibit more conformity than the American within the family unit, so might he also manifest greater dependency within this unit. Conversely, as he asserts his individuality outside the family unit, he would correspondingly engage in more independent behavior apart from this basic group.[31]

Hanks and Phillips see the individual's independence urges played out within the general context of dependence, that indeed the very strivings for independence carry within them the necessity for increased dependence. Driven toward independence in the social expectation of becoming master of his own family, a young Thai male must paradoxically depend on others to provide for him while he attempts to assert this independence. The Thai system of affiliation with a leader or kinsman who grants favors in return for obedient service tends to encourage dependence and postpone urges of independence. It stresses the benevolent aspects of a superior, particularly his kindness to his subordinates.

"The urges for independence are gradually satisfied, in small steps, first as one rules it over one's younger siblings and later as one becomes master of one's own household. . . . Yet every independent position has its counterpart of dependence. Even at the peak of independence both peasant and government official must reckon with other superiors . . . ," Hanks and Phillips note.[32]

They add that the Thai personality may then be understood in terms of a variety of adjustments to a social system "which maximizes dependence and friendly . . . relations while it minimizes the hostile and prematurely independent relationships."

Thais and Americans, then, share a sense of self-reliance; the major distinction would seem to lie in the stronger dependency strain also present in the Thai personality. Thus there probably would be more instances of dependency behavior among Thai than among Americans, although neither would manifest the all-compassing dependency found in some other cultures.

Concrete examples of traces of dependency in Thai conduct would be the following situations. When Thais eat in a restaurant, one person—usually the most senior member of the group in terms of age or status—will "*liang*" (treat) the others. The junior members of the group in a sense "*phûeng*" (depend) on their "patron" in a manner which parallels the traditional benefactor system. The American concept of "Dutch treat" is virtually unknown.

Another Thai custom which illustrates a more dependent approach vis-à-vis the American pattern is the manner of accompanying another person either to a new situation or to a railroad station or airport for a sendoff. For example, if a person has not gone to a particular apartment building or to meet with his program officer before, often he will expect someone to take him there—or at least deeply appreciate it if someone does. This is particularly true of most Thai women, who generally do not like to travel about on their own. As for the sendoff custom (*paj sòng*), friends and coworkers will drop everything to escort a departing acquaintance to the bus, rail, or air terminal.

One final aspect of the more independent American and the more dependent Thai approach can be seen in the way that an American young person will want to establish his independence by moving away from his parents while he is in his late teens or early twenties. Thai children will generally stay with their parents much longer and do not feel the same need to assert their independence by a physical move.

Thus Thais, like Americans, seek a measure of self-reliance or independence, but they also maintain—at least in certain situations—a greater sense of dependence.

RELATING THOUGHT TO ACTION

William James would have felt right at home in Thailand, for as Fred Riggs points out, "The Thai were pragmatists long before the philosophy of pragmatism was invented."[33] When it comes to a distaste for verbose theoreticians, ivory-tower abstractions, and heavy doses of dogma, Thais and Americans are clearly on the same wave length. Both peoples are highly pragmatic, and the Thai—their acute realism rooted in common-sense Buddhism—have perhaps out-pragmatized the nation that gave birth to the philosophy."

"(T)he Thai . . . generally think in concrete and particularistic terms. They are little concerned with general abstractions; they live in the 'here and now' which they try to make as comfortable and free of problems as possible," according to Jean Barry.[33]

Unlike China's Confucian-trained intellectuals who wrestled with the problem of how to reconcile Chinese cultural values with Western materialism and science, "the Thai tend to accept anything which appeals directly to them as having value regardless of whether or not it conflicts with other accepted values. . . . Truth is not perceived in either/or terms, and propositions are judged on the basis of their empirical usefulness."[33]

Julian Wohl and Amnuay Tapingkae, who did a study on the "Values of Thai University Students," found a striking difference between the "relatively practical, realistic manner" of the Thai students and the more metaphysical orientation of a comparable group of Burmese students.[34]

> In contrast to the Burmese students, references to philosophical, moral, or religious concepts are virtually absent. Unlike the Burmese students, (the Thai) do not indulge in vague generalizations about the nature of man, the moral order of the universe, desirable states of mind and being, or moralistic assertions and prescriptions for living. (The Thai) comments with respect to intangible, desirable personal qualities have almost exclusively the family as a concrete reference point from which they seek esteem and love, and for which they wish to be virtuous, honorable and dutiful.

Based on their analysis of the essays the Thai students wrote for the study, Wohl and Amnuay summarized the values of the students "as functional, not esthetic; materialistic, not idealistic; practical, not theoretical; secular, not religious; rational, not romantic."[34]

This realistic, pragmatic pattern is observed in the general Thai distaste for the Buddhist doctrine of mystical contemplation. "The Thai are not mystically inclined, and the elaborate Indian physical techniques of inducing contemplation are absent."[35] Realism tinged with a sober-minded skepticism was noted among Thai university students by a British professor of literature, who gave several examples from examination papers the students turned in to him:

"If the poet always sings the truth, he would have little raw material to produce his work because there are not (many) truths."

"Poetry makes the world, the nature, have more technique (sic) colors than it really has."

"If men study poetry which is too romantic, it may lead to sadness at the end."

The professor concluded, "These wise comments indicate the realism of the Thais, their only mildly regretful acceptance of things-as-they-are. It is not so much a cynical or pessimistic attitude as a Buddhistically modest view of this world of dew, this world of small expectations."[36]

He compared this strong disinclination for flights of fancy with the "ingenious profundity evinced by Japanese students of literature, whose respect for poetry is so immense that it sometimes leads them to ignore the poem. . . . Thai and Singaporean students are alike in their fondness for 'coming down to earth'—and bringing literature with them. Japanese and Indians prefer to soar aloft in the vast inane."[36]

This coming down to earth is clearly illustrated in Thai proverbs on veracity, such as, "What people say, divide by five," and "Ten mouthfuls are not so good as an eyeful (i.e., ten people may lie or exaggerate; it's better to see for yourself)."[37]

Content to look for small pleasures, the Thai generally do not have the strong drive for learning typical of, among others, the Japanese and Chinese. "There is, however, a prestige associated with study in Europe or the United States; and then, travel is pleasurable. . . . (M)any Thai are not so much interested in going abroad for the love of learning, but rather in order to visit some well known American or British institution," according to Embree.[38]

Though this practical, modest approach is not superficially inspiring, it seemed wise-beyond-its-words to the aforementioned literature professor. "There are not many truths in the world, and the Thai is in happy but not arrogant possession of the most important of them," he said.[36]

Not surprisingly, the Thai have not been great ideologues in matters political, mirroring once again the pragmatic American pattern, which has driven political scientists to distraction trying to come up with more than a dime's worth of ideological difference between the Republicans and Democrats. "Ideology has played a very minor role in Thai politics, and the electorate has typically been apathetic," notes Mosel.[39]

It is to the Thai brand of Buddhism that one must turn, however, to gain a deeper grasp of the fundamental roots of Thai pragmatism. Buddha is said initially to have laid down for his disciples a set of regulations and rules of conduct (*vinaya*), a modification of which is adhered to by monks today. Significantly, these rules are considered lofty by secular standards, and the layman is thus bound only by five basic precepts: (1) Do not kill any living creature; (2) do not steal; (3) do not act unchastely; (4) do not lie; and (5) do not drink intoxicating beverages.

Strict adherence to even these five precepts is not demanded, and Thais seem to tolerate an often wide discrepancy between religious values and social behavior. "We suggest that this is not the consequence of some innate Thai moral or intellectual fault but the practical consequence of a social order in which the vast majority cannot afford the luxury of hoeing to a firm, orthodox, religious line as fervently as can the society's few well-positioned and economically secure," contends Norman Jacobs.[40]

The average Thai is not nonreligious, in fact quite the contrary, but he does live in a social order which makes important nonreligious demands which cannot be avoided; in responding to these demands, he picks and chooses what he can accept religiously as against what he must accept nonreligiously, according to Jacobs. "This ability to choose is facilitated by a religious system which postulates no absolute dogma, makes no absolute demands on him, and hence, in turn, engenders no religious discomfort (guilt) when he does not conform."

Take, for example, the killing of animals, which clearly runs afoul of the first precept. Yet the Thai remain a nation of fishermen, eating fish daily; and they do not forego meat when they can afford it. Thus interesting rationalizations have developed to satisfy both religious belief and physical hunger. "(F)ish die because they are out of the water, not because someone took them out of the water and killed them; once dead, they should not go to waste." Concerning the eating of meat, legalistically a Thai Buddhist could search out a non-Buddhist to kill for him. Or if this would still cause him discomfort since he was the one responsible for the killing, he could send instead for an animal or fowl which was already dead; thus no guilt would attach to him. A more general justification is that if an individual kills, it is for food or protection (clubbing rats and snakes, for example) in order to preserve a higher form of life, man. "(The Thai) will not take life willfully and to no purpose, (but) if an individual feels he has to kill, he will kill and not worry about it afterwards."[40]

Likewise the Buddhist precept against intoxicants is not observed by many. "A merry party, a wedding, a festive day, is hardly considered to have been properly celebrated unless there has been a large amount of beer, wine, and whiskey consumed. ... This is not to say that drunkenness is a social problem in Thailand; it is relatively minor. But no tabu against the use of intoxicants is generally observed."[35]

Though certainly more strict than the layman, even the monk believes he must be practical when the situation warrants. "Although forbidden to him, he will eat meat if it is offered in his bowl; he rationalizes that he must eat what is placed there, even if it be the legendary leper's thumb.

If for any reason a monk cannot eat his second meal before noon, he will not necessarily miss it. He can have his assistant tell him that the time is not yet noon."[40]

Jacobs quickly adds, however, that such practices do not imply religious indifference or religious cynicism. "Rather the Thais are merely responding to accepted, alternative, religiously sanctioned norms in a religious system which permits selective conformity to ritual and doctrine."[40] Such selective conformity finds sanction in the ideal of the middle way between extreme conformity and extreme laxity which the Buddha himself preached and by the doctrine that knowledge must be used for experience and that experience must be realistic. Further justification is found in the Kalama Sutra, which argues that those rules which impede the successful adaptation of the religion's veritable truths to the contemporary social situation can and should be discarded.[40]

Despite such general doctrinal principles as karma, merit, and nirvana, there are no absolute, clearly defined, doctrinaire roots in the Thai (Buddhist) religious-value system or in diffused religious form in the Thai social-value system, according to Jacobs.[40] Since Buddhism neither confirms nor denies any abstract, absolute dogma, it may be characterized as a religion of ethical relativity.

> In the Thai version of Buddhism, in particular, actions are judged virtuous or not in terms of their specific consequences in specific situations, subject to review against a standard of only a few broad principles (including) whether or not actions will cause trouble to others, encourage social conflict, and destroy social harmony.... Certainly there is nothing in this... system which would force Thais to consider taking an absolute Lutheran, irreversible stand, "come what may," sacrificing practical interests to some abstract value "no matter what...."

The practical, pleasure-seeking Thais even have some reservations when it comes to the ultimate Buddhist ideal of nirvana, just as many Christians have found it easier to identify with a materially comfortable limbo than an ethereal heaven. A story is told of the Thai boy who hoped that he would not accumulate too much merit; he did not want to take a chance of achieving bodiless existence (nirvana). "The average (Thai) layman ... trusts that he will always have enough merit to avoid the more painful hells, and to escape the inclusion in his career of the life of a draught-ox or other long-suffering beast, and he hopes either for rebirth as a man in a better worldly condition than the present or for a few million years of rest among the pleasures of one of the Lower Heavens."[41] This attitude is confirmed by a second observer, who points out that "in most cases (the Thai) makes merit in the hope not of attaining nirvana but of re-entering the world of humans on terms more favorable to himself."[42]

If this sounds somewhat akin to the American's notion of "enlightened self-interest," it should not be surprising; for both peoples—bridging a gap of considerable cultural and geographical distance—can find a common ground of understanding in the philosophy of pragmatism.

NOTES

1. Embree, "Thailand—A Loosely Structured Social System," *American Anthropologist,* 52:181-193 (1950).

2. Mulder, in Evers (ed.), *Loosely-Structured Social Systems: Thailand in Comparative Perspective,* p. 20, Yale University, 1969.

3. In Evers (ed.), *Loosely-Structured Social Systems: Thailand in Comparative Perspective,* p. 21, Yale University, 1969.

4. Kirsch, in Evers (ed.), *Loosely-Structured Social Systems: Thailand in Comparative Perspective,* p. 46, Yale University, 1969.

5. Phillips, in Evers (ed.), *Loosely-Structured Social Systems: Thailand in Comparative Perspective,* p. 30, Yale University, 1969.

6. Benedict, "Thai Culture and Behavior," Cornell University Data Paper, 4, p. 30, 1943.

7. Piker, "Relationship of Belief System to Behavior in Rural Thai Society," *Asian Survey,* 8:384 (1968).

8. Hanks and Phillips, "A Young Thai from the Countryside," in Kaplan (ed.), *Studying Personality Cross-Culturally,* pp. 655-656, Harper & Row, 1961.

9. Blanchard (ed.), *Area Handbook for Thailand,* p. 218, Human Relations Area Files, 1957.

10. Embree, "Thailand—A Loosely Structured Social System," *American Anthropologist,* 52:183 (1950).

11. Pramoj, *Myang Maya,* p. 326, Kawnaa Publisher, 1965.

12. Barry, "Thai Students in the U.S.: A Study in Attitude Change," Cornell University Data Paper 66, p. 78, 1967.

13. Smith, "Thai Family—Nuclear or Extended," *Journal of Marriage,* 35:136 (1973).

14. Blanchard (ed.), *Area Handbook for Thailand,* p. 172, Human Relations Area Files, 1957.

15. Blanchard (ed.), *Area Handbook for Thailand,* p. 27, Human Relations Area Files, 1957.

16. Stewart, "American Cultural Patterns: A Cross-Cultural Perspective," p. 69, Regional Council for International Education, 1971.

17. Tapingkae, "The Buddhist Theories of the Learner and of the Teacher," in Tapingkae (ed.), *Education in Thailand—Some Thai Perspectives,* p. 10, U.S. Department of Health, Education, and Welfare, 1973.

18. Mosel, "Thai Administrative Behavior," in Siffin (ed.), *Toward the Comparative Study of Public Administration,* p. 301, Indiana University, 1957.

19. Benedict, "Thai Culture and Behavior," Cornell University Data Paper 4, p. 27, 1943.

20. Blanchard (ed.), *Area Handbook for Thailand,* p. 217, Human Relations Area Files, 1957.

21. Piker, in Evers (ed.), *Loosely-Structured Social Systems: Thailand in Comparative Perspective,* p. 69, Yale University, 1969.

22. Barry, "Thai Students in the U.S.: A Study in Attitude Change," Cornell University Data Paper 66, p. 78, 1967.

23. Ayal, "Value Systems and Economic Development in Japan and Thailand," *Journal of Social Issues,* 19:35, 46 (1963).

24. Ingersoll, "Fatalism in Rural Thailand," *Anthropological Quarterly,* 39:205 (1966).

25. Phillips, "Fatalism in Rural Thailand," *Anthropological Quarterly,* 39:205 (1966).

26. Mosel, "Thai Administrative Behavior," in Siffin (ed.), *Toward the Comparative Study of Public Administration,* p. 287, Indiana University, 1957.

27. Rubin, "Effects of Institutional Change upon a Dependency Culture—Commune Council 275 in Rural Thailand," *Asian Survey,* 13:270 (1973).

28. Blanchard (ed.), *Area Handbook for Thailand,* p. 28, Human Relations Area Files, 1957.

29. Piker, in Evers (ed.), *Loosely-Structured Social Systems: Thailand in Comparative Perspective,* p. 394, Yale University, 1969.

30. Piker, in Evers (ed.), *Loosely-Structured Social Systems: Thailand in Comparative Perspective,* p. 72, Yale University, 1969.

31. Stewart, conversation with author.

32. Hanks and Phillips, "A Young Thai from the Countryside," in Kaplan (ed.), *Studying Personality Cross-Culturally,* p. 654, Harper & Row, 1961.

33. Barry, "Thai Students in the U.S.: A Study in Attitude Change," Cornell University Data Paper 66, p. 121, 1967.

34. Wohl and Tapingkae, "Values of Thai University Students," *International Journal of Psychology,* 7:23 (1972).

35. Benedict, "Thai Culture and Behavior," Cornell University Data Paper 4, p. 35, 1943.

36. Enright, "Thai Personalities," *Encounter,* 32:27 (1969).

37. Benedict, "Thai Culture and Behavior," Cornell University Data Paper 4, p. 35, 1943.

38. Embree, "Thailand—A Loosely Structured Social System," *American Anthropologist,* 52:181 (1950).

39. Mosel, "Thai Administrative Behavior," in Siffin (ed.), *Toward the Comparative Study of Public Administration,* p. 311, Indiana University, 1957.

40. Jacobs, *Modernization without Development—Thailand as an Asian Case Study,* p. 276, Praeger, 1971.

41. Benedit, "Thai Culture and Behavior," Cornell University Data Paper 4, p. 34, 1943.

42. Piker, "Relationship of Belief Systems to Behavior in Rural Thai Society," *Asian Survey,* 8:384 (1968).

CULTURE SHOCK AND THE PROBLEM OF ADJUSTMENT IN NEW CULTURAL ENVIRONMENTS

Kalvero Oberg

Reprinted from *Readings in Intercultural Communication,* vol. II, 1972, David S. Hoopes, ed., Society for Intercultural Education, Training and Research, Washington, D.C.

Culture shock might be called an occupational disease of people who have been suddenly transplanted abroad. Like most ailments, it has its own symptoms and cure.

Culture shock is precipitated by the anxiety that results from losing all our familiar signs and symbols of social intercourse. Those signs or cues include the thousand and one ways in which we orient ourselves to the situation of daily life: when to shake hands and what to say when we meet people, when and how to give tips, how to make purchases, when to accept and when to refuse invitations, when to take statements seriously and when not. These cues, which may be words, gestures, facial expressions, customs, or norms, are acquired by all of us in the course of growing up and are as much a part of our culture as the language we speak or the beliefs we accept. All of us depend for our peace of mind and our efficiency on hundreds of these cues, most of which we do not carry on the level of conscious awareness.

Now when an individual enters a strange culture, all or most of these familiar cues are removed. He or she is like a fish out of water. No matter how broad-minded or full of good will you may be, a series of props have been knocked from under you, followed by a feeling of frustration and anxiety. People react to the frustration in much the same way. First they reject the environment which causes the discomfort. "The ways of the host country are bad because they make us feel bad." When foreigners in a strange land get together to grouse about the host country and its people, you can be sure they are suffering from culture shock. Another phase of culture shock is regression. The home environment suddenly assumes a tremendous importance. To the foreigner everything becomes irrationally glorified. All the difficulties and problems are forgotten and only the good things back home are remembered. It usually takes a trip home to bring one back to reality.

Some of the symptoms of culture shock are excessive washing of the hands, excessive concern over drinking water, food dishes, and bedding; fear of physical contact with attendants, the absent-minded stare; a feeling of helplessness and a desire for dependence on long-term residents of one's own nationality; fits of anger over minor frustrations; great concern over minor pains and eruptions of the skin; and finally, that terrible longing to be back home.

Individuals differ greatly in the degree in which culture shock affects them. Although not common, there are individuals who cannot live in foreign countries. However, those who have seen people go through culture shock and on to a satisfactory adjustment can discern steps in the process. During the first few weeks most individuals are fascinated by the new. They stay in hotels and associate with nationals who speak their language and are polite and gracious to foreigners. This honeymoon stage may last from a few days or weeks to six months, depending on circumstances. If one is very important, he or she will be shown the show places, will be pampered and petted, and in a press interview will speak glowingly about goodwill and international friendship.

But this mentality does not normally last if the foreign visitor remains abroad and has seriously to cope with real conditions of life. It is then that the second stage begins, characterized by a hostile and aggressive attitude toward the host country. This hostility evidently grows out of the genuine difficulty which the visitor experiences in the process of adjustment. There are house troubles, transportation troubles, shopping troubles, and the fact that people in the host country are largely indifferent to all these troubles. They help, but they don't understand your great concern over these difficulties. Therefore, they must be insensitive and unsympathetic to you and your worries. The result, "I just don't like them." You become aggressive, you band together with your fellow countrymen and criticize the host country, its ways, and its people. But this criticism is not an objective appraisal. Instead of trying to account for the conditions and the historical circumstances which have created them, you talk as if the difficulties you experience are more or less created by the people of the host country for your special discomfort.

You take refuge in the colony of your countrymen which often becomes the fountainhead of emotionally charged labels known as stereotypes. This is a peculiar kind of offensive shorthand which caricatures the host country and its people in a negative manner. The "dollar grasping American" and the "indolent Latin Americans" are samples of mild forms of stereotypes. The second stage of culture shock is in a sense a crisis in the disease. If you come out of it, you stay; if not, you leave before you reach the stage of a nervous breakdown.

If the visitor succeeds in getting some knowledge of the language and begins to get around by himself, he is beginning to open the way into the new cultural environment. The visitor still has difficulties but he takes a "this is my problem and I have to bear it" attitude. Usually in this stage the visitor takes a superior attitude to people of the host country. His sense of humor begins to exert itself. Instead of criticizing, he jokes about the people and even cracks jokes about his or her own difficulties. He or she is now on the way to recovery.

In the fourth stage, your adjustment is about as complete as it can be. The visitor now accepts the customs of the country as just another way of living. You operate within the new surroundings without a feeling of anxiety, although there are moments of social strain. Only with a complete grasp of all the cues of social intercourse will this strain disappear. For a long time the individual will understand what the national is saying but he is not always sure what the national means. With a complete adjustment you not only accept the food, drinks, habits, and customs, but actually begin to enjoy them. When you go home on leave, you may even take things back with you; and if you leave for good, you generally miss the country and the people to whom you became accustomed.

CROSS-CULTURAL AWARENESS

Robert G. Hanvey

From Robert G. Hanvey, *An Attainable Global Perspective*, 1976. Reprinted with permission of the author and the publisher, Center for Global Perspectives, New York (218 East 18th St., New York 10003).

Cross-cultural awareness may be one of the more difficult dimensions to attain. It is one thing to have some knowledge of world conditions. The air is saturated with that kind of information. It is another thing to comprehend and accept the consequences of the basic human capacity for creating unique cultures—with the resultant profound differences in outlook and practice manifested among societies. These differences are widely known at the level of myth, prejudice, and tourist impression. But they are not deeply and truly known—in spite of the well-worn exhortation to "understand others." Such a fundamental acceptance seems to be resisted by powerful forces in the human psychosocial system. Attainment of cross-cultural awareness and empathy at a significant level will require methods that circumvent or otherwise counter those resisting forces. Let us think afresh about what such methods might be, with a full recognition of how difficult the task will be and a corresponding willingness to discard ideas that don't work.

DOES UNDERSTANDING FOLLOW CONTACT

One of the cherished ideas of our own times and of earlier times is that contact between societies leads to understanding. The durability of this notion is awesome considering the thousands of years of documented evidence to the contrary. Consider the following example. When the

French began to explore North America they came into contact with a number of aboriginal groups. At various times they attempted to muster the males of these groups into fighting units. The Indians clearly had no aversion to fighting; they were warriors, skilled in the use of arms, proud of triumphs over an enemy. But they would not take orders. French commanders had no control and the so-called chiefs of these groups depended on persuasion, which might or might not be successful. Every individual Indian warrior made his own decisions about whether to join a raid or war party, worked out his own battle strategy, and left the fray when he chose.

This kind of contact between the French and the Indians provided the French with detailed information on the ways of their Indian allies—information they noted scornfully in their journals, sometimes sputtering in rage and frustration. But the behavior they described was incomprehensible to them. By virtue of the concrete experiences that the French had with the Indians, the French had rich data—but no understanding. The French were able to see Indian behavior only in the light of their own hierarchical social system, where it is natural for the few to command and the many to obey. Social systems that worked on other principles were literally unimaginable.

Of course, now we are more sophisticated. What happens when the nature of the contact between groups is not one of exploitation or domination but rather one of sympathetic assistance, and where there is at least some preparation for the cultural differences that will be encountered? Here is an account of Peace Corps experience in the Philippines:

> Most human relationships in the world are governed by a pervasive fatalism, in the Philippines best described by the Tagalog phrase, *bahala na,* which means, "never mind" or, "it will be all right" or, "it makes no difference." Americans, more than any other people in history, believe man can control his environment, can shape the forces of nature to change his destiny. That peculiarity, which is essentially Western, is quintessentially American.
>
> Most of the peoples of the world also value dependency and harmony relationships within the in-group. Rather than stress independence in relationships—freedom from restraint and freedom to make choices—they emphasize reciprocity of obligation and good will within the basic group and protection of that group against outsiders. It is the group—family, tribe or clan—which matters and not the individual. In the Philippines, this phenomenon is perhaps best described by the term *utang na loob* which means a reciprocal sense of gratitude and obligation.
>
> The value of independence in relationships and getting a job done makes us seem self-reliant, frank, empirical, hardworking, and efficient to ourselves. To Filipinos, the same behavior sometimes makes us seem to be unaware of

our obligations, insensitive to feelings, unwilling to accept established practices, and downright aggressive. . . .

Nearly all volunteers had to struggle to understand and deal with Filipino behavior that, when seen from our peculiar stress on independence in relationships as opposed to Filipino *utang na loob,* was deeply distressing. . . . Filipinos wanted to be dependent on others and have others dependent on them; they were often ashamed in the presence of strangers and authority figures; they were afraid of being alone or leaving their families and communities; they showed extreme deference to superiors and expected the same from subordinates; they veiled true feelings and opinions in order not to hurt others or be hurt by them. . . .

It is one thing to study and understand *utang na loob.* It is another to have a principal treat you as a status figure and to insist that you tell him how to run his school, or to have children in your class cower in what seems to be shame, or to have neighbors who care much more that you should like them and that you should have a pleasurable experience than that you should get your job done.

Filipinos, with their incessant hospitality and curiosity, repeatedly made it plain that for them the main job of Peace Corps volunteers was to enjoy themselves and to enhance pleasure for those around them, an approach to life best described by the Filipino phrase, *pakikisama.* . . . Nothing was more difficult for volunteers to understand or accept than that Filipinos wanted them for pleasure in relationships and not to achieve the tasks to which they had been assigned. . . .

It was not just the Filipino's stress on *utang na loob* and *pakikisama* which interfered with getting the job done. It was also *bahala na,* the widespread fatalism of the barrio which showed itself in the lack of emotion at the death of little children, the persistent and nearly universal beliefs that ghosts and spirits control life and death, and the failure of Filipinos to keep promises and appointments. Why should the job matter when fate governs human existence? . . .

During the first two years, four volunteers resigned and twenty-six others were sent home, usually by mutual agreement, because they were not able or willing to cope with the extraordinary psychological burdens of being Peace Corps volunteers. Some volunteers developed a "what's the use" attitude and failed to appear at school, or made short unauthorized trips away from their barrios. Withdrawal was sometimes followed in the same volunteer by extremely hostile behavior against the Philippine Bureau of Public Schools, Washington, and the Peace Corps staff. Some volunteers, particularly those in the first group, wished there was some honorable way for them to cut short their tour of duty without an overwhelming sense of personal failure.[1]

The American Peace Corps volunteers, like the French officers of the 17th Century, could not escape the powerful influence of their own culture, especially since that culture was so deeply embedded in the very definition of the mission. The task was to render assistance. And success was measured by some kind of closure, "getting the job done." Filipino behavior stood in the way of getting the job done. There were distractions, delays, and detours. And the positive reinforcements that a busy, efficient American would have received in his home setting were nowhere to be found. The result: puzzlement and frustration equivalent to that of the French in their relations with Indian groups.

ACHIEVING UNDERSTANDING

But some volunteers did solve the cultural puzzle.

> A male volunteer from South Carolina, D was as much admired by Filipinos and volunteers as any volunteer in the project. Almost from the first, he accepted people for what they were, learned the dialect, made friends, and seemed to enjoy that more than anything else. After two years, he wrote, "I consistently believed and followed a life based on getting away from all identity or entanglement with the Peace Corps. My reasons were . . . to figure out a little bit about what was going on in the Philippines, to see what was really significant in my own place, to try to understand life here, and to learn to function in a way that could be meaningful to me and the community. I burrowed into life here unmindful of anything but my community and involvement and survival. . . ."
>
> Although everyone had thought that he epitomized the ability of a volunteer to live deeply in the culture after just six months, he wrote toward the end of his third year, "I have continued to change here and have now sort of reached a point of being able to feel with others. This is different from understanding how they feel. I am able to be a part of them as they do things with each other and me . . . " (Fuchs, p. 253).

D was a success in both Filipino and Peace Corps terms. So was another volunteer.

> A male volunteer from Massachusetts ran what appears to have been highly successful in-service training classes on English and science for teachers. He also had effective adult education classes and a successful piggery-poultry project. He seemed to blend into his community almost from the beginning, becoming one of the first volunteers to learn the dialect from his region and use it extensively. He enjoyed serenading at night with the gang from the *sari-sari* store and drank tuba with the older men who, as he put it "had the pleasure of learning they could drink the American under the proverbial table" (Fuchs, p. 250).

These two cases teach us some useful things. Both volunteers genuinely joined their communities. They learned the language, sought to "burrow in." Most importantly, they accepted the Filipinos on their own terms and made friends with them, presumably long before their own understanding of the local culture had developed. D wrote, "The people are different, but willing to take me in. . . ." Somehow or other, the Filipino traits that so frustrated other volunteers were not an obstacle to these two. Instead, these two accepted not only the worth of the Filipinos but the worth of their ways, enough to practice them joyfully. And out of that long practice came D's remarkable statement that he was now able to feel *with* others.

Did the two volunteers "go native"? In a sense. Perhaps the most important respect in which this is true lies in the acceptance of the worth and authority of the local community's standards of conduct. These volunteers *participated* in Filipino life. That participation was reinforced in two ways. First, it must have been intrinsically enjoyable to these particular young men. It was satisfying to drink tuba with the local males. Second, that participation must have won social approval from the Filipinos *and that approval must have mattered* to these volunteers. Conceivably the approval of Peace Corps staff became less important (remember that D chose to shake off "entanglement" with the Peace Corps) as the approval of the local community became more important.

The sequence of events seem to go like this:

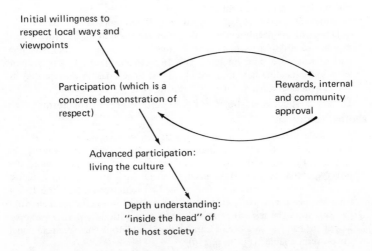

Initial willingness to respect local ways and viewpoints

Participation (which is a concrete demonstration of respect)

Rewards, internal and community approval

Advanced participation: living the culture

Depth understanding: "inside the head" of the host society

It is worth noting that it was only after three years of intense, 24-hour-a-day experience that D felt that he was inside the Filipino head, seeing and feeling in Filipino ways. This, of course, should be no surprise, especially to Americans with their centuries of experience in the difficulties of immigrant assimilation. Stories of immigrants are replete with the difficulties of adjustment, the persistence of old-country ways and attitudes, the stress between parents and the children born in the new country. Many immigrants never made the cultural shift emotionally, even after decades of living in the new setting. But many did.

RESPECT AND PARTICIPATION—MISSING ELEMENTS

What the Peace Corps examples—and the American immigrant experience—show us is that it is not easy to attain cross-cultural awareness or
understanding of the kind that puts you into the head of a person from
an utterly different culture. Contact alone will not do it. Even sustained
contact will not do it. There must be a readiness to respect and accept,
and a capacity to participate. The participation must be reinforced by
rewards that matter to the participant. And the participation must be
sustained over long periods of time. Finally, one may assume that some
plasticity in the individual, the ability to learn and change, is crucial. In
general, the young will be more flexible and able to achieve this.

This kind of cross-cultural awareness is not reached by tourists nor, in
the days of empire, was it reached by colonial administrators or
missionaries, however long their service on foreign soil. In American
schools, despite integration and black and Chicano study programs,
whites do not achieve such an awareness of minority world-views. The
missing elements are respect and participation. The society offers limited
gratifications for reinforcement of respect for minorities—and very
limited penalties for disrespect. And it offers absolutely no rewards to
those of the white majority who might seek to participate in minority
behavior patterns. The situation for the minority groups is somewhat
different; there are social rewards for participating in the majority
culture and many individuals shuttle more or less successfully between
the two worlds or work out some kind of synthesis.

OPTIONS

If cross-cultural awareness of a profound sort is extremely difficult to
attain, what are the options? Are there lesser varieties of awareness that
might nonetheless be said to contribute to a global perspective? Are there
better methods than have typically been employed to reach awareness? Is
the goal itself worthwhile; i.e., does cross-cultural awareness matter?

Let me talk to that last question first. Yes, cross-cultural awareness
does matter, for the following major reason if for no other. Several
million years of evolution seem to have produced in us a creature that
does not easily recognize the members of its own species. That is stated
in rather exaggerated form, but it refers to the fact that human groups
commonly have difficulty in accepting the humanness of other human
groups.

> we call a group of primitives in northern North America Eskimos; this name,
> originated by certain Indians to the south of the Eskimos, means "Eaters of
> Raw Flesh." However, the Eskimos' own name for themselves is not Eskimos

but in Inupik, meaning "Real People." By their name they provide a contrast between themselves and other groups; the latter might be "people" but are never "real."[2]

This practice of naming one's own group "the people" and by implication relegating all others to not-quite-human status has been documented in nonliterate groups all over the world. But it is simply one manifestation of a species trait that shows itself in modern populations as well. It is there in the hostile faces of the white parents demonstrating against school busing. You will find it lurking in the background as Russians and Chinese meet at the negotiating table to work out what is ostensibly a boundary dispute. And it flares into the open during tribal disputes in Kenya.

It must, once, have been an adaptive trait. Perhaps, in ways that we now tend to deprecate, it still is. We call it chauvinism rather than self-esteem. Clearly, there are positive effects associated with a strong sense of group identity. Loyalty is a virtue everywhere, disloyalty abhorred everywhere. The inner harmony of groups is strengthened if aggression can be displaced, diverted to external targets. And if aggression is to be justified, then it helps if the enemy is not quite human. It helps even more if the enemy can be shown to be engaging in practices that are so outrageously different from one's own that they can be credibly labeled inhuman.

There was a time when the solidarity of small groups of humans was the basis for the survival of the species. But in the context of mass populations and weapons of mass destructiveness, group solidarity and the associated tendency to deny the full humaneness of other peoples pose serious threats to the species. When we speak of "humans" it is important that we include not only ourselves and our immediate group but all four billion of those other bipeds, however strange their ways.

This is the primary reason for cross-cultural awareness. If we are to admit the humanness of those others, then the strangeness of their ways must become less strange. Must, in fact, become believable. Ideally, that means getting inside the head of those strangers and looking out at the world through their eyes. Then the strange becomes familiar and totally believable. As we have seen, that is a difficult trick to pull off. But there may be methods that will increase the probability of success. Further, there are lesser degrees of cross-cultural awareness than getting inside the head; these more modest degrees of awareness are not to be scorned.

LEVELS OF CROSS-CULTURAL AWARENESS

We might discriminate between four levels of cross-cultural awareness as follows:

Level	Information	Mode	Interpretation
I	Awareness of superficial or very visible cultural traits: stereotypes	Tourism, textbooks, National Geographic	Unbelievable, i.e., exotic, bizarre
II	Awareness of significant and subtle cultural traits that contrast markedly with one's own	Culture conflict situations	Unbelievable, i.e., frustrating, irrational
III	Awareness of significant and subtle cultural traits that contrast markedly with one's own	Intellectual analysis	Believable, cognitively
IV	Awareness of how another culture feels from the standpoint of the insider	Cultural immersion: living the culture	Believable because of subjective familiarity

At level I, a person might know that Japanese were exaggerated in their politeness and gestures of deference. At level II are those who know, through either direct or secondhand experience, of cultural traits that significantly (and irritatingly) contrast with one's own practices. The French in their relations with some Indian tribes and the Peace Corps volunteers who failed to adjust might be at this level. So, too, might those who despair over the seeming inability of many developing countries to control population growth. At level III are those who might know, for example, that the really distinctive aspect of the Japanese social hierarchy has nothing to do with the forms of politeness but rather exists in the keen sense of mutual obligation between superior and inferior. The level III person accepts this cultural trait intellectually; it makes sense to him. Peace Corps volunteers might have had this kind of intellectual understanding before actual contact with host cultures. After that contact, some of them slipped to level II and some moved to level IV.

According to this scheme, "believability" is achieved only at levels III and IV. And I have argued that believability is necessary if one group of humans is to accept other members of the biological species as human. I have also noted the rigors of the climb to level IV. This seems to leave level III as the practical goal. But is level III enough?

My position is that level III is indeed more attainable than level IV, and it is a reasonably worthy goal. But not quite enough. We should try to attain at least some aspects of level IV awareness. We can. There are new methods to be explored. And there is a more general reason for encouragement. The evolutionary experience that seemed to freeze us into a small-group psychology, anxious and suspicious of those who were not "us," also made us the most adaptive creature alive. That flexibility, the power to make vast psychic shifts, is very much with us. One of its manifestations is the modern capacity for empathy.

BEYOND EMPATHY

Daniel Lerner in *The Passing of Traditional Society* writes:

> Empathy . . . is the capacity to see oneself in the other fellow's situation. This is an indispensable skill for people moving out of traditional settings. Ability to empathize may make all the difference, for example, when the newly mobile persons are villagers who grew up knowing all the extant individuals, roles and relationships in their environment. Outside his village or tribe, each must meet new individuals, recognize new roles, and learn new relationships involving himself. . . .
>
> High empathic capacity is the predominant personal style only in modern society, which is distinctively industrial, urban, literate and participant. Traditional society is nonparticipant—it deploys people by kinship into communities isolated from each other and from a center. . . .
>
> Whereas the isolate communities of traditional society functioned well on the basis of a highly constrictive personality, the interdependent sectors of modern society require widespread participation. This in turn requires an expansive and adaptive self-system, ready to incorporate new roles and to identify personal values with public issues. This is why modernization of any society has involved the great characterological transformation we call psychic mobility. . . . In modern society *more* individuals exhibit *higher* empathic capacity than in any previous society.[3]

If Lerner is correct, modern populations have a dramatically different outlook, a dramatically different readiness for change, than traditional populations. That difference must have been learned—and by millions of people. If the latent capacity for empathy can be learned or activated, then it may not be too much to work toward a psychic condition that reaches a step beyond empathy. Magoroh Maruyama, an anthropologist-philosopher, describes that next step as *transspection*.

> Transspection is an effort to put oneself in the head . . . of another person. One tries to believe what the other person believes, and assume what the other person assumes. . . ." Transspection differs from analytical "understanding." Empathy is a projection of feelings between two persons with one epistemology. Transspection is a trans-epistemological process which tries to learn a foreign belief, a foreign assumption, a foreign perspective, feelings in a foreign context, and consequences of such feelings in a foreign context. In transspection a person temporarily believes whatever the other person believes. It is an understanding by practice.[4]

Empathy, then, means the capacity to imagine oneself in another role within the context of one's own culture. Transspection means the capacity to imagine pupils in a role within the context of a foreign culture. Putting Lerner and Maruyama together, we might chart the psychic development of humanity as follows:

Traditional peoples	Unable to imagine a viewpoint other than that associated with fixed roles in the context of a local culture.
Modern peoples	Able to imagine and learn a variety of roles in the context of a national culture.
Postmodern peoples	Able to imagine the viewpoint of roles in foreign cultures.

Or, we might show the sequence of development in a more graphic way, as involving a movement from the constrictions of local perspectives through the expanded psychological flexibility necessary for role learning in large, heterogeneous national societies, to the advanced versatility of "global psyches" that travel comfortably beyond the confines of the home culture. (The gray zone is home culture.)

The modern personality type did not develop because it was planned. It emerged in the context of changing social conditions. The postmodern personality type, similarly, is not likely to be produced by educational strategies. But if there is a broad social movement, an essentially unplanned intensification of human interaction on the world stage, then educators and other interested parties can play their minor but nonetheless useful roles in the unfolding drama. For educators, that will mean providing students with maximum experience in transspection. And maximum experience means more than time. It means a climate in which transspection is facilitated and expected—and in which the expectations are reinforced. Under such circumstances the schools might produce a slightly higher proportion of persons with the kind of psychic mobility displayed by D, the Peace Corps worker who could feel *with* others. That would be a gain.

If more and more individuals reach the vantage point of level IV awareness, there will be another kind of gain. Dispelling the strangeness of the foreign and admitting the humanness of all human creatures is vitally important. But looking at ourselves from outside our own culture is a possibility for those who can also see through the eyes of the foreigner—and that has significance for the *perspective consciousness* discussed earlier. Native social analysts can probe the deep layers of their own culture, but the outside eye has a special sharpness: if the native for even a moment can achieve the vision of the foreigner, he will be rewarded with a degree of self-knowledge not otherwise obtainable.

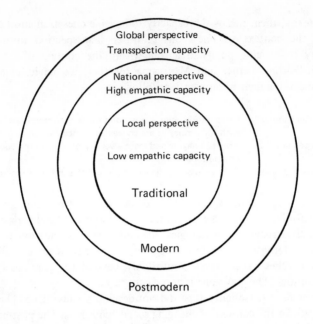

Global perspective
Transspection capacity

National perspective
High empathic capacity

Local perspective

Low empathic capacity

Traditional

Modern

Postmodern

NOTES

1. Lawrence H. Fuchs, "The Role and Communication Task of the Change Agent—Experiences of the Peace Corps in the Philippines," in Daniel Lerner and Wilbur Schramm (eds.), *Communication and Change in the Developing Countries,* pp. 242-245, East-West Center Press, Honolulu, 1967.

2. Wendell H. Oswalt, *Understanding Our Culture,* p. 19, Holt, Rinehart and Winston, Inc., 1970.

3. Daniel Lerner, *The Passing of Traditional Society,* pp. 50, 51, Free Press, 1958.

4. Magoroh Maruyama, "Toward a Cultural Futurology," Cultural Futurology Symposium, American Anthropology Association national meeting, Training Center for Community Programs, University of Minnesota, 1970.

COMMUNICATION OVERSEAS

Lorand B. Szalay and *Glen H. Fisher*

Reprinted by permission of Lorand B. Szalay, Institute of Comparative Social and Cultural Studies, and Glen H. Fisher, Foreign Service Institute. This material has been reproduced for instruction purposes at the Foreign Service Institute, Department of State. The graphic material has been provided by the Institute of Comparative Social and Cultural Studies, Inc., 4430 East West Highway, Suite 900, Washington, D.C. 20014.

When we travel abroad or undertake an overseas assignment, we expect some degree of communication problems. Our attention is fixed on the foreign language itself, on language lessons, and on how much English will be spoken. But the mistake most of us make is to assume that our problems in communication stem only from language differences, and that the problem can be resolved by completing a language course and learning how to translate our English thoughts into the appropriate foreign language.

We do realize, when we consider communication in a sense broader than language, that difficulty in getting meaning across is not limited to those who must speak across a language barrier. There are breakdowns in communication within our own country, and even within our own families where there is no language difference. Yet in using a foreign language or an interpretation, we dismiss our problems not too thoughtfully by simply saying "it loses something in translation." If our concern is really communication, the obvious question is: "Just what is it that is lost?"

Although our modern advances in communications technology have been impressive, and even revolutionary in nature, our understanding of the human dimension in communication is relatively limited. As communication involves ideas, images, and symbolic meaning, communication problems arise in any situation in which the life experiences of the communicators are not the same. These differences can range from simple matters of age and sex to living in differing cultures and speaking in entirely different languages.

Thus, while speaking and understanding the local language in a country we visit are certainly useful, one has to go beyond the words themselves and accepted translations to become aware of a complex series of psychological processes which, in final analysis, determine the course of human communication. The mechanical process of sending communications signals is comparatively simple: Signals emitted by the sender are picked up and decoded by the receiver. This, however, is only the first step in a very complex, psychological process of human communications. Whether the words we use faithfully perform their intended communication function depends mainly on the subjective reaction they elicit in the mental processes of the listener. If in decoding the signals the receiver attaches the same meaning to the words as the speaker had in mind when he used them, then the communication is a success. Usually it does not work out this perfectly. The communication is often only a partial success as the result of some degree of discrepancy between the psychological meanings attached to the words by the communicator and the receiver, respectively. The factors which impinge on psychological meaning can be varied and profound.

Important differences in effective meaning occur even at the primary levels within a society. When adults talk with their teenagers about the drug scene, the success of the discussion will depend greatly on the adults' ability to talk about drugs in a way that carries meaning in terms of adolescent concerns, interests, and actual experiences—and vice versa. In other words, the critical factor in this communication process is the subjective meaning which each attaches to the word "drug." The dictionary meaning is of limited use: "A substance with medical, physiological effects." This does not take into account the fact that adults and teenagers bring their own world of experiences and associations into the meaning of the word. Nor, for that matter, does it show how Christian Scientists, drug addicts, and physicians define the word from their own subjective experiences. The meaning of the word, then, is determined in large part by each person's characteristic *frame of reference*.

Further, there are additional ways to convey subjective meanings along with the choice of words, for communication in everyday life is normally a face-to-face verbal interaction process which is supported by many nonverbal elements. These include a variety of feedback mechanisms such as gestures, facial expressions, tone of voice, and the context of the interaction itself. Most of this goes on largely spontaneously and without conscious direction, although the whole speaking and listening process is highly complex and involves sophisticated communications skills. The speaker must be able to read all types of cues which indicate his listener's reactions, agreement, disagreement, lack of understanding, and so forth. With this ability he is able to choose a strategy in manipulating all the subtle factors which will convey his meaning. Every day we use these skills as a matter of course, and a good communicator learns to empathize enough with his listener to sense which approach will be effective. A successful salesman or politician, for example, develops almost a sixth sense to know what to emphasize to a potential customer or client, or what meaning or connotation to signal to achieve the desired impression. By experience, the salesman learns to adjust his sales pitch to the frame of reference of each type of customer.

The objective then, whether sought with conscious intent or not, is to capture the frame of reference. Even within a single country one finds groups of people whose frames of reference differ greatly. In these cases we are often able to communicate reasonably well, as both speaker and listener are familiar with these differences as a matter of normal experience and are able to shift frames of reference to accommodate the difference. But when we must communicate with people whose culture is foreign to us, the range of differences grows, and we are less prepared, on the basis of direct, firsthand experience, to cope with the mental framework confronting us. Therefore, a new communications task is involved simply to comprehend the subjective meaning of the words used in communication after the translation is made. Still greater effort is needed to read the nonverbal cues. And to the extent that subjective meanings reflect differences in underlying philosophy, assumptions, world view, or habits of logic, the complexity of the task is compounded.

CROSS-CULTURAL COMMUNICATION:
A PROCESS OF ADAPTING TO NEW FRAMES OF REFERENCE

In adjusting to an overseas communication situation, the first problem we must overcome is "egocentric bias." This involves the tacit assumption that if we say something that makes good sense to us, it should make sense to everyone else—a bias that is about as unrealistic as it is widespread. In some cases in our own culture, as when talking to children or to mental patients, we are more aware that our statements may not be automatically understood. But on the whole, our failures to communicate in our own society have not been dramatic enough to modify our conviction that what we are saying is based on a type of universal validity. Without previous foreign travel, one is hardly attuned to recognizing his own egocentric bias or—perhaps better for this discussion—ethnocentric bias. And foreign experience does not necessarily disabuse a person of this bias unless he is sensitized to some degree to note more specifically the kind of communication problems which rise out of cultural differences.

People in every country of the world develop their own particular interests, perceptions, attitudes, and beliefs—that is, a characteristic frame of reference within which they organize and interpret their life experiences. How much people in a particular country differ from Americans in this regard is hard to judge. The psychological factors involved are difficult to define, observe, and predict. Nevertheless, tuning in on this difference is essential to communication across a language barrier.

That language and its meaning are so much a function of culture is understandable, for language is one of the most fundamental systems of culture and human society. It serves its purpose as it provides the means to express, share, and transmit the ideas and experiences of the people who practice the corresponding culture. Thus anthropologists have suggested that making a transition from one language to another actually involves going from one culture world to another. They further have noted the close association between language structure and content and characteristic habits of perceiving and reasoning on the part of its native speakers. How much particular language forms determine or limit patterns of thinking and perceiving is much debated, but disassociating language from some cultural context is a cognitive impossibility.

A MODEL FOR CONTRASTING
CULTURAL FRAMES OF REFERENCE

If, as we have shown, communication is fundamentally a psychological process, we need something more than the usual dictionary technique for establishing the effective meaning of words and phrases. To translate with optimum communication we need more than an English-Spanish dictionary, for example, or an English-Japanese phrase book. Psychological meanings are not those found in dictionaries. In contrast to the limited dictionary meaning based on convention and formal rules of use, psychological meaning refers to the entire subjective reaction elicited by a particular concept. This subjective association can be thought of in terms of components, of which one would naturally be the dictionary meaning. For example, "education" is "the process of schooling," but many other meanings would be attached to "education" based on what activities it involves, how it is valued, what purposes it serves. These components, which vary in saliency or "dominance," would determine which aspects of education are considered most important to the individual and therefore deserve special attention from the viewpoint of analyzing the communication process. If, for instance, you were urging technical education on people whose concept of education emphasized the social prestige of law and medical degrees, your communication would fall short of the mark.

Let us follow this sample word "education" in a further example in order to demonstrate the way in which these meanings can be conceptualized and charted to make this kind of analysis more explicit—to build a picture of what is involved in analyzing varying components of meaning, and varying dominance of these components. Consider the differences in psychological meaning which our word "education" would have for a priest and a football coach, confining the contrasts to American society for the moment. Based on what is commonly known of these two occupations, we can assume that they will agree on the importance of some of the possible components of meaning, and disagree on others, or at least assign differing importance to them. They would probably agree on school attendance, but disagree on the most desirable types of schools or curricula. They may agree on character development as a part of education, but the priest might more likely stress morality and the role of the church in the nurturing of character, while the coach might be more concerned with discipline, physical fitness, training, fame, desire to win fairly, and the like in building character.

To visualize this divergence in frames of reference, a visual aid is available in the techniques which have been used in an analytical approach called Associative Group Analysis (AGA). This is a word-association technique which, among other products, produces "semanto-graphs," as will be demonstrated below. When the technique is applied cross-culturally, the procedure is to select statistically valid sample groups of native speakers of the two languages concerned, and ask them to respond by free association to stimulus words in their respective languages—such as "socialism," "father," or "education" for the English speakers and the accepted translations for the other language group. When these methods are carefully applied and the results are analyzed, it is possible to chart salient differences in the components of subjective meaning, and differences in dominance or strength of these subjective meanings. Note how a semantograph would chart the differing frames of reference for the priest and coach above, even without a language barrier (see Figure 1).

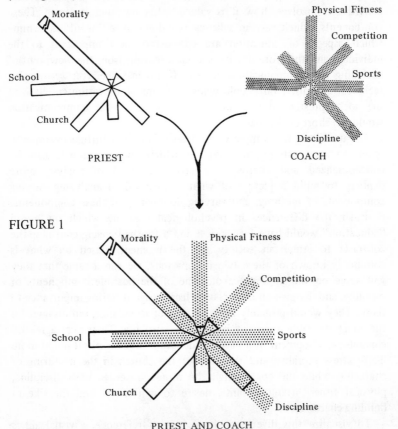

FIGURE 1

In Figure 1, we see how the composition of the subjective reactions of the priest and coach to "education" compare in schematic form. The length of the bars expresses the importance and the strength of particular meaning components. The longer the bar, the more important that aspect or association with education is to that person. When the bars coincide and are long, both persons share and give importance to that component. Such provides the basis for easy communication between the priest and the coach. Nonshared elements, i.e., bars which do not coincide or agree in length, tend to increase the difficulty of communication.

This illustration shows the combination of subjective meaning reactions as well as the formal dictionary component. The subjective elements derive from the frame of reference of the person interpreting "education." For the priest, education contains strong religious elements (morality, virtue, church). The coach's subjective concept, reflecting his frame of reference, emphasizes sports, competition, and training. Combined, these two frames of reference form a *semantograph*. The radial direction of the bars is arbitrary, with the stronger components for one frame of reference on the left, the other on the right, and accommodation made for overlapping connotations or subjective meanings.

It is important to note that when this method is used in research work, the components are isolated by a free-association method. Therefore, this serves as evidence to which a knowledge of normal experience or cultural background can be added to gain an understanding of the contrasting frames of reference involved in a communication process. The above illustration suggests an additional important hypothesis: If the subjective, psychological meanings of individual words or themes such as education are influenced by the major components of a person's frame of reference, we may also expect these subjective meanings to tell us something about a more general characteristic frame of reference which would supply meaning for other words and themes in other communication situations. Thus the coach might carry over some of the same or consistent meaning components into his psychological reaction to words like "school," "teacher," or "sports." If this is tested and found to be the case, we find that something of an enduring and repetitive frame of reference has been described, and that this would allow one to predict that these meaning components would have a bearing in other instances in what we might call an "education domain."

All this becomes complicated beyond the intentions of this discussion. In technical application this approach is the basis for research into the contrasting meanings of translated language. It is also being used for developing lexicons which allow one to look up the meaning components for key words and phrases, to note the cultural context consistent with the psychological meanings presented and appreciate the consistency in frames of reference from one subject to the next.

Empirical research in this direction has only begun. But the logic of the approach itself may provide a useful intellectual orientation for anyone working with a foreign language and concerned with communication rather than merely accepted translation. Therefore, the following comparisons of American and Korean meanings are presented as samples of the kind of results obtained when the AGA analysis is applied in an actual communications research project. In this case they provide insight into the nature and scope of cultural differences which affect communication between native speakers of English and Korean. The key words and phrases presented here are drawn from an extensive project. The explanation of the analytic technique and computations may be found in the large prototype communication lexicon which was produced covering social, national, and motivational domains.

Empirical research is needed to achieve the level of analytic completeness attempted in the samples which follow, something which is out of the question in routine communications situations. However, much is to be gained by carrying around in one's head a picture of a semantograph—circles, bars, components, and all—as a reminder of what one is searching for when learning or using a new language, for it is in recognizing the existence of differing patterns of underlying meaning that the full dimensions of a cross-cultural communication process can be seen.

In order to convey to the reader the nature and range of cultural meanings, two groups of themes, one on family and one on political systems, will be presented.

"FAMILY"

To illustrate some consistent cultural trends in the area of "family," the analysis of the following four themes is presented: FAMILY, FATHER, FILIAL DUTY, and ANCESTORS.

FAMILY
Summary of Main Components of Cultural Meanings

1. CHILDREN, BROTHER, SISTER (U.S.: 593; K: 737). This component reflects preoccupation with *siblings* (K: 251) and *children* (U.S.: 133; K: 19) and is stronger for Koreans, although it is also weighty for the Americans. Both groups think more in terms of brother and sister rather than *son* and *daughter*.

2. RELATIVES (U.S.: 218; K: 465). Koreans pay a great deal of attention to various *family members* (K: 168) and *relatives* (K: 104; U.S.: 83), especially those belonging to the older generation: *grandmother* (K: 61; U.S.: 13) and *grandfather* (K: 74; U.S.: 8).

3. HAPPINESS, FUN (U.S.: 166; K: 183). FAMILY as a source of emotional satisfaction is about equally emphasized by Americans and Koreans: *happiness* (U.S.: 94; K: 58), *harmony* (K: 74), and *fun* (U.S.: 29).

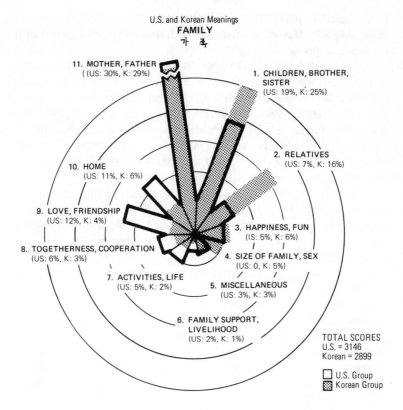

U.S. and Korean Meanings
FAMILY
가 족

11. MOTHER, FATHER
((US: 30%, K: 29%)

1. CHILDREN, BROTHER, SISTER
(US: 19%, K: 25%)

2. RELATIVES
(US: 7%, K: 16%)

10. HOME
(US: 11%, K: 6%)

9. LOVE, FRIENDSHIP
(US: 12%, K: 4%)

3. HAPPINESS, FUN
(IS: 5%, K: 6%)

8. TOGETHERNESS, COOPERATION
(US: 6%, K: 3%)

4. SIZE OF FAMILY, SEX
(US: 0, K: 5%)

7. ACTIVITIES, LIFE
(US: 5%, K: 2%)

5. MISCELLANEOUS
(US: 3%, K: 3%)

6. FAMILY SUPPORT, LIVELIHOOD
(US: 2%, K: 1%)

TOTAL SCORES
U.S. = 3146
Korean = 2899

☐ U.S. Group
▦ Korean Group

U.S. GROUPS

The main emphasis is on the nuclear family: MOTHER, FATHER, and CHILDREN. RELATIVES receive less attention. Beyond the people included in the U.S. image of the FAMILY, emotional ties and life conditions receive increasing attention. LOVE and FRIENDSHIP are the important ties accounting for the climate in the HOME, involving TOGETHERNESS, shared ACTIVITIES, and HAPPINESS.

KOREAN GROUPS

In the Korean's image of FAMILY, the role of parents, MOTHER AND FATHER, is about as pervasive as in the American's image. Nonetheless, CHILDREN and also RELATIVES occupy a more important part of this image for Koreans than for Americans. They emphasize more the older and the male members of the FAMILY (*father, grandfather, brother*). The emotional climate, HAPPINESS, and harmony are given distinct attention. There is some concern expressed with the SIZE OF THE FAMILY.

4. SIZE OF FAMILY, SEX (U.S.: 15; K: 136). Koreans show stronger concern with the family size, sex differences, and *family planning* (33).

6. FAMILY SUPPORT, LIVELIHOOD (U.S.: 58; K: 28). This is a small, primarily U.S. component, in which the family *car* (40) represents the largest response.

7. ACTIVITIES, LIVING (U.S.: 147; K: 62). The common events, activities, and shared family experiences play a somewhat greater role in the U.S. image: *dinner, reunions, outings, picnics, vacations.*

8. TOGETHERNESS, COOPERATION (U.S.: 192; K: 77). This component further reinforces the impression of stronger U.S. emphasis on family unity, on living and working together: *togetherness* (U.S.: 89), *close* (U.S.: 31), *unit* (U.S.: 25). The Koreans mention family *cooperation* (34), *dependence* (10), and *intimacy* (10).

9. LOVE, FRIENDSHIP (U.S.: 367; K: 120). The emotional ties of *love* (U.S.: 184; K: 91) and *friendship* (U.S.: 82) apparently play a stronger role in the U.S. image of the family. The emphasis on friendship appears to be especially characteristic of the American group.

10. HOME (U.S.: 111; K: 49). This strong, primarily U.S. component is consistent with the content of the previous components emphasizing love, togetherness, and shared life.

11. MOTHER, FATHER (U.S.: 951; K: 840). This is the strongest component for both groups. *Mother* (U.S.: 328; K: 287) appears to have a slightly greater role for Americans, while the *father* (U.S.: 257; K: 318) is slightly more emphasized by the Koreans. There are also more U.S. references to *wife* (U.S.: 203; K: 36), which reflects that a greater percentage of the U.S. subjects were married at the time of the testing.

FATHER
Summary of Main Components of Cultural Meanings

1. HOME, FAMILY, RELATIVES (U.S.: 324; K: 331). In both images there is a strong component expressing that father is a part of the *home* (U.S.: 131; K: 112) and *family* (U.S.: 83; K: 23). While family is a narrower concept for Americans, it involves a more extensive network of relationships for the Koreans: *uncle, nephew, grandfather, ancestor.*

2. MAN (U.S.: 112; K: 301). The Koreans greatly emphasize the manliness of the father (*male* 260, *man* 41). What this exactly means becomes more apparent from some of the following categories.

3. LEADER, PROTECTOR (U.S.: 140; K: 204). For the Koreans the father is *master of the family* (108), who because of his role and age assumes an elevated position. This leadership role receives much less emphasis from the U.S. groups (*leader* 49, *head of house* 29).

4. RESPECT, FILIAL DUTY (U.S.: 103; K: 172). The idea of *respect* for the father (U.S.: 80; K: 61) is shared by both groups. *Filial*

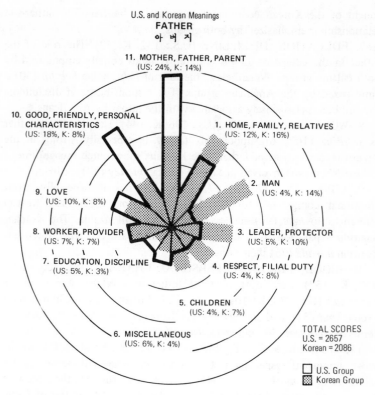

U.S. and Korean Meanings
FATHER
아 버 지

11. MOTHER, FATHER, PARENT
(US: 24%, K: 14%)

10. GOOD, FRIENDLY, PERSONAL
CHARACTERISTICS
(US: 18%, K: 8%)

1. HOME, FAMILY, RELATIVES
(US: 12%, K: 16%)

2. MAN
(US: 4%, K: 14%)

9. LOVE
(US: 10%, K: 8%)

8. WORKER, PROVIDER
(US: 7%, K: 7%)

3. LEADER, PROTECTOR
(US: 5%, K: 10%)

7. EDUCATION, DISCIPLINE
(US: 5%, K: 3%)

4. RESPECT, FILIAL DUTY
(US: 4%, K: 8%)

5. CHILDREN
(US: 4%, K: 7%)

6. MISCELLANEOUS
(US: 6%, K: 4%)

TOTAL SCORES
U.S. = 2657
Korean = 2086

☐ U.S. Group
▨ Korean Group

U.S. GROUPS

The U.S. image of FATHER shows a few differences in emphasis. His relationship to MOTHER is emphasized as the critical tie underlying the American family. His most outstanding characteristics are that he is GOOD and FRIENDLY. LOVE is the prevalent tie. He is a WORKER and PROVIDER and has an important role in EDUCATION and in maintaining DISCIPLINE. In this sense he is a LEADER and PROTECTOR.

KOREAN GROUPS

In the Korean context, FAMILY implies an extended network of relatives. The elevated position of the FATHER in this network derives apparently from his traditional role as the master of the family. This idea is supported by the high cultural values placed on men (manliness) and age (elderliness). From the part of the children, this role is accepted with the attitude of FILIAL DUTY. The image of FATHER conveys the idea of authority and strength, which, as the reactions show, does not preclude love.

---

duty (79) and *dignity* (20), however, constitute characteristically Korean values of considerable importance.

5. CHILDREN (U.S.: 102; K: 146). In both the American and Korean context, the image of the father involves having children. The

weight of the Korean component is somewhat heavier. The father-son relationship is emphasized by both groups.

7. EDUCATION, DISCIPLINE (U.S.: 132; K: 72). The role of the father in the education of his children is about equally emphasized by both culture groups. Nonetheless, the idea of *help,* being *helpful* (50) is emphasized by the American groups. The responsibility of disciplining the children is also closely associated with the father by Americans.

8. WORKER, PROVIDER (U.S.: 196; K: 144). The role of the father as *working* (102) to support his family is especially strong in the American perception of father. The Koreans show much recognition of the *hardships* (46) involved in earning enough *money* (47) for living.

9. LOVE (U.S.: 276; K: 172). FATHER has an especially strong emotional component for the U.S. group (*love* 223). The Korean references to *love* (99) are less weighty but still sizable. The Koreans mention separation from their father (*wish to see* 55); the Americans mention *missing* (26) their father.

10. GOOD, FRIENDLY, PERSONAL CHARACTERISTICS (U.S.: 477; K: 157). Americans view the father in a relationship based on *friendship* (U.S.: 70; K: 10) and *fun* (U.S.: 26) and describe him as *good* (106), *kind* (53), and *strong* (39). The Koreans characterize the father in terms of *sternness* (44) and *graciousness* (28).

11. MOTHER, FATHER, PARENT (U.S.: 629; K: 293). One of the most important aspects in the American image of father is his relationship to *mother* (U.S.: 346; K: 189). This suggests the American focus on the nuclear family is built on the close dualistic ties of father and mother, in contrast to the Korean concept of family, which involves extended family ties.

FILIAL DUTY
Summary of Main Components of Cultural Meanings

1. PARENTS, MOTHER, FATHER (U.S.: 56; K: 1004). This largest Korean component involves especially heavy references to *parents* (461) in general and to *father* (219) and *mother* (226) in particular. References to *grandparents* (98) are distinct but less sizable.

2. SON, DAUGHTER, FAMILY (U.S.: 38; K: 317). Heavy Korean references to *son* in particular suggest that this attitude toward the parents involves at least tacitly the son more than the daughter. *Ancestors* and *ancestor worship* (34) are also a part of FILIAL DUTY to the Koreans.

3. SINCERITY, RESPECT, LOVE (U.S.: 138; K: 277). This is again primarily a Korean component. While the U.S. groups emphasize *love* (53), the Koreans focus on *sincerity* (88) and *respect* (70).

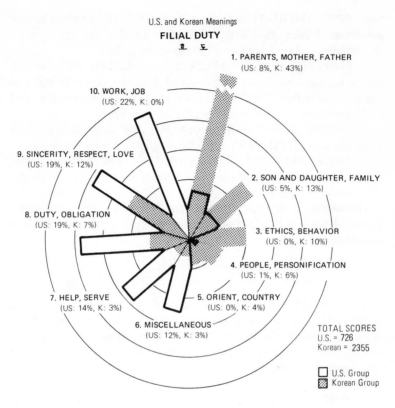

U.S. and Korean Meanings
FILIAL DUTY
孝 도

1. PARENTS, MOTHER, FATHER
(US: 8%, K: 43%)

10. WORK, JOB
(US: 22%, K: 0%)

9. SINCERITY, RESPECT, LOVE
(US: 19%, K: 12%)

2. SON AND DAUGHTER, FAMILY
(US: 5%, K: 13%)

8. DUTY, OBLIGATION
(US: 19%, K: 7%)

3. ETHICS, BEHAVIOR
(US: 0%, K: 10%)

4. PEOPLE, PERSONIFICATION
(US: 1%, K: 6%)

7. HELP, SERVE
(US: 14%, K: 3%)

5. ORIENT, COUNTRY
(US: 0%, K: 4%)

6. MISCELLANEOUS
(US: 12%, K: 3%)

TOTAL SCORES
U.S. = 726
Korean = 2355

☐ U.S. Group
▨ Korean Group

U.S. GROUPS

For Americans this theme is generally unknown and relatively meaningless. With its rudimentary denotation, it refers to the attitudes of LOVE, *responsibility,* and *obligation.* As an activity, it suggests HELP, mainly menial performance. The idea of DUTY elicits strong identification with WORK, JOB. As is apparent, the U.S. interpretation of FILIAL DUTY is preconditioned mainly by its component parts ("filial" and "duty") and is little related to the original concept.

KOREAN GROUPS

As the four times larger score expresses, this concept is more culturally meaningful for the Koreans. It refers to a particular relationship toward the PARENTS by the children: SON AND DAUGHTER. This relationship involves the attitudes of SINCERITY and RESPECT as well as the virtues of *loyalty, obedience, service,* and *sacrifice.* It has its historic roots in the Confucian ETHICS with contemporary implications for PEOPLE and their interpersonal relationships.

4. ETHICS, BEHAVIOR (U.S. 0; K: 232). The largest response, *Confucius* (48), reflects the ethical origin of this concept. Other strong associations were *courtesy* (24), *piety* (29), and *honesty* (18). No U.S. reference was made to this ethical-religious component.

6. DUTY, OBLIGATION (U.S.: 138; K: 167). The strongest Korean duties are *loyalty* (54) and *obedience* (50); for the U.S. groups, *responsibility* (45) and *obligation* (25) score the highest.

7. PEOPLE, PERSONIFICATION (U.S.: 7; K: 143). This predominantly Korean component focuses on characterisic personifications of this virtuous attitude. *Sim chong* (51) is mentioned as a classical symbol of filial piety, since she sacrificed her life for this cause.

8. ORIENT, COUNTRY (U.S.: 0; K: 83). The Koreans express their awareness that FILIAL DUTY is fundamentally an oriental concept.

9. HELP, SERVE (U.S.: 129; K: 69). The American emphasis is on *help* (33) and *menial* work (28); the Koreans stress the idea of *serving* (37), *sacrifice* (9), and *devotion* (9).

10. WORK, JOB (U.S.: 135; K: 0). This purely U.S. component indicates that duty has a strong English connotation of *work* (93) and manual labor.

ANCESTORS
Summary of Main Components of Cultural Meanings

1. FOREFATHERS, GRANDPARENTS, RELATIVES (U.S.: 546; K: 824). This is an especially strong Korean component with almost exclusive concentration on the male lineage: *grandfather* (420), *great grandfather* (77), *forefather* (125). The U.S. group refers more to family with emphasis on grandparents, both *grandfather* (126) and *grandmother* (47).

2. RITES, VENERATION, WORSHIP (U.S.: 39; K: 384). This primarily Korean component expresses semi-religious attitudes and behavior such as *veneration* (84) and *respect* (34). These are manifested in *rites* (198), having religious, ethical foundation in Confucianism.

3. GRAVE, DEAD (U.S.: 91; K: 233). This predominantly Korean component also is related to the ceremonial aspects of ancestor worship and respect: visiting the *graves* (106). This component indicates that ancestors are an active part of the Koreans' daily lives.

4. LEGENDARY FIGURES (U.S.: 0; K: 144). References to famous personalities of history and legend are exclusively Korean.

6. PREHISTORIC MAN, APE (U.S.: 73; K: 35). The main U.S. focus is on ancient and subhuman predecessors to man as identified by disciplines such as anthropology and zoology with regard to phylogenetic evolution: *Adam* (10), *cave man* (19), *Neanderthal* (13), *Java man* (11).

7. HISTORY, TRADITION (U.S.: 152; K: 84). The U.S. emphasis is on *history* (69) and historical heritage (*Mayflower*); the Korean is more on *tradition* (28) and *custom* (5).

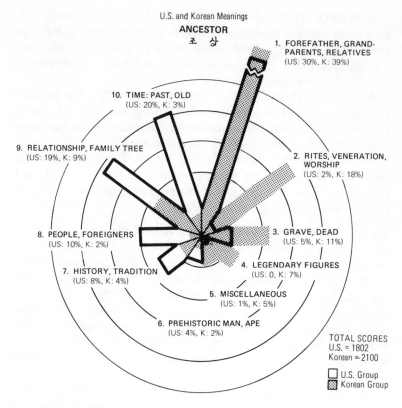

U.S. and Korean Meanings
ANCESTOR
조 상

1. FOREFATHER, GRAND-
   PARENTS, RELATIVES
   (US: 30%, K: 39%)

10. TIME: PAST, OLD
    (US: 20%, K: 3%)

9. RELATIONSHIP, FAMILY TREE
   (US: 19%, K: 9%)

2. RITES, VENERATION,
   WORSHIP
   (US: 2%, K: 18%)

8. PEOPLE, FOREIGNERS
   (US: 10%, K: 2%)

3. GRAVE, DEAD
   (US: 5%, K: 11%)

7. HISTORY, TRADITION
   (US: 8%, K: 4%)

4. LEGENDARY FIGURES
   (US: 0, K: 7%)

5. MISCELLANEOUS
   (US: 1%, K: 5%)

6. PREHISTORIC MAN, APE
   (US: 4%, K: 2%)

TOTAL SCORES
U.S. = 1802
Korean = 2100

☐ U.S. Group
▨ Korean Group

U.S. GROUPS

As a primary meaning, ANCESTOR refers to progenitors, particularly GRANDPARENTS and *great grandparents,* with emphasis on consanguine RELATIONS–deceased relatives belonging to the FAMILY TREE. More distant in the past are those Americans who played a major part in HISTORY (*Mayflower*) and also FOREIGNERS, the immigrants from other countries and continents. ANCESTOR also refers to an even more distant category: PREHISTORIC MAN, APE. This explains why the American attitudes toward ANCESTORS are weak and mixed, while the dimension of TIME: PAST, OLD acquires salience.

KOREAN GROUPS

As expressed by the substantially higher score, this theme is more dominant for the Korean groups. It refers to FOREFATHERS, with emphasis on male predecessors. The Koreans also show concern with the VENERATION of ANCESTORS, involving moral, religious principles and attitudes frequently labelled as "ancestor worship." As overt manifestations this includes services at the GRAVE, RITES. All the ideas related to this concept are viewed as an element of the Korean cultural HISTORY, TRADITION. Ancestors are not old, forgotten relatives, but command contemporary influence and recognition as an active part of the daily lives of Koreans.

8. PEOPLE, FOREIGNERS (U.S.: 187; K: 33). This primarily U.S. component contains numerous references to *people* (85) and foreign nations—*Europe* (10), *Ireland* (24), *Germany* (15)—reflecting the multinational background of Americans. The only Korean response refers to ANCESTORS as *human beings* (33).

9. RELATIONSHIP, FAMILY TREE (U.S.: 335; K: 196). The U.S. focus is on *relatives* (216) in the sense of consanguinity, as is reflected by the *family tree* (48) and *descendants* (52). Comparable Korean reactions refer to *ties* (25), *generations* (55), and *genealogy* (58).

10. TIME: PAST, OLD (U.S.: 354; K: 59). This is mainly a U.S. component emphasizing the time dimension of the *past* (97), an idea not entirely free from connotations of remoteness and irrelevance— *long ago* (32), *unknown* (6).

Trends of Cultural Interpretation in the Area of Family   There are some consistent response trends which reveal culturally characteristic patterns of family structure, role relations, as well as value orientations.

The U.S. focus is on the father and mother. This is also true for the Koreans, but they place greater emphasis on children than do the Americans. Emphasis on the father and mother suggests a horizontal relationship, while emphasis on parents and children suggests a fundamentally vertical relationship. The Koreans' description of the father as master, leader, and head of the family indicates the father's roles within the Korean family.

Sex differences produce strong role differentiation between mother and father within the Korean family where maleness and age constitute preferential status. There is consistently more emphasis on male relatives and on the older generation by Koreans than by Americans.

The generally stronger emphasis on relatives by the Koreans reflects that the extended family is more characteristic of the Korean culture while the nuclear family limited to parents and children is more characteristic of the American.

The organizational characteristics of the family predispose different types of relationships between the members of the family. The Americans emphasize love and friendship as the main family ties. This implies that the existence of the American family is dependent on the personal feelings the members attach to each other. On the other hand, the fact that the Koreans place less emphasis on feelings suggests that the Korean family is a more stable, institutionalized unit, whose permanence is taken for granted.

Compared to Americans, the Koreans refer more to filial duty and respect, which suggests more traditional ties and interrelations that involve subordination rather than equality. The greater Korean emphasis

on tradition is consistent with their strong concern with ancestors—
another case in which Koreans see a superior (ancestor) and subordinate
(Korean individual) relationship. The similar type of relationship
between the Korean parent and child is consistent with the idea of
education as a strong function of the Korean family.

The Americans make consistently heavy references to goodness and
kindness and features of likability and sociability. For the Americans, the
idea of home is especially central, which is a framework for living
together—working, providing as well as entertainment and fun.

"POLITICAL SYSTEMS"

Three themes have been selected on "political systems" to show how
Koreans and Americans perceive important political concepts differently.
They are GOVERNMENT, CAPITALISM, and SOCIALISM.

GOVERNMENT (See page 74 for chart.)
Summary of Main Components of Cultural Meanings

1. NATION, COUNTRY, PEOPLE (U.S.: 183; K: 512). This largest
Korean meaning component suggests that the most salient aspect of the
GOVERNMENT is that it represents the *nation* (216). The focus here is
not on the faithful representation of the will of the people, but on
government as a symbol of the nation, protecting the country's interests
and enhancing its prestige. For the U.S. group, however, GOVERNMENT
is closely related to the *people* (U.S.: 134; K: 124).

2. PRESIDENT, EXECUTIVE BRANCH (U.S.: 187; K: 473). The
most important element of the government is the executive branch,
headed by the *president* (U.S.: 76; K: 173), which receives especially
emphatic attention from the Korean groups.

3. LEGISLATIVE, JUDICIARY BRANCHES (U.S.: 143; K: 167).
The main difference between the two cultural groups is that the
American references to legislative bodies include *Congress* (80), *Senate*
(34), and *House* (12); the Koreans refer only to the *National Assembly*
(118), which is unicameral.

5. POLITICS (U.S.: 108; K: 99). The U.S. group appears to pay more
attention to *politics* (U.S.: 59; K: 31) and *elections* (U.S.: 39; K: 22). At
the same time, the Koreans pay distinct attention to the *government
party* (34) and its *opposition* (12), which represent an alien notion to the
independent U.S. party system.

6. ARMED FORCES (U.S.: 126; K: 16). This distinct component is
characteristic of the American groups. It shows that the Americans
perceive the armed forces as a part of the government.

Main Meaning Components for U. S. and Korean Groups

GOVERNMENT

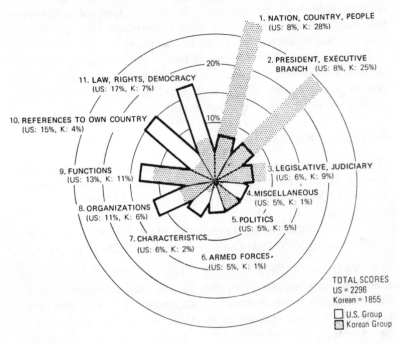

1. NATION, COUNTRY, PEOPLE
(US: 8%, K: 28%)

2. PRESIDENT, EXECUTIVE
BRANCH (US: 8%, K: 25%)

11. LAW, RIGHTS, DEMOCRACY
(US: 17%, K: 7%)

10. REFERENCES TO OWN COUNTRY
(US: 15%, K: 4%)

9. FUNCTIONS
(US: 13%, K: 11%)

8. ORGANIZATIONS
(US: 11%, K: 6%)

7. CHARACTERISTICS
(US: 6%, K: 2%)

6. ARMED FORCES.
(US: 5%, K: 1%)

5. POLITICS
(US: 5%, K: 5%)

4. MISCELLANEOUS
(US: 5%, K: 1%)

3. LEGISLATIVE, JUDICIARY
(US: 6%, K: 9%)

20%

10%

TOTAL SCORES
US = 2296
Korean = 1855

☐ U.S. Group
▨ Korean Group

U.S. GROUPS

A central idea expressed by this cultural group is that the GOVERNMENT exists for the people and must provide LAW, RIGHTS, and DEMOCRACY for the individual. The American group is well aware of the complex, differentiated structure of their government (ORGANIZATIONS, AGENCIES–OFFICIALS). The executive branch seems most representative of the government, followed closely by the legislative; only slight mention is made of the judicial branch. The CHARACTERISTICS of government are more negative than positive. The ARMED FORCES are also considered to be a part of the U.S. government.

KOREAN GROUPS

NATION, COUNTRY, PEOPLE, the largest Korean meaning component, suggests that GOVERNMENT is conceived at a collective, national level. The Korean idea of GOVERNMENT seems to be centered around the executive branch–more specifically, on the president and his cabinet. The government is thus fundamentally identified by its top leadership as representatives of the nation. This idea of leadership embodies offices more than personalities. The functions of the government are expressed mainly in terms of administration, management, and policy-making.

7. CHARACTERISTICS (U.S.: 137; K: 42). The Americans are especially concerned with the size (*big, large* 26) and strength of the GOVERNMENT; the critical sentiments outweigh the positive (*corrupt, red tape, inefficient, injustice*).

8. ORGANIZATIONS (U.S.: 256; K: 121). This component reflects strong concern with the bureaucratic, administrative organizations of the government. It is nearly twice as large for the American as for the Korean groups.

9. FUNCTIONS (U.S.: 303; K: 208). This category reflects a somewhat stronger U.S. concern. The largest U.S. responses are *taxation* (79) and *rule* (64); the largest Korean response is *administration* (87).

10. REFERENCES TO OWN COUNTRY (U.S.: 335; K: 66). This is the second largest American category, probably because of the heavy response *U.S.* (271). The concept of "U.S. government" represents a high-frequency idiom which establishes a close connection between U.S. and government.

11. LAW, RIGHTS, DEMOCRACY (U.S.: 393; K: 139). The central idea of this largest U.S. component is that GOVERNMENT stands for the people, for their personal legal rights, for freedom. The large U.S. response *law* (102) implies that the power and activities of a democratic government are controlled by law.

CAPITALISM (See page 76 for chart.)
Summary of Main Components of Cultural Meanings

1. MONEY (U.S.: 169; K: 398). This primarily Korean category suggests that the financial aspects of CAPITALISM are the most salient: *money* (U.S.: 129; K: 336), *capital* (U.S.: 21; K: 21).

2. OWN AND OTHER NATIONS (U.S.: 236; K: 315). For both groups, the country most representative of the idea of CAPITALISM is the *United States* (U.S.: 211; K: 205). Koreans also make sizable references to their own country (76).

3. RICH AND POOR (U.S.: 6; K: 309). By contrasting richness (118) with poverty (37) this large Korean component carries negative connotations. It has more social than economic implications of inequality.

4. DEMOCRACY, FREEDOM (U.S.: 94; K: 232). In this primarily Korean component, a close connection is seen between CAPITALISM and the political ideals of *democracy* (U.S.: 27; K: 132): *freedom* (U.S.: 67; K: 39), *equality* (K: 20), *rights* (K: 15).

5. NATION, COUNTRY, SOCIETY (U.S.: 90; K: 143). CAPITALISM is viewed as an economic system characteristic of particular countries. This component is slightly stronger for the Korean than the U.S. groups.

Main Meaning Components for U.S. and Korean Groups

CAPITALISM

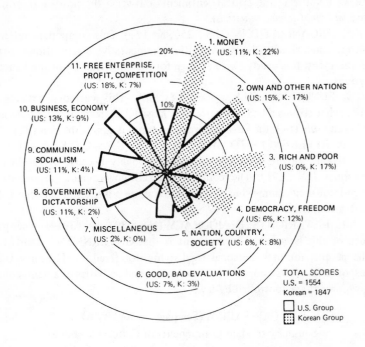

1. MONEY
(US: 11%, K: 22%)

11. FREE ENTERPRISE,
PROFIT, COMPETITION
(US: 18%, K: 7%)

10. BUSINESS, ECONOMY
(US: 13%, K: 9%)

9. COMMUNISM,
SOCIALISM
(US: 11%, K: 4%)

8. GOVERNMENT,
DICTATORSHIP
(US: 11%, K: 2%)

7. MISCELLANEOUS
(US: 2%, K: 0%)

6. GOOD, BAD EVALUATIONS
(US: 7%, K: 3%)

2. OWN AND OTHER NATIONS
(US: 15%, K: 17%)

3. RICH AND POOR
(US: 0%, K: 17%)

4. DEMOCRACY, FREEDOM
(US: 6%, K: 12%)

5. NATION, COUNTRY,
SOCIETY (US: 6%, K: 8%)

TOTAL SCORES
U.S. = 1554
Korean = 1847

☐ U.S. Group
▦ Korean Group

U.S. GROUPS

The combined focus on NATION, COUNTRY, SOCIETY, and particularly on OWN AND OTHER NATIONS, suggests that for the U.S. groups the large-scale, systemic aspects of CAPITALISM are the most prevalent. Their OWN NATION is the foremost representative of CAPITALISM. FREE ENTERPRISE, PROFIT, COMPETITION are the main operational principles of the system, which is based on THE ECONOMY, BUSINESS and MONEY. Components with sociopolitical content such as DEMOCRACY, FREEDOM and RICH AND POOR have low salience. For Americans, CAPITALISM is mainly an economic concept.

KOREAN GROUPS

The Koreans have not only an economic but also a highly sociopolitical conception of CAPITALISM. The categories dealing with NATIONS (OWN AND OTHER NATIONS and NATION, COUNTRY, SOCIETY) suggest that Koreans also think of CAPITALISM as a system characteristic of specific nations. They view the United States as the main representative of CAPITALISM and, to a lesser extent, also associate their own country with CAPITALISM. Their heavy focus on DEMOCRACY, FREEDOM and on the strong contrast of the RICH AND POOR indicates that for Koreans CAPITALISM has more sociopolitical connotations than for Americans.

6. GOOD, BAD EVALUATIONS (U.S.: 105; K: 50). Responses indicating positive evaluation of CAPITALISM are mostly American (*good, ideal, needed*); the negative, mostly Korean (*corruption, cruel, unfair*).

8. GOVERNMENT, DICTATORSHIP (U.S.: 169: K: 30). This is almost exclusively a U.S. component, particularly stressed by U.S. workers, who apparently view their government as capitalistic or as promoting the interests of the capitalists.

9. COMMUNISM, SOCIALISM (U.S.: 167; K: 65). For both groups there is a strong contrast between CAPITALISM and *communism*. Although the CAPITALISM-*socialism* contrast is also strong for the U.S. groups, it appears negligible for Koreans.

10. BUSINESS, ECONOMY (U.S.: 201; K: 169). This component indicates that CAPITALISM is primarily an economic system, which to the Americans operates on the principles of free enterprise, profit, and competition. The Koreans emphasize economy more.

11. FREE ENTERPRISE, PROFIT, COMPETITION (U.S.: 283; K: 130). Concern with the economic principles fundamental to CAPITAL-ISM is reflected in this largest U.S. component. The Koreans show relatively little interest in or awareness of these principles. Outside the U.S., the meaning of CAPITALISM is primarily excessive control of government.

SOCIALISM (See page 78 for chart.)
Summary of Main Components of Cultural Meanings

1. DEMOCRACY, EQUALITY (U.S.: 22; K: 323). This strongest Korean component shows that the Korean groups view and evaluate SOCIALISM in the context of democratic principles, especially *equality* (U.S.: 16; K: 46) and *freedom* (K: 51). For the U.S. groups this context is negligible.

2. NATION, RACE (U.S.: 21; K: 67). This is a small and primarily Korean category. The Korean response *race* (14) is used in the sense of ethnic national identity.

3. IDEA, BELIEF (U.S.: 59; K: 45). This small component indicates that the U.S. groups view SOCIALISM more as a matter of *belief* (42), while for the Korean students, it is more a *theory* (24).

4. CAPITALISM (U.S.: 55; K: 39). This is a small but distinct response category. Capitalism, perhaps even more than democracy, represents a partial opposite of SOCIALISM. This interpretation is supported by the small response *anticapitalism*.

6. PROGRAMS, ISSUES (U.S.: 145; K: 107). Social and economic programs, such as *welfare* (U.S.: 32) and *social security*, receive the most

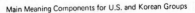

Main Meaning Components for U.S. and Korean Groups

SOCIALISM

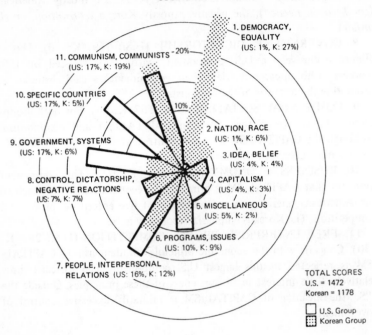

1. DEMOCRACY, EQUALITY
(US: 1%, K: 27%)

11. COMMUNISM, COMMUNISTS –20%–
(US: 17%, K: 19%)

10. SPECIFIC COUNTRIES
(US: 17%, K: 5%)

10%

9. GOVERNMENT, SYSTEMS
(US: 17%, K: 6%)

2. NATION, RACE
(US: 1%, K: 6%)

3. IDEA, BELIEF
(US: 4%, K: 4%)

8. CONTROL, DICTATORSHIP, NEGATIVE REACTIONS
(US: 7%, K: 7%)

4. CAPITALISM
(US: 4%, K: 3%)

5. MISCELLANEOUS
(US: 5%, K: 2%)

6. PROGRAMS, ISSUES
(US: 10%, K: 9%)

7. PEOPLE, INTERPERSONAL RELATIONS (US: 16%, K: 12%)

TOTAL SCORES
U.S. = 1472
Korean = 1178

☐ U.S. Group
▦ Korean Group

U.S. GROUPS

There is clear evidence that the meaning of SOCIALISM is complex and controversial. First of all, the Americans strongly identify socialism with COMMUNISM. However, among the SPECIFIC COUNTRIES mentioned, there are more non-Communist than Communist countries. Fundamentally, SOCIALISM for the U.S. groups refers to a political system run by a strong centralized GOVERNMENT, which carries heavy connotations of CONTROL, DICTATORSHIP. However, it is also associated with active socioeconomic PROGRAMS and denotes friendly INTERPERSONAL RELATIONS as well.

KOREAN GROUPS

As shown by the lower total scores for the Korean groups, the theme SOCIALISM may be less meaningful than for the U.S. groups, but it is no less controversial. It shows similarly strong association with the two major competing doctrines (DEMOCRACY AND COMMUNISM). The students identify it more with COMMUNISM, the workers and peasants with DEMOCRACY. Accordingly the students mention mostly Communist COUNTRIES and express more negative attitudes (CONTROL). There is no indication of concern with an extensive role of the GOVERNMENT. References to economic PROGRAMS are more general, and they do not include specific programs; for example, those comparable to Medicare.

attention from the U.S. groups. The main Korean responses *economy* (U.S.: 7; K: 20) and *money* (23) are more general and have a stronger economic focus.

7. PEOPLE, INTERPERSONAL RELATIONS (U.S.: 230; K: 143). The U.S. emphasis is on the proper attitudes required for friendly and happy relations. The Korean responses are less concrete and more moralistic.

8. CONTROL, DICTATORSHIP, NEGATIVE REACTIONS (U.S.: 106; K: 79). This primarily American component expresses their negative evaluations focusing on oppressive, dictatorial characteristics of SOCIAL-ISM: *bad, wrong, unfair, oppression.*

9. GOVERNMENT, SYSTEMS (U.S.: 246; K: 68). The extremely strong association with *government* (140) reflects that in the American interpretation SOCIALISM implies a system characterized by strong government and centralized power.

10. SPECIFIC COUNTRIES (U.S.: 256; K: 64). The heavy U.S. responses suggest that SOCIALISM is viewed primarily as a form of governmental system characteristic of particular foreign countries. *U.S.S.R.* (U.S.: 75; K: 27) and *England* (U.S.: 92) emerge as the most characteristic representatives.

11. COMMUNISM, COMMUNISTS (U.S.: 252; K: 223). This is the largest U.S. and second largest Korean category. It shows a very close relationship between SOCIALISM and *communism* (U.S.: 144; K: 136). However, this does not mean that the two themes are synonymous, as distinct differences appear in other categories.

Trends of Cultural Interpretation in the Area of Political Systems   There are some consistent trends of interpretation within this problem area of "political systems" as well. The U.S. groups place consistently greater emphasis on government. Government has a higher dominance for Americans; it is a key issue in viewing socialism as well as capitalism. These systems are apparently perceived as implying first of all a particular system of government. Government control and dictatorship appear as especially central concerns for the Americans.

For the Koreans government appears to be more a national issue than a matter of power and political organization. Their references to nation, race, and president are consistently stronger, whereby it has to be mentioned that race is a reference to their own ethnic national identity. There is a Korean tendency to capitalize on high offices and on the executive branch with less emphasis on the other branches, functions, organizations.

Americans emphasize generally more functions, organizations, and the political process, while there is a stronger Korean emphasis on political isms and ideology.

Similarly, Americans stress consistently more human rights, people, and economic principles of free enterprise and competition; the Korean emphasis is generally more on society and social principles. An exception to this rule appears to be in the case of capitalism, but even here the heavy Korean references to money, rich, and poor appear to have not only economic but social and political connotations as well.

The preceding comparisons of U.S. and Korean meanings show that there are distinct differences as well as similarities between the two cultures. Themes representing important concerns for Americans do not always represent equally important concerns for the Koreans. Nonetheless, some words (or themes) seem to have broad universal meanings, such as FATHER and FAMILY. These themes show relatively large areas of agreement between cultures. On the other hand, there are concepts that are more characteristic of specific cultures, such as FILIAL DUTY or ANCESTORS. These themes with relatively little cross-cultural overlap show greater cultural differences.

Generally, the more concrete concepts such as FATHER and FAMILY retain a similar meaning for both cultures, while more abstract themes such as FILIAL DUTY or SOCIALISM show greater cross-cultural variation. Moreover, even if there is a universally agreed upon core meaning, as in the case of FATHER, there will still be differences in the subjective meanings of the word for each culture. Even though the biological meaning of FATHER (i.e., the male progenitor) is universal, the subjective meaning also involves his roles, relations, and functions as head of the family, educator, and provider, which differ from culture to culture. In certain cultures, for instance, the mother's oldest brother is the head of the family, provider, and educator, while the biological father is only an occasional guest. Thus, psychological or cultural meanings of even such fundamental concepts as father and mother are also dependent on the broader framework of interpersonal relations.

Furthermore, the more a concept refers to interpersonal relations, the greater will be the differences in cultural meanings. In instances where the concept denotes primarily relationships that are largely culture-specific, as in the case of FILIAL DUTY, it becomes a question of whether the original Korean word and its U.S. translation really represent the same concept. The relationship referred to by the concept FILIAL DUTY is so fundamentally characteristic of the Confucian philosophy that without conveying this, the label FILIAL DUTY naturally remains meaningless to an American; or worse, it becomes filled with character-istically U.S. interpretations: for example, "duty" implying menial jobs, work.

At first glance, the meaning differences shown by the single specific examples may appear discouraging, suggesting there is often a gap between what we want to say and the meanings other people really attach to our translated message, even if the translation is precise according to the dictionary. Such meaning differences also suggest that learning the foreign language will not make us effective communicators unless we also learn the cultural meanings of the foreign words. Because a reasonable fluency in a foreign language requires learning at least a couple of thousand words, it would appear that learning these subtle, psychological differences is a hopelessly demanding task.

However, by considering the larger, more general areas as a whole, the problem of cultural differences becomes more manageable. There is no need to learn all the single psychological differences in meaning related to each word of the vocabulary.

First, there are some common trends in the U.S. and Korean interpretations of these specific themes. A component that appears important in the interpretation of one word tends to emerge with similar importance in the interpretation of related words. For instance, the fact that the extended family is a characteristic social structure in the Korean culture emerges clearly from the large number of relatives mentioned in the context of each word analyzed on "family." The Americans, on the other hand, consistently had a narrower focus on parents and children— the nuclear family. The consistency of findings across the themes from the area of family therefore suggest that information from a sample of themes representing a particular problem area can be extended to other themes from the same area.

In order to obtain general knowledge in the most economical way, groups of words representing several important fields of concern can be used. From the findings based on single themes, consistent trends of cultural interpretations will emerge.

The preceding examples show that words are not isolated and independent units of language but organized elements of the culture's frame of reference. Psychological meanings both depend on and faithfully reflect the important dimensions of this frame of reference.

USING CULTURAL MEANINGS TO COMMUNICATE EFFECTIVELY

The important question is how to systematically organize such knowl-edge so that it becomes useful to people trying to familiarize themselves with another language and culture. Because the information is on meanings, the construction of a new type of dictionary seems to be a logical solution.

In this new concept, a communication lexicon differs fundamentally from a conventional dictionary in that it is not designed for word-by-word translations. Its purpose is to describe the cultural frame of reference through its natural units of meaning, which happen to be the natural units of the language as well. It contains information on well-established images, patterns of thought, and attitudes characteristic of the people of a particular culture. To approach a particular problem area, the lexicon can indicate (1) how to select themes of dominant concern within a given problem area and (2) what to emphasize and in which context to discuss it so that it will communicate, that is, bear on the experiences and concerns of a particular foreign people.

The practical problems encountered while abroad are countless and often unforeseeable. Thus it would be impossible to anticipate all the potential problems in communication and interaction and to provide a specific solution for each. However, a general approach toward improving communications is outlined below.

First, we must realize that cultural differences do exist and that we cannot assume the translations of our ideas in another language will convey the same meaning. The objective, concrete meanings may be understood, but it is the subjective meanings associated with the ideas that will actually determine how effective our communications will be. Naturally, this works both ways. Just because a representative of another country speaks English fluently does not mean there will not be communication problems.

Second, it is the culture and life experiences that produce different patterns of thinking, or frames of reference. The cultural frame of reference influences the meanings of the words that the native speaker uses to communicate his ideas.

Finally, the culture can be studied through the meanings of words used to communicate within the culture. By analyzing the psychological meanings of words representing those concepts that are most important to a people, we can focus on the natural priorities of a particular culture and equip ourselves with data of fundamental relevance and broad applicability. We will then possess the important information about a particular cultural frame of reference that will enable us to communicate effectively with that people.

VERBAL SELF-DISCLOSURE:
TOPICS, TARGETS, DEPTH

Dean C. Barnlund

From *Public and Private Self in Japan and the United States,* by Dean C. Barnlund. Copyright © 1975 by The Simul Press, Tokyo, Japan. Canadian and United States distributor, ISBS, Inc., Portland, Oregon. Reprinted by permission of The Simul Press and the author.

Anyone who stands at an urban intersection or in the lobby of a large office building soon senses some pattern in the migrations of people. There are times when they flow together, congregating in dense masses, and times when they disperse and flow apart. Even within such aggregations there are minor currents: some people seek each other out, others meet by accident, and some consciously avoid each other; there are some who never converse, others who speak briefly, and still others who talk at great length.

If we were to look within these encounters we would find further regularities. Conversations usually begin with rituals of greeting. People prolong the relationship, if they desire, through an exchange of prosaic and predictable commonplaces. These conversational pastimes sometimes extend to more serious talk and a deeper sharing of private thought and personal feeling. Each person contributes remarks that will maintain rapport, disclose his experience, and fulfill his needs. From each encounter flows a mixture of consensus or confusion, trust or suspicion, excitement or boredom, affection or animosity.

Probably there are no more basic questions one can ask of a person or a culture than these: To *whom* does one speak or not speak? About *what* may one talk or not talk? How *completely* is inner experience shared or withheld? Answering each of these questions should help to expose the structure of human relationships and the norms that govern interpersonal communication in Japan and the United States.

PERSON ACCESSIBILITY

In one of the many insightful cartoon episodes of *Peanuts* Lucy declares, "I love humanity! It's people I can't stand!" And so it is with many human beings. No one seeks to talk to every passerby. No one is a friend to everyone. There is simply not enough time or energy to maintain deep relations with all our neighbors. Nor do most people want to do so.

All people are not equally attractive companions. "Interpersonal valence" is a term that reflects the lines of attraction or rejection that develop among the members of any group or society. Each person and each culture generates criteria for the selection of communicative partners. Any personal quality—age, sex, occupation, education, status, power, talent, beauty—may contribute to or detract from the potential attractiveness of another human being.

What part, if any, do cultures play in the selection of conversational partners? Do Japan and the United States favor communication with the same sorts of people? Are members of one culture closer to their parents, and are members of the other closer to their peers? How do these two societies evaluate conversation with females or males, mothers or fathers, acquaintances or strangers?

TOPIC ACCESSIBILITY

How, also, do cultures influence the content of conversations? The catalog of topics that might be appropriate for conversation is infinite. Yet each person develops his own topical priorities and prejudices, ranking subjects according to their attractiveness to him. Some people prefer to talk about work or family life, others to discuss politics or sex. Some prefer "small talk," enjoying an exchange of information about ordinary daily events, while others prefer "big talk," finding greater stimulation in a discussion of larger philosophical issues.

It would not be surprising to find that people are drawn particularly to those with similar interests. A person who enjoys talking about sports and one who likes to discuss music may not be equally enthralled about meeting an olympic medal winner and a member of a chamber orchestra. If someone—out of ignorance or reticence—is uncomfortable talking about existentialism or birth control, he may simply avoid people who are likely to bring up those subjects.

Cultures not only influence the choice of acquaintances, but mediate also the content of conversation. Each society, to some extent, expresses its values by encouraging or discouraging the exploration of certain subjects. Some topics are approved and freely discussed while others are literally forbidden. A society that attaches great value to business, to the arts, or to family life might be expected to promote somewhat different attitudes toward these areas of discourse. At one time or another in history entire cultures have felt it proper or immoral to discuss religion, sex, evolution, politics, race relations, even dress and diet. Are similar topics approved and disapproved in Japan and the United States? Or do they differ on what is proper and improper for people to talk about?

Every person, within his own circle of acquaintances, also forms different kinds of communicative alliances. Friends are seldom alike in their experience, knowledge, talent, or emotional sensitivity. If this is true, then people may discriminate in what they talk about with each of their acquaintances. Financial matters, for example, may be discussed with parents, but sexual problems only with friends. Or once deep attachments are formed, do people explore without limit any subject that concerns them? Do these two cultures encourage selective communication—limiting the discussion of specific topics to specific target persons—or do they encourage unlimited communication with all associates? If they do support topical discrimination, do both societies favor the same topical priorities with parents, peers, or strangers?

LEVEL ACCESSIBILITY

There is another dimension to verbal interaction. It has to do with the depth of talk. No matter what topic happens to be in focus, comments may reflect varying degrees of personalization, the extent to which the self is revealed in any remark. A statement may refer to external realities, the outer public world, or to inner realities, the private world inside our skins. Or it may comment on the relations between these two worlds. Remarks of the first type tell very little about the speaker while remarks of the second type tell a great deal more about the person who makes them. Any message, in short, may be highly self-disclosing or only slightly self-disclosing.

If time were no limitation, every statement could be subjected to this sort of scrutiny. The remark, "You're driving too fast," is a statement about the world outside the self. It claims objective validity. "I get scared going this fast," reflects the inner state of the speaker. The same distinction may be seen in "The company's reorganization plan is sound" compared with "I am excited about my new assignment." The former is a depersonalized judgment, the latter a statement with the self squarely in the center. The mother who says, "The children are going through a difficult phase," and the one who says "I feel inadequate with my children," are conveying quite different information. One tells us about the children, the other about the personal meaning this behavior has for the mother. It reflects her inner experience and informs us as much about her as it does about her children.

In *The Transparent Self* Sidney Jourard emphasizes the difference between people who are "transparent" and those who are "opaque." Some people allow others to know them intimately by often revealing their inner thoughts and feelings, while some hide themselves so others rarely glimpse what they are like inside.[1] Most people, however, are not equally disclosing of themselves on all topics since their emotional comfort and self-knowledge are not equal on all topics. They may speak quite frankly on some subjects, those that seem safest, and speak cautiously or deceitfully on subjects that are dangerous. People are not equally honest with all their acquaintances because it is not common to feel equally comfortable with parents, friends, business associates, and complete strangers.

We might expect that cultures, like human beings, would differ in the level of self-disclosure they feel is appropriate in conversation. They may prescribe different levels of frankness for different topics: heretical religious views were repressed during the Middle Ages just as firmly as racial doubts remain undiscussed in South Africa today. Societies may differ, also, on the degree of intimacy or distance they feel is appropriate for conversations between people and their parents, their friends, their associates, and strangers. Singular levels and forms of self-expression may be cultivated in Japan and the United States.

SELF-DISCLOSURE SCALE

Sidney Jourard and Paul Lasakow have perfected a Self-Disclosure Scale which permits simultaneous measurement of three related variables: topic of conversation, target person, and depth of self-disclosure.[2] For this study the questionnaire was slightly abridged to reduce its length but without altering its basic structure. The form that was used identified six potential communicative partners: Mother, Father, Same Sex Friend, Opposite Sex Friend, Untrusted Acquaintance, and Stranger. The scale enables one to obtain a picture of the relative intimacy of communicative relationships with six persons who occupy significant places in the interpersonal experience of each respondent.

With each target person the respondent is asked to indicate the level of his or her communication. An appropriate symbol is used to indicate the level of disclosure on a variety of topics with each partner. The symbols and their meanings are as follows: 0—Have told the person nothing about this aspect of myself; 1—Have talked in general terms about this item; 2—Have talked in full and complete detail about this topic; X—Have lied or misrepresented myself to this person. From these scores one can easily calculate the relative accessibility of the self to a variety of other people across a number of conversational topics.

The relative depth of disclosure to these target persons was determined on six broad topics commonly discussed in interpersonal encounters: (1) *Opinions* about political, religious, and social issues, (2) *Interests* in food, music, television, and books, (3) *Work* goals and difficulties, special talents and limitations, (4) *Financial* status, including income, savings, debts, and budget, (5) *Personality,* specific assets and handicaps, sources of pride or shame, (6) *Physical* attributes including feelings about one's face and body, illnesses, sexual adequacy. In each critical area five specific questions sought to fix the location of conversational norms and the limits felt appropriate for each of these general topics. The scales have been used successfully over a period of years to study differences in the disclosure patterns of males and females, members of various races, and people belonging to different cultures.

This questionnaire was given to 120 Japanese and 120 American college students. All were single, were between 18 and 24 years of age, and were equally divided between males and females. Each was asked to read the thirty questions carefully, think of a specific person within each target category (Mother, Father, Same Sex Friend, Opposite Sex Friend, Untrusted Acquaintance, Stranger), and report his actual or probable verbal behavior with each. The tests were completed anonymously, and subjects were given unlimited time to finish.

TOPICAL PRIORITIES

What subjects do members of each of these cultures prefer to talk about, or avoid, when they meet? The answers to this question are somewhat surprising. Instead of a cultural difference in topic preferences, the results revealed immense consistency in what is considered an appropriate or inappropriate topic for conversation.

Among Japanese respondents matters of interest and taste were the most fully discussed topics, followed by opinions about public issues, and attitudes toward work or studies. Financial matters, aspects of personality, and feelings about one's body ranked lower. Males and females displayed similar topical orientations, although females ranked work-related questions second while males ranked them third. But this difference was slight and insignificant.

American respondents supplied a very similar, but not identical, pattern of response. Matters of taste and interest again scored as the most appealing subjects, but attitudes toward work and studies scored second. Opinions on public issues ranked third, while financial status, aspects of personality, and feelings about physical adequacy followed in that order. But, again, the difference in the relative ranking of attitudes toward work and opinions about public issues was small. And the degree of cultural consistency was very striking. American males and females agreed completely in their topical preferences.

Hence it appears that there are only small and inconsequential differences between Japanese and Americans (and between males and females) with regard to conversational focus: members of both nations seem to prefer to discuss their tastes in food, books, television programs and films, and prefer to talk less about their personal traits and physical or sexual adequacy.

It might be expected that opinions on public issues, since they are the most remote from the self, might be the most favored topics for conversation. But apparently not. Tastes and interests were. There may be several reasons for this. It may be that matters of taste rarely provoke deep or fundamental conflicts in values, and hence are less likely to produce arguments or friction. Or it may be that such differences, since they need not be reconciled, stimulate curiosity rather than animosity. For whatever reason, they constituted the most likely conversational material in both countries.

Scores on the specific questions that make up the six general areas provide further information on verbal disclosure. Among Japanese the most fully explored questions were those relating to tastes in food, music, reading, television and film. Next most fully discussed were opinions on race and male-female relations. The least popular specific questions dealt with feelings about sexual adequacy, facts about sexual behavior, feelings about the appearance of the body and face, and events that arouse shame or guilt. All but the latter two fall into the broad category of attitudes toward the physical self, and the exceptions relate to the adequacy of the psychic self. Males and females differed only slightly in their response even to specific questions on the scale.

Similarly among Americans the most thoroughly explored specific questions concern taste in food, music, television and film, attitudes on race and career goals. Males and females showed only slight differences even with regard to disclosure on specific questions. Americans and Japanese reflected nearly identical patterns of disapproval for conversations relating to personal and sexual matters. And, again, male and female responses revealed no differences sizable enough to be reliable.

Interestingly the level of talk within each broad area was consistent no matter which specific question was considered. But there was one notable exception to this rule. Questions about sex, for example, appeared under three different topical categories. "My personal opinions about sexual morality" appeared as a question under Opinions on Public Issues, "Facts about my present sex life" appeared under Personality, and "Feelings about my own sexual adequacy" apppeared under Physical Attributes. In every case the specific question on sex received the lowest score within the general topic area and, in the last two cases, the lowest scores of any items on the test. This pattern seems to confirm that discussion of the body and its functions is one of the least desirable topics of conversation in both cultures. Sex, even when discussed as a public problem, is seen as a relatively unattractive topic. This may be because it can easily lead to an exploration of attitudes that are highly personal and private. When questions relating to the body and to sexual behavior are set aside, the next lowest specific scores (with the exception of past episodes involving shame or guilt) for both Japanese and Americans referred to money—savings, debts, budgets.

The evidence is overwhelming in support of similar orientations among Japanese and Americans with regard to what is appropriate and inappropriate to talk about. There are slight differences between the cultures on specific questions within the broader categories, but these appear random and inconsequential. Differences between males and females also seem small and, given traditional concepts of their roles, quite understandable.

TARGET PREFERENCES

If conversational topics can be ranked, is there also a hierarchy of conversational partners? Are the people who occupy our interpersonal worlds equally attractive as associates, or do they vary systematically in attractiveness? Does this change according to topic, or does it remain the same regardless of topic? The data obtained from the Self-Disclosure Scale permit these questions to be explored.

A clear hierarchy of target persons emerged from the findings. The Japanese ranked friends highest as communicative partners, parents next, and strangers and untrusted acquaintances last. Within these categories same sex friends were clearly preferred to opposite sex friends, mothers ranked next (scoring nearly as high as friends of the opposite sex), but fathers scored substantially lower. Among the least attractive conversational partners, unknown people were preferred slightly over untrusted acquaintances. While the decline in scores among the most attractive partners (same sex friend, opposite sex friend, mother) was regular, the drop between these and father, stranger, and untrusted person was more precipitous.

All potential target persons scored substantially higher with Americans, but essentially the same hierarchy existed. Friends were communicated with most fully, parents next, and strangers and untrusted people least. Also, the scores decreased gradually and a radical drop did not appear until one reaches the scores for strangers and untrusted people. Again, unknown persons were preferred to untrusted ones.

There are some interesting, though subtle and unreliable, differences in the responses of males and females in both samples. Japanese males appeared to disclose most to male friends, but more fully to friends of either sex than to their mothers. Japanese females disclosed most to the same sex friend, but next to their mothers. There was substantial disclosure to opposite sex friends, but it was less complete than to mothers. Americans, both male and female, communicated more fully with friends of either sex than they did with either parent.

Verbal disclosure to fathers may differ in the two cultures: Americans appeared to communicate almost equally with mothers and fathers; Japanese seemed to differentiate between the amount of disclosure with each parent. Whereas disclosure to American fathers was nearly indistinguishable from other intimates, disclosure to Japanese fathers dropped off considerably and approaches the level of American disclosure with strangers. Americans revealed more of themselves to strangers and untrusted associates, but, like the Japanese, preferred the former to the latter as communicative partners.

Choice of topic and choice of partner would not seem to be independent of each other. They should interact. It would seem reasonable that most people would seek out specific persons when they wish to discuss certain topics, and seek other partners to discuss other topics. But the data from this investigation raise doubts about that presumption, for there was considerable consistency across all topics for all target persons. That is to say, there was little evidence of either avoidance of or emphasis upon particular topics with particular acquaintances. Generally tastes and opinions were the most fully discussed in both cultures with all people. And physical attributes and personal traits were the least discussed, again with all people.

These generalizations may obscure some exceptions to this rule. Some Japanese respondents, for example, seemed to prefer to discuss financial matters with their mothers, next with male friends and female friends. They preferred to talk about bodily characteristics, excepting sexual behavior, with mothers before male or female friends. Among Americans, financial matters seemed more likely to be discussed with mothers, secondly with fathers, rather than with peers of the same or opposite sex. Unlike their Japanese counterparts, Americans did not appear to find discussion of physical attributes easier with mothers or fathers than with the same or opposite sex friend. But evidence of selective communication is too haphazard to be taken seriously.

Thus it appears there is a communicative bias operating in both countries that encourages greater personal disclosure to same and opposite sex friends, favors somewhat less disclosure to parents, and restricts interaction still more with unknown and untrusted people. Each sex seems somewhat to prefer communicating with members of the same sex, but this preference is much stronger among Japanese than Americans. The Japanese seem to differentiate more sharply between communicating with mothers and fathers while Americans seem to perceive both parents as more equally attractive partners.

LEVEL OF PERSONAL INVOLVEMENT

The order of topical priorities and hierarchy of communicative partners seem generally consistent in both cultures. But what is most critical is the depth of personal disclosure that is encouraged within interpersonal encounters. How much of themselves do Japanese and Americans reveal in their conversations? The data obtained from the Self-Disclosure Scale provide a simple and clear index of self-revelation.

The scoring of the Self-Disclosure Scale is such that a score of 0 indicates that respondents "Have told nothing about this aspect of myself," a score of 100 indicates they "Have talked in general terms about this aspect of myself," and a score of 200 indicates they "Have talked in full and complete detail about this item."* Scores falling between 0 and 100 would suggest a low level and between 100 and 200 a high level of self-disclosure. With so broad a range of topics and so

---

*To simplify the presentation of the results on the Self-Disclosure Scale raw scores have been multiplied by 100 to convert them into whole numbers.

diverse a set of communicative partners it would be surprising if scores averaged above 150.

For the Japanese the average level of disclosure across all topics and all target persons was 75. The average disclosure score for Americans was 112. Scores of males and females in both cultures were very similar: Japanese males and females obtained exactly the same scores on self-revelation; Americans showed a slight sex difference, males averaging 113 and females averaging 110. (The small differences in disclosure levels of American males and females is traceable to relatively greater openness of males with strangers.) But these differences were so small they cannot be taken very seriously.

However, it may be more representative of a culture to consider the level of communication only with "trusted acquaintances." Although conversations with strangers may be suggestive of the range of social interaction, it seems questionable to incorporate this figure in appraising the general level of disclosure in daily conversation. Disclosure to untrusted people, too, seems to constitute a special rather than typical instance of personal interaction. A better and more representative estimate of the normal depth of disclosure may be secured by eliminating these two categories of target persons.

When these are omitted from the calculations, the average level of conversation with trusted acquaintances (mother, father, male friend, female friend) rises from 75 to 100 for the Japanese and from 112 to 144 for Americans. A slight sex difference appeared in both samples, but again of such small size as to be discounted.

With regard to overall levels of interpersonal communication the findings seem clear. Interpersonal distance, as estimated by self-disclosure, was substantially greater among Japanese than among Americans. The degree to which persons shared their experience—private opinion and private feeling—was considerably higher among Americans. And this appeared to be true whether potential partners included or excluded unknown and untrusted persons.

For Japanese the average level of disclosure rose to 100 only with trusted acquaintances. This indicates, on the average, that Japanese express themselves only "in general terms" with their closest associates—parents and intimate friends. For the United States the comparable figure was 144. While this figure does not suggest a total sharing of the self, it does indicate a level of expression that varies between talking "in general terms" and talking "in full and complete detail about onself." In order to reach this level approximately half of all communication with intimates would have to involve a full sharing of the self.

The precise boundaries of the "public self" and the "private self" in Japan and the United States may now be estimated using the data on self-disclosure. The generalized models suggested earlier can now be drawn more precisely. (These appear in Figures 1 and 2.) In the typical Japanese the area of the "private self" extends from the "unconscious" to the point at which the person reveals his inner feelings in only "general terms" (100). For the typical American the "private self" extends from the "unconscious" to a point midway between disclosing his inner experience "completely" or in "general terms" (144). Thus the total area of the self accessible to others through communication is significantly smaller in Japan than in the United States. (It is possible to represent the boundary of the public and private self in each topical area—for a culture or an individual—by making the contour of this boundary conform precisely to the profile of scores in each topical area and for each conversational partner.)

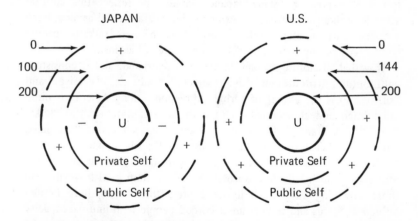

Figure 1   Precise Boundary of Public Self

It is when individual questionnaires are examined that the full impact of these findings is felt. Depersonalized averages tend to obscure extreme cases and blunt somewhat the human significance of these overall figures. Many people reported no disclosure of self on a number of topics; many others reported no instances of deep disclosure to any person. There were more than a few, especially among the Japanese sample, whose average level of self-expression was not near 100, but closer to 0, who on *nearly all topics* and with *nearly all people* reported they "Have told the person nothing about this aspect of myself." As one data processor remarked while scoring some of the questionnaires, "Have these people ever revealed anything about themselves to anyone? Are they known to any other human being at all?" This is a stronger indictment of Japanese conversational manner than that offered by Robert Guillain, but it is similar in tone. He notes that the Japanese enjoy social contacts, but contacts that are more pleasant than deep: "Beyond polite phrases, the Japanese speaks very little, particularly about himself."[3]

The avoidance of frank or full disclosure of interior experience is reflected not only in the findings of this study but in many commentaries on social behavior in Japan. James Moloney, for example, remarks that "There are vast areas of behavior about which the ordinary Japanese may be unwilling to talk freely."[4] Conversation, according to Bernard Krisher, is founded on an "economy of words," with couples often spending a lifetime together without ever discussing their feelings with one another.[5] There appears to be strong cultural resistance to excessive verbalization and a compensating reverencing of silence and less explicit forms of expression. Many Japanese aphorisms reflect this cultural attitude. Talkative persons, for example, are characterized as resembling a "paper carp in May." Like these inflated banners, talkative people consist only of huge open mouths with nothing but air inside.

If verbal disclosure among Japanese is restricted, and is consistent with cultural attributes such as "reserved," "cautious," "evasive," and "silent," so is the extent of verbal expression among Americans more uninhibited and equally consistent with cultural traits such as "talkative," "frank," and "self-assertive." If one society favors a "restrained self," the other favors an "unrestrained self"; where one encourages "contraction," the other encourages "expansion." Those in the United States who are inarticulate, verbally vague or clumsy with words, and those unwilling to contribute or express their views, have limited influence. Status and respect are accorded people with unusual capacity for defining problems and mobilizing support for their solution. An appetite or aptitude for expressing the self verbally seems differently valued in these two cultures.

LEVEL OF DISCLOSURE BY TOPIC

Interpersonal encounters move through a more or less patterned sequence. People talk first in more formal ways. The subject matter is more distant than self-revealing (Tastes). Gradually, after an appropriate period of exploratory testing, conversants move to more personal levels of talk (Opinions, Work). Finally, as mutual trust grows between them, they may drop their defenses and exchange more private feelings (Personal and Physical). Not only does the topical focus change with time, but also the level of disclosure deepens on each topic. If so, the findings of this study suggest that among Japanese this is often an incomplete process; the topical progression is interrupted earlier and is less often carried to the point of deep mutual sharing. Though the same overall pattern undoubtedly appears in American conversations, they seem to move more quickly and more consistently to the final stages. Clearly neither culture always completes this process; each favors some restriction upon the sharing of inner meanings.

The average level of verbal disclosure can easily be computed for each topical area. The figures presented in Table 1 reinforce the earlier conclusion drawn from overall averages. Americans showed a consistently higher level of self-revelation on all topics. In fact, their level of disclosure on the least appealing topic in both cultures equaled or surpassed the level of disclosure of Japanese on all but the most preferred topic. That is, Americans shared nearly as much of themselves with regard to physical and sexual adequacy as the Japanese did with regard to their preferences in food, music, reading materials, and television programs.

Table 1   Average Disclosure on Conversational Topics

	Japanese	American
Average Disclosure on All Topics (To All Persons)	75	112
Average Disclosure on All Topics (To Intimates)	100	144
Average Disclosure by Topic (To Intimates):		
Interests/Tastes	126	163
Work/Studies	113	162
Opinions on Public Issues	107	151
Financial	96	143
Personality	90	129
Physical	69	113

Again, individual patterns of communication within specific topics were revealing, and convey some of the uniqueness of the responses. What often appeared among both Americans and Japanese might be called "communicative blanks." Though most respondents talked with some intimacy to some people on some topics, there were areas of private experience that were blotted out completely. Some, for example, avoided discussing illness or debts or sex with anyone, while others avoided conversations that touched upon race relations or Communism or work handicaps. (Somewhat surprising was the finding that Americans disclosed slightly more to each other on the subject of sexual standards than on the subject of Communism.) It seems, then, that some people confine interaction to well-worn conversational ruts, often avoiding alternative topic material. Both healthy and symptomatic communicative patterns may be identifiable in these individual profiles of self-disclosure.

LEVEL OF DISCLOSURE TO SIGNIFICANT PERSONS

Finally, we may examine the relation between levels of disclosure and the persons with whom one converses. As noted earlier, both countries tended to rank potential communicative partners in similar ways. The precise averages for disclosure to all target persons, trusted target persons, and each of the specific persons identified in this study are presented in Table 2.

Table 2   Average Disclosure to Target Persons

	Japanese	American
Average Disclosure to All Partners (All Topics)	75	112
Average Disclosure to Intimates (All Topics)	100	144
Average Disclosure to Specific Target Persons:		
Same Sex Friend	122	157
Opposite Sex Friend	103	153
Mother	100	138
Father	75	126
Stranger	27	58
Untrusted Acquaintance	22	38

Again, the overall level of disclosure, regardless of whether all target persons or only trusted ones are included, was substantially lower among the Japanese than among the Americans. On the whole, the Japanese talked only in the most general terms even with their own parents and closest friends. The overall average for Americans with all target persons, including unknown and untrusted people, exceeded the level of personal exchange of Japanese in even their most intimate relationships. The figures for specific target persons, of course, elaborated this general trend. The extent of personal disclosure for the Japanese was roughly similar for male friend, female friend and mother, but then dropped sharply. For Americans the communication levels with male friend and female friend were nearly identical, and similar for father and mother. The level dropped more sharply only with strangers and untrusted people.

Yet it is important not to overlook the diversity that lies behind cultural norms. In both samples there were some who communicated deeply with their mothers, but others who communicated with them superficially. If some discussed a wide set of topics with their closest friends, there were others who were more discriminating about what they talk about with their same or opposite sex friends. Where some did not explore any topic with strangers in depth, others appeared to be more open with strangers than with their own parents. Still, despite such individual variability, the consistency within each cultural group was striking and the contrast between them was substantial.

DISCLOSURE TO FATHERS

Disclosure to fathers appeared to constitute a special instance of interpersonal communication. According to Jourard there is less sharing of the self with fathers than with mothers and peers in many cultures. If so, our data did not confirm that conclusion among Americans, but strongly reinforced that generalization among Japanese. There was substantially less disclosure to fathers than to any other intimate associates inside or outside the family. Americans apparently shared their private thoughts and feelings nearly as much with strangers as Japanese did with their own fathers. These findings tend to substantiate the saying that there are four things Japanese fear most: earthquakes, thunder, fire, and fathers. The inclusion of fathers on a list of purely physical occurrences appears to be more than accidental. At any rate the evidence supports Benedict's characterization of Japanese fathers as "depersonalized objects" and Doi's description of Japan as a "fatherless society."

A study of the communicative orientations of high school students corroborates these results. With regard to the question "With whom can you share your troubles most freely and frankly?" Japanese students ranked in order of attractiveness "mothers," "intimate friends," "older brothers and sisters," "younger brothers and sisters," and "fathers." When asked to identify the person with whom they shared the least communicatively, fathers were the nearly unanimous choice. These students reported saying little to their fathers beyond "Good morning" and "Goodnight." In contrast, mothers were the persons with whom the most was shared conversationally.[6]

When asked to identify the chief role of their father among those of "Friend," "Teacher," "Adviser," "Boss," "Partner," or "None of these," Japanese college students rarely chose "Friend." Many found none of the terms really suitable in describing his role. Among those who did, most preferred "Boss" or "Adviser." Only 11 percent regarded him as a "Friend."[7] Hiroyoshi Ishikawa reports a similar sentiment reflected in college students' perceptions of their fathers. They described him as "alone" or "isolated," a remote figure surrounded by forbidding walls that reduced conversation to commonplaces.[8]

CONCLUSION

Conversation is an activity sustained by two or more persons who use their private experience as a resource on which to build some sort of human relationship. The kind of relationship, of course, depends on their desire and capacity to maintain a deep or shallow linkage with each other. The findings of this study, reflected in the accompanying visual summary [Figure 2], suggest there is both universality and distinctiveness in the verbal style cultivated in each culture. (Comparisons along any dimension can be made simply by glancing down the columns to compare the extent of disclosure with each communicative partner, or across the rows to contrast the level of disclosure on each topic.)

These charts reveal that both cultures cultivate a similar set of attitudes toward people who are the potential receivers of messages. As communicative partners, peers are preferred to parents, parents are preferred to strangers. Within these categories there is a slight preference for same sex over opposite sex friends, but a more marked preference, especially in Japan, for mothers over fathers. Neither culture encourages verbal intimacy with strangers. Both societies also promote similar orientations toward a wide range of topics. In both, people tend to talk more about their tastes, opinions, and work than about their financial affairs, personal traits, and physical or sexual adequacy.

But here the similarity ends. These two countries appear to differ sharply in the depth of conversation they feel is appropriate in interpersonal encounters. Among Japanese there is substantially less disclosure of inner experience while among Americans substantially greater disclosure on all topics and with all persons. Where the former share their private thoughts in only a general way, among the latter these are revealed much more completely. Americans, for example, reveal themselves more completely on the most superficially explored topics

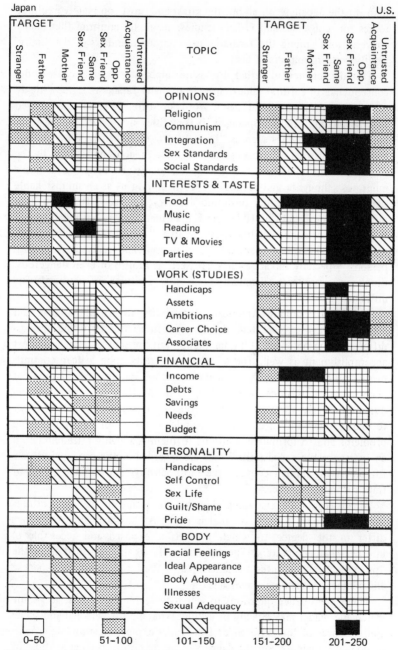

Figure 2   Summary of Topic, Target, and Level of Disclosure

than do the Japanese on all but the safest and most completely explored topics of conversation. Other studies seem to confirm that many conversations among the Japanese, even among members of the family, chiefly concern matters of taste.

This discrepancy in verbal disclosure appears as both a cause and a consequence of cultural values. Speech, to many Japanese, is not a highly regarded form of communication. Words are often discounted or viewed with suspicion. Talk is disparaged. It is realities, not words, that regulate human affairs. Sayings such as "By your mouth you shall perish" reflect this basic mistrust of language as a vehicle of communication. In the words of Inazo Nitobe, "To give in so many articulate words one's innermost thoughts and feelings is taken among us as an unmistakable sign that they are neither profound nor very sincere."[9] This thought is put more bluntly still by Hidetoshi Kato when he says, "In Japan speech is not silver or copper or brass—but scrap."[10] Intuitive communication, through means other than words, is praised and revered. Articulate persons, especially talkative ones, are seen as foolish or even dangerous. Eloquence can even disqualify one for positions of authority or influence.

In contrast, among Americans the ability to articulate ideas and feelings is highly respected. Speech is seen as not only the species-differentiating potential of human beings, but the source of their greatest accomplishment as well. The social system rests upon a deep commitment to discussion as the primary mode of inquiry, of learning, of negotiation, and of decision making. Valued ideals and critical procedures are nearly always codified in constitutions and contracts in order to clarify them and to minimize misunderstanding. An ability to define problems and to formulate solutions to them is a highly prized and even an indispensable social skill. Words are regarded as the principal vehicle for preserving human contact, the most sensitive and flexible means of transmitting experience.

In any case, the character of verbal disclosure in the two cultures provides support for the original hypothesis: Japanese and Americans differ in the degree to which the self is exposed and accessible in interpersonal encounters. The "public self" as distinguished from the "private self" constitutes a smaller area of the total self among Japanese and a larger area among Americans.

There are further questions to which these findings point, and some which the reader may already be asking: What are the personal and social consequences of this difference? Does fuller expression stimulate growth or does it impair it? Are the dangers of overexposure as great as those of underexposure? Is someone capable of communicating at deeper levels likely to communicate better interpersonally or interculturally? These questions can be explored, but first it would be helpful to know more of the character of nonverbal interaction and of the prevailing forms of defensive communication in these two cultures.

NOTES

1. Sidney Jourard, *The Transparent Self,* Van Nostrand, Princeton, 1964.

2. Sidney Jourard and Paul Lasakow, "A Research Approach to Self-Disclosure," *Journal of Abnormal and Social Psychology,* 56 (1958).

3. Robert Guillain, *The Japan I Love,* Tudor Press: New York, n.d., p. 11.

4. James Moloney, *Understanding the Japanese Mind,* p. 126, Philosophical Library, New York, 1954.

5. Bernard Krisher, "Who Are the Japanese?" *Newsweek,* July 17, 1972, pp. 12-13.

6. Keiko Hida, Shizue Nomonto, and Midori Shigeta. "Family Communication." Research Project, International Christian University, 1968.

7. Miwako Kaihara, "A Comparative Study of Selected Communication Patterns in Japan and Costa Rica." Senior Thesis, International Christian University, 1972.

8. Hiroyoshi Ishikawa, "Father Is Complic ted Person," *Japan Times,* Jan. 1, 1973.

9. As quoted in Bernard Rudofsky, *The Kimono Mind,* p. 157, Tuttle, Tokyo, 1971.

10. Hidetoshi Kato, "Mutual Images: Japan and the United States Look at Each Other," paper presented at the Conference on Intercultural Communication, International Christian University, 1972.

OUT OF HOUSE AND HOME

John C. Condon and Fathi Yousef

From *An Introduction to Intercultural Communication* by John C. Condon and
Fathi S. Yousef, © 1975 by the Bobbs-Merrill Company, Inc., reprinted by
permission of the publisher.

Although we designate food, clothing, and shelter as life's "necessities,"
across cultures we find extraordinary variety in each of these categories.
So much variety, in fact, that what makes the mouth water in one
culture turns the stomach in another; the variation in dress, even within
what might be considered a single culture over a relatively short period of
time, hardly needs to be mentioned. Housing, too, offers considerable
variety even within a single culture, and it may be that people fantasize
about their "dream home" even more than they do about food or
clothing. The number of popular and folk songs which recall or idealize
home is extensive. What should be obvious is that the symbolic values of
these three far outweigh their survival functions for most persons. What
is less obvious and more intriguing is the extent to which such
"necessities" reflect and influence cultural patterns of communication.

In some societies dietary customs have been credited with reflecting
and promoting more basic values: spokesmen for vegetarian societies, for
example, have often contrasted their values with those of the aggressive,
predatory meat-eating peoples.[1] The influence of clothing on lifestyle
and outlook is also a frequent source of conscious cultural distinction;
Charles Reich's paean to bell-bottom trousers in *The Greening of
America* is one of the more recent, as he claims it is impossible to take
yourself too seriously while wearing that fashion.[2] (He overlooks the
long tradition of bell-bottom trousers in the Navy.) In this chapter we

will concentrate on the possible influence on patterns of communication of house structure and its use by a family.

"First we shape our buildings and then they shape us," Churchill observed, and it is in this spirit that we approach the subject. Our parents and those who lived before we were born helped shape the home into which we were born, and to some extent that home has influenced us. The same can be said for the language we are "born into" or for any aspect of our culture, of course. But homes are both more personal (each home being notably different, to members of the same culture) and more subtly influential.

Before beginning our brief discussion of house and home styles in several different societies, we must acknowledge the fact that these are described in general terms and without any effort to be comprehensive about any one of them. It is also true that homes in some societies are easier to generalize about than those in others, simply because of greater cultural homogeneity and a relative lack of economic, social, or regional variations. We have tried to limit our observations on house and home styles to a few characteristics that seem to be especially revealing of cultural values and related patterns of communication.

We are indebted to Dr. Ben Goodwin, and Professor Leland Roloff for developing the first of these themes in the American context.[3] Over a period of many years, Goodwin, a psychiatrist in Dallas, Texas, found patterns of behavior in his patients which seemed to be consistent with home styles; the source of such data and the need to generalize into some kind of composite house/home styles should caution us, but the concept of the approach seems valid.

TWO STYLES OF HOMES IN THE UNITED STATES

The authority-centered home   In this home there is some "authority" which serves as a standard by which most or many important matters are judged. The authority may be a person, father or grandfather, or it may be a religion or a religious book, such as the Bible. It may be education or some symbol of that, such as a weighty set of *The Great Books*. It might be the family business or the family name. But there is a sense of a fixed authority, a core, around which communication is centered. (Note that this need not be an *authoritarian* home.) While this home is described as one type of American home, arising from Goodwin's observations, it shares much in common with many European homes. Comparisons with a German home will be described later.

In this home there is often a clear distinction between family areas of the home and guest areas; typically there is a livingroom or parlor where guests are received and entertained, and this room is ordinarily not used by family members. In this room are displayed the treasures of the home: antiques, heirlooms, a portrait, perhaps, and the most sacred and salient symbols of the family.

Ideally in this home the family dines together. Children are expected to be present for dinner, and it is at dinner that the children are socialized into the family and its values. Conversation proceeds typically in a question and answer form, the parents asking the questions, the children supplying the answers: "What did you learn at school today? You came home at 4:30, but school is out at 3:15; where did you go after school! Have you started on your homework yet? Did you do the chores?" The children give the answers. Goodwin notes that among his patients who come from such a background there is often tension associated with eating.

There are to be no secrets in this family; anything and everything of importance is to be discussed within the home. Mother or father feel free to check on the children's reading materials, and to open and read letters received by the children, and to approve or censor what is found. That which takes place outside of the home, away from the eyes and ears of the parents, is suspect. The house has doors and the doors have locks, but one must not go into a room and lock the door: "What are you doing in there? Why did you close the door? You don't have to close the door; if we're making too much noise for you to study we will be quiet. Open the door."

For these reasons, the bathroom becomes an important room for intrapersonal communication—for being alone and "thinking" or even talking out loud. The bathroom (and toilet) is the only place where one can be alone without arousing suspicion, and the bathroom provides the added advantage of a mirror for "mirror talk" while shaving or putting on makeup.

The kitchen is often a setting for "negotiation" between children and their mother, particularly when it is necessary to talk father into something. As many questions and problems and requests by children are likely to be answered by, "ask your father" or "ask your mother," and as mother is more accessible physically and psychologically than father, mother's area in the kitchen is extremely important. (It is interesting that in a study of word values conducted independently, the word "kitchen" was found to rank among the most highly valued words by Americans.)

The parents' bedroom is a setting for *little intimate communication.* Largely off-limits to the children and often symbolically divided between mother's and father's areas (separate closets or wardrobes, often with mother's "little shrine of perfumes," as Roloff describes it, and father's tie rack, comb and brush set), even the sides of the bed (or twin beds) also limit communication between the parents. (In the bathroom, "His" and "Hers" towels may reflect the division.)

Outside of the home, the best place for the children to be—from the parents' point of view—is the school. There the parents assume that control is maintained, and, moreover, competitive values are sharpened. Competition is regarded as essential to the development of character and appears to influence even patterns of speech.

There is more to be said about this kind of home, but this may be sufficient to contrast this authority-centered home with another style, the social-centered home.

The Social-centered Home   The social-centered home is embued with an air of social activity, and the entire home is prepared for sociality. In contrast to the authority-centered home, where the parents have clear authority over their children, in the social-centered home the parents often act as assistants to their children's social interests: "Would you like to have a party this week? I will help you plan some games, and Dad can bring the other children here in the car if you like."

There is a great informality about the home, so that there are no clearly marked divisions between "family" and "company" areas. A guest is as likely to be invited to the kitchen as to the livingroom. Movement within the house is free and casual, so that almost no room is likely to be more of a center for communication than any other. In sharp contrast to the authority-centered home, the family is not likely to take meals together: The very social activities may prevent everybody from being home at the same time. The kitchen sometimes resembles a central information exchange, with messages substituting for conversation: "Johnny—sorry, but I have to go to a meeting—there are leftovers in the refrigerator, fix yourself something for supper. Dad has bowling tonight. Mom." "Mom: Peter came home with me and we made sandwiches. We have play rehearsal tonight. See you about 9:30. Johnny. P.S. Betty called and said she will be home late."

Along with such activities as Scouts, community projects, sports, and music lessons, party-going and dating is urged upon the children at an early age. And one of the significant results of all this socializing is that serious conversations are more likely to take place away from home than within the home. Thus, Goodwin notes, when persons from such home backgrounds marry, they often find it difficult to talk to each other at home! They are so accustomed to going out to parties, dances, and dinners where they are with other people, that the two alone in a home are not prepared for significant conversations. And so they may continue the pattern of socialization very soon after marriage, inviting friends over and going out to parties. A wife may receive some important information secondhand, overhearing her husband saying something to a friend before she herself is told: "Mat, I heard you telling Mrs. Bensen that you thought we might go to Mexico this summer. You didn't tell me that before." "Didn't I? Oh, I guess I didn't—well, what do you think of the idea?"

Although both of these *models,* oversimplified and stated very briefly, might characterize American homes, there are clearly different values reflected in each: The authority-centered home seems more traditional and may be associated with older, established families. The social-centered home seems much more typical of the dominant suburban middle class. (Those who have read Reich's *Greening of America* may identify the former with his "Consciousness I," the latter with the values of his "Consciousness II.") The social-centered home is particularly characteristic of those values most associated with American culture: informality, openness, constant busyness, "other-directed," and what some critics might call "superficiality" or fragmentation.

It is no accident that the social-centered home flourishes in a consumer society such as the United States, with billions of dollars spent on home furnishings and leisure activities (including what is surely the largest producer of "games" of all kinds). The social-centered home is likely to be in a constant state of rearrangement, and every change becomes the subject of display for visitors. For this reason, too, the kitchen (which is likely to be the most expensive room in the house, with all the gadgets and luxury utensils) is a more interesting and information-filled room than any other.

Many visitors to the United States are invited to homes as part of any number of "people-to-people" programs, and the kind of homes they are most likely to visit are those of the social-centered type (since inviting foreign visitors is yet one more social activity and an excellent expression of this concept of a home). For many visitors such a home is in startling contrast to their own homes. For many of these guests, the visit is likely to be startling, discomfitting. American norms of informality and blurring of host-guest relationships are unique in the world: "Make yourself at home," Americans say, and as this is a most peculiar home, it may be very difficult for a guest to feel at home. To be invited to the kitchen, even to be invited to help prepare a meal or to fix a drink, even to answer the door and invite others inside ("tell whoever it is to come in, and introduce yourself—I'll be out in a few minutes").

Similarly, the American abroad is likely to be surprised—sometimes delighted, sometimes disappointed—when he finds that this house and home values and behavior are not appropriate. He may never be invited to a home in the first place, and this he may interpret as unfriendliness. Or if invited, he may be treated so much as a guest that he feels uncomfortable about all the special attention he is getting. He is afraid that he is causing his hosts too much trouble for he would never go to such trouble for his guests. He is likely to be curious about the house, particularly if he is a first-time visitor in the country, and he may ask if he can see the kitchen and sleeping rooms. But in some countries this is like a visitor arriving at an American home and asking if he could inspect the toilet.

Probably the ideal home for most Americans is one which is occupied by only one nuclear family and one in which each member of the family has his own private room. (Recently there has been a reaction against this norm by some younger members of the society in the so-called "counterculture" who value community living, but even within most of these communes, the members join voluntarily and tend to be of about the same age and with very similar outlooks toward life. Few communes will contain three or even two generations, and in this sense even the counterculture is still an extension of many of the dominant American values.)

In many societies, however, the concept of a family is not restricted to parents and children; grandparents, in-laws, uncles, and aunts all may be considered when one thinks of a family. And the home may include many such relations. In Africa it is a common problem for young people who have come from the countryside to find work in the city to soon be visited by other members of their family, who simply move in on them. House complexes, if not a single house, are very likely to accommodate a large number of family members. And within a home, the divisions and organization of space are likely to be very different.

THE SWAHILI HOME

A common style of home in the coastal cities of Tanzania is what is sometimes called the Swahili house. To the outsider, the house looks like a small single-family dwelling, rectangular in shape, with a single door in the middle of the front of the house. When one enters the door, however, he looks down a long hallway often with three doors opening on each side of that corridor. In each of these six rooms, usually, there is a family; as many as six families, often from fifteen to twenty-five people, living in this single house. At the rear of the home is a common area for cooking, and another area for a toilet and possibly a place for bathing as well.

The six families may or may not be related, may or may not even be from the same tribe, and thus within the house there may be several different languages spoken. Obviously the values of privacy, community, and many other related values are very different for persons growing up in a Swahili house than for those growing up in a suburban American home. We might assume that this Swahili home is a product of a low standard of living, a point in the socioeconomic process leading to single-family homes. But such an interpretation is clearly biased by values of individuality, privacy, contractual friendships, and the like. The Swahili home bears resemblance to many living patterns in the country where all aspects of life are shared among neighbors and members of the extended family.

The socialist program of President Julius Nyerere (*"Ujamaa"*—literally "familyness") is built upon these values which are reflected and reinforced in such living styles. In this case it is possible to extend the influence of home style even to political systems for an entire nation. Nyerere sometimes quotes the Swahili proverb, *Mgeni siku mbili; siku ya tatu mpe jembe,* which means you should treat a guest as a guest for two days, but on the third day, give him a hoe, so he can work like one of the family. Sharing a home, sharing work and problems, and sharing in celebrations and in the simple pleasures of life are all related. Mother rarely prepares her meal alone; she is almost always cooking with the other mothers. The men, who keep away from the women's territory, may sit outside of the home and talk and watch the people pass by the house. Social organizations, community dances, and other such functions are similarly communal and divided among ages and sexes but not usually among individual family units.

Neighboring houses, too, are extensions of the principle. If there is a thief or a fire or a wedding or a baby born, everybody in the neighborhood feels obliged to assist in any way possible. And if a visitor comes, the host is sure to take the visitor around the neighborhood to meet the neighbors just as he would introduce members of his own family. To fail to do so would be impolite. Or worse, if a family remained unto themselves they might not receive the help from the community when problems arose.

Much of this description from East Africa is quite similar to what would be described in traditional communities in most of the world. There are unique patterns to each society, but the spirit of community, of sharing, of a lack of private property and privacy appear throughout the world as the rule rather than as the exception.

THE JAPANESE HOME

With the exception of some apartments and very small living quarters, most "Western homes" clearly distinguish between a living room, a dining room, and a bedroom. Each is characterized by its own furniture. In the traditional Japanese home, however, a single room can serve all three of these functions, and thus it is sometimes difficult to speak of the bedroom or the dining room, for it may depend more on the hour of the day than the areas themselves. One reason this is possible is that traditionally very little furniture is used in the home; there are no beds as such, for example, but instead *futon* (thick sleeping mats with a comforter-like top) are spread out when it is time to sleep, and folded up and put into special closets when not being used; cushions rather than chairs are used for sitting, and these, too, are easily moved or removed as required. Where Western homes may have several tables (a coffee table, a dining table, study table) a single low table may serve several of these purposes and may also be put out of the way when it is time for the *futon* to be spread. The lightness and airiness, and the sense of space characteristic of Japanese aesthetics is thus expressed in the practical day-to-day living. Moreover, the doors which separate most rooms are also lightweight sliding doors which thus can be removed entirely when necessary, unlike the fixed, hinged Western doors; and therefore a room may be made to seem larger or smaller as needed by closing or removing these doors.

These sliding doors (both the thicker, elegant *fusuma* and the translucent, this *shoji*) have no locks. One cannot go into his own room and lock the door. The sliding glass doors and windows which open out onto the garden or street do have locks and there is also an additional set of wooden doors (*amado* or "rain doors"), which completely block out all vision. These, too, are always closed and locked at night.

Although we cannot prove any cause or even significant correlations between home structure and cultural patterns of communication, we would expect less individualism within the Japanese home, and a stronger separation of the home from the outside than would be true in the West. And, of course, this is exactly what is usually said about Japanese culture.

This aspect of home structure seems very consistent with contrasting values of Japanese and Western peoples. That is, the family as a whole, rather than the individual, is highly valued in Japan. As the action of any one member of the family reflects on the entire family, individual choices and decisions must be made with great care and after considerable discussion within the family. Moreover, several scholars have noted that there is no word for privacy in Japan, at least not in the sense that we can speak of a *private room* or a *private car*. And while Americans are likely to speak of *"my* house," Tanzanians (and many others with similar related values) will always say *"our* house"; in Japanese it is the word for house itself (*"uchi"*) which serves as the pronoun for possession: *uchi no kuruma,* for example, meaning "our car" (or "my car") literally translates as "the house's car."

Although it is impossible to treat all the characteristics of homes in any culture in so short a discussion as this, it might be worth considering a few other characteristics of the traditional Japanese home style, for in many ways it provides a striking contrast with Western homes.

Bath and Toilet   In Japan, the bathing area and the toilet are always in separate rooms (except in some Western-style hotels or apartments); the American euphemism "bathroom," meaning toilet, is thus very confusing to Japanese who take care to distinguish the two as the clean place and the dirty place. In the past, and to a great extent today even in Tokyo there is no large hot-water tank to provide hot running water. Thus in the evening when it is time for a bath, the *ofuro* or Japanese bathtub is filled with cold water, and a small stove is lit which heats the water. Preparing for a bath at home thus requires as much as an hour just heating the water.

Unlike Western bathing, the Japanese style is to do all the soaping and scrubbing and rinsing outside of the tub; the tub itself is for soaking and relaxing. In this way the same bath water can serve the entire family. (Perhaps the Western counterpart is taking a shower before entering a public swimming pool.) We mention these details not because bathing customs are interesting in themselves, but because even in the bath the individualistic versus family orientation is clearly reflected. An entire family may bathe together, and it is very common for mothers to bathe with their children or for older children to bathe together.

When family members bathe in sequence in Japan, the traditional order of bathing also reflects and reinforces the authority structure of the home. The most important person, father, bathes first. The water is of course hottest and cleanest for the first person who bathes, and thus the order of the bath also reflects cultural values. In Japan the traditional pattern was quite simple: father bathed first because he was the most important person; then the older sons bathed, with the children and wife being the last.

Values are further reinforced by that shared hot water. If one should be the first to bathe and find the water too hot, it is improper to add cold water to lower the temperature, for this makes the water still colder for the next person who may prefer it even hotter. The bathing pattern thus also reinforces in such a subtle way values of group-consciousness, conformity, acceptance of what is provided. No claim is made that cultural values arise from such routines as bathing, but neither are they separable. To some extent for the child growing up, cultural values are introduced in such ways.

While bathing is generally regarded as relaxing and refreshing in the West, there are also those children who avoid taking baths whenever possible ("Do I have to? I took a bath last night."). This attitude is not found in Japan where the bath is consistently associated with relaxation and family ties, rather than the "hurry up I'm waiting to take a bath" attitude sometimes felt in Western families. (The English musical review of several years ago, *At the Drop of a Hat,* by Michael Flanders and Donald Swann, contained a delightful song called "In the Bath." The song extolled the pleasures of bathing and concluded by encouraging all of the political leaders in the world to get together in a bathtub, for this was surely the best of all places to be friendly—and agreeable. Something of that attitude is characteristic of Japan, not so much within a home as at the thousands of bathing spas throughout the country which are favorite meeting places for friends and social groups.) One American girl recently married to a Japanese man confided: "Whenever my husband and I get into a fight, we always find it easiest to make up in the bath. It is impossible to be angry in the bath."

At Home and Away   It is very unusual to telephone a Japanese home and receive no answer. Somebody is always at home it seems; it is still very rare for a wife to work. (*"Okusan,"* the polite word used when referring to any mature woman except one related to the speaker, means literally "deep in the middle of the home," the traditionally valued place for a woman.) And when the wife must go shopping or take a child to school, her mother-in-law, who is likely to live in the home, will answer the telephone. And if there is no mother-in-law in the home, then things may be arranged so that the house is occupied by somebody else.

So Near, So Far   The Japanese language contains many expressions for organizations of houses. One has obligations toward the neighbors which date back centuries. During the Second World War, this pattern was applied by the military government to make a whole neighborhood of ten houses culpable for the criminal act of any member of any of the homes. The positive virtues of neighborliness remain (except in the tall, grim apartment buildings of large cities) in forms such as offering service on special occasions (such as weddings) or giving gifts to families returning from a vacation. The traditional patterns of obligations extend to neighbors on either side of the house plus the neighbor across the street.

This relationship is similar to the East African pattern in its sense of obligations to neighbors. It differs sharply, however, in the individual's view of his own home, which is far more private in Japan than in any of the other homes described here. For a visitor, even a neighbor, to be invited into a Japanese home brings with it even more obligations: serving tea, food, the obligation of a return visit, and probably gift exchanges as well. Therefore, the inside of one's house is regarded as very different from the outside. Again the language reveals the importance of this distinction: *uchi no* (literally means "the house's," but it is used to mean "our") affairs, business, problems, is contrasted with *soto* (literally, "outside," but covering everything else that is not *ours*). Nearly everything in Japan, it seems, from problems to friends, is distinguished in this way.

All of these observations may help to explain the puzzlement felt by foreign visitors in Japan when they find they are treated with generosity and kindness but almost never are allowed to feel "at home." Emotionally and quite literally they must always be *yoso no hito,* "people outside our house."

THE MIDDLE EASTERN HOME

The nature of social interaction in the Middle East is reflected in the structure of the average home in the area. In urban or rural settings, a room is usually set aside for receiving and entertaining guests. That room is the pride of the family. Valued heirlooms, pictures of the dear, living or dead, and cherished souvenirs are displayed in the *salon,* an Arabicized word from the French. By the same token, the room's furnishing reflects the family's degree of education, affluence, and modernity. The taste, the quality of furnishings, and the degree of Westernization that the room reflects are a mirror of the family's status and the light in which it likes to be viewed. For example, the family that seats its guests on rugs and hassocks reflects a different structure of internal relationships from the family that seats its guests on sofas and armchairs. The message reflects an advertised measure of identification with the Western, the modern. Although the *"salon"* is a very important room in the home, it is not the most frequently used. It is, paradoxically, both focal and peripheral. It is the center of the family's formal social interaction with visitors, while it is physically located on the periphery of the home.

In the Middle Eastern home, a door usually opens into a family room with a hallway and a number of rooms that are open either on the family room or on the hallways. In the back, close to the kitchen, are the bathroom facilities.

In most homes all rooms look alike. The use and function of every room is decided upon by the family. However, the *salon* is usually the room farthest away from all others and the closest to the door leading to the outside. Actually, in older buildings, the *"majlis"* or the salon or the guest room (which is a literal translation in certain Arabic dialects), a door leading to the outside opens directly into this room on one end and another door opens to the inside of the home. In such a layout the guest knocks at the door and is either led into the *salon* through the home or asked to please wait until the other door leading immediately to the salon is opened for him. The behavior reflects two of the primary cultural values of the area. The first is the preoccupation with the concept of face, facades, and appearances. The guest is exposed only to the most shining, formal, and stylized part of the home and gets to meet only the members whom the family intends for him to meet. On the other hand, relationships in the Middle East reflect contextual varieties of guest-host interactions with territorial expectations of welcome and hospitality on the part of the guest and situational obligations of maintaining the traditional image of an open house on the part of the host. Thus, in receiving the guest in the most distinguished part of the home and in having him meet only the members of the family dressed for the occasion, the guest is honored and the family status is reflected.

With close association and the development of friendship, a guest comes to be accepted by the family and received in the family room or what is commonly referred to in the Middle East as the *sitting room.* However, between the time a guest is received in the salon and the time he is accepted as "one of us," a translation from the Arabic expression, certain social processes take place in terms of the guest's relationship to the family. The pace at which the guest meets the members of the opposite sex in the host family, and the length of the interaction reflect the internal sociocultural norms of the family. For example, it is not unusual in the Middle East for two men to have known each other for a number of years without either of them having met the female members of the other's family, even though they may know a lot about each other's life. This is in contrast to a modern, Westernized fmaily in which a guest may meet most of the members during his first visit.

Until a guest is accepted and received informally in the family room his movement is usually restricted to the salon. Unlike the custom, in the United States, for example, where a guest wanting to use the toilet just gets up and heads toward the bathroom perhaps mumbling an "excuse me" or perhaps not, in the Middle East, the guest asks for permission to go to the bathroom and for guidance to it. The request allows the host to go out first and check to make sure that the way to the bathroom is clear. That is, he makes sure that there are no family members that the host doesn't want to introduce to the guest, that those around are decent, and that the place is tidy and in agreement with the image that the host would like to create. Consequently, because of all these little inconveniences, it is uncommon for a salon-only guest to go to the bathroom in a host's house. The situation is of course different in the case of a guest who is invited to a meal.

In one sense, the most exclusive place in the Middle Eastern home is the kitchen. Its territory is the domain of the household members and mainly the females in the family. To that extent it is the most intimate place in the Middle Eastern home. A guest, whether male or female, has to have achieved the highest degree of familiarity with a family to be admitted to their kitchen.

Depending upon the socioeconomic level of the family, the home may have a sitting room and a family room with one of them the equivalent of a North American den. The use and functions, however, are different. In the Middle East, it is not too frequent that all members of the family gather together in the sitting room. In fact, when the older members are in the sitting room, the young may stay away in the "den" or in their bedrooms out of deference, unless there is something specific that they want to discuss with their parents or aunts or uncles. In behavioral terms, deference is reflected in subduing physical noise or keeping it away from the ears of the elders in the family. Hence the different connotations of silence in certain contexts, for example, for the Middle Easterner and the North American.

In the Middle East, however, the men usually congregate together in the early evening and night hours in indoor or outdoor cafés. Meanwhile, the women visit together, and the young have uninhibited access to all parts of the home, since it is usually the presence of the father or the elder male members in the family that regulates movement and noise in the home. However, with the introduction of television, and the appeal of contemporary programs, family togetherness has begun to center around the television set. Even popular cafés in the Mideast have had to acquire television sets to help maintain their appeal.

The allocation and use of private space in the Middle Eastern home reflect the value system and lines of authority within the family. In some homes, for example, only the elder male members of the family may have access to the whole home. That is, only they are allowed to disturb or invade the privacy of any member of the family who might be alone in his room working, sulking, or visiting with a friend. Also, it is not unusual to find that only the mother has access to the father if he is alone in his room behind a closed door.

The Middle Eastern home, like others, reveals the authority system within the home, the roles and norms of behavior for each sex, and a culture's outlook toward friends and neighbors. The home is a miniature replica of its society and a propagator of many of its values and patterns of communication.

THE GERMAN HOME

Doors, hedges, fences: these physical features of a German home reflect an emphasis on privacy which is pervasive throughout German life.[4] Add to privacy formal and regimented behavior, tempered by a love of the outdoors, and you have much that is at the heart of the German home and basic to many characteristically German patterns of communication. Two centuries of industrialization, plus the devastation and forced migration wrought by the war, have not lessened the ideal of a *Heimat,* a place of one's own, a family home, even if the ideal must sometimes be accommodated to the realities of small apartment living in the larger cities.

In contrast to the kind of neighborhood fostered by the American social-centered home, one which is likely to stress good schools, good companions for the children, and friendly neighbors on the block, in Germany a "good neighbor" is likely to be one who is quiet, knows his place, doesn't object when children make noise, and keeps his own sidewalk clean. Good fences make good neighbors. There is no place here for the welcome wagon, and relatively little "dropping by" for a chat. Even leases are likely to enforce some of these qualities. A lease will often specify who may use the garden or the yard in the back of the house, if there is one, and at which hours. It will probably require the tenant to sweep and wash the stairwell outside of the apartment, and quite possibly the front steps and the sidewalk, too. Time periods for making noise may be prescribed: no running water after 10 P.M.

Even in smaller towns in Germany, formality and social distance are notable in home style and house construction. The door to the average home is made up of two parts, and usually only the top part, about waist height, is opened to receive goods or for conversing with neighbors. When housewives gather for the *Kaffeeklatch,* which is really a gossip session, they usually refer to each other—and to those about whom they are speaking—as Frau or Fräulein so-and-so, not by first names. Thus here, too, the formality of a proper social distance is maintained.

People in small towns and in large cities throughout Germany share a great love for the outdoors; the outside is a central part of the concept of an ideal home. However, the outdoors is a private nature and not at all like the expansive front lawns and floor-to-ceiling picture windows glorified in so many American home magazines. Yards are in the back and well shielded from neighbors by shrubbery. Even in city apartments, balconies are very common and well planted. Some city apartments often lack a dining room or a dining-kitchen, the balcony serves to stretch the available space and helps to give the illusion of being in contact with nature. Yards are used for gardening as well as for dining.

Germans eat meals or snacks outdoors at all hours of the day. Garden restaurants, such as the familiar Biergarten, are among the most frequent settings for communication. Indeed, except for family and very close friends, homes are not used for entertaining guests. Restaurants usually have a special table marked by the sign, *"Stammtisch"* (regular's table) for patrons who come every evening to talk, dine, and drink.

For the woman who stays at home, the morning is probably spent in doing housework and shopping and preparing for the midday meal, *Mittagessen,* the main hot meal usually served around 1 P.M. As in most countries outside the United States, both the limitations of space as well as cultural values require shopping daily. When the meal is served, the whole family should be present. School has ended by this time, many shops close, and father has at least an hour free from work. (Increasing problems of traffic threaten this pattern in Germany as elsewhere, however.) Only a serious problem justifies the absence of any member of the family. There is little tolerance for a child's declining to join the family because he says he is not hungry or has promised to eat elsewhere.

After the meal, although school is over, schooling is not. German schools are demanding, and thus mother and child (or children) will spend the afternoon bound together in school work. The parent is a taskmaster (or mistress). Home offers no respite for the child. Headaches, tension, even nervous breakdowns are cause of concern in Germany, but much of the child's day at home is spent under such pressure. And everything may be reviewed again in the evening when father returns. (Except for the hours involved, this description of schooling in the German home is nearly identical to that of contemporary Japan, we might note.)

As we have indicated in our comments on house and home styles in other cultures, the physical plan of the German home also seems to reflect and help maintain many basic cultural values which recur in communication patterns. The ideal German home has foyer or entryway that leads visitors into the house without exposing them to specific rooms and a resultant loss of privacy for the family members. The living room, or *Wohnsimmer,* is the most formal room in the house, and it shares much in common with such rooms in the other homes described (except for the case of the social-centered home in the United States). Whatever the family considers an heirloom is there: a wall scroll showing the family tree, an antique statue, a piano, a Bible, or a wall full of books. Here guests are entertained. If there are children in the family who are old enough to be quiet, they may be expected to appear immediately, greet the guests, and stay quietly for the length of the visit. They speak when spoken to; they are to be seen but not heard. Thus their behavior in the living room is usually quite different from that of many American children who can drop in and say "Hi" and then leave in order to pursue their own interests.

As we have already indicated, a balcony or a back yard may also be a center of social activity, each well hidden from public view and as overflowing with flowers as is possible. Similar guarantees of privacy are provided by heavy drapes on the windows, or with the drapes opened but lighter white sheer curtains drawn. (We recall that Freud's colleague and a noted psychoanalyst himself, Theodore Reich, has also written about the importance of curtains. Reich noted that curtains or drapes were the first things a woman wanted in a house, and he interpreted this in terms of female sexuality and modesty. A better guess might be in terms of German values of privacy.)

The typical bedroom closely resembles that described for the authority-centered home in the United States. The rooms tend to be smaller than those in the American model, but twin beds are far more common than double beds. In fact, double beds are sometimes referred to as *"Französische Betten"* (French beds), and many Germans find the idea of such a bed tantalizing if not quite erotic.

Closed doors and massive furniture are themes already explored by Edward Hall in *The Hidden Dimension.* He sees the double doors often used in offices and hotels as evidence of the German search for privacy via soundproofing as well as physical barriers. In this respect the German sense of privacy within a home or office is completely different from that found in Japanese homes, where walls and doors must be among the thinnest in the world. However, in regard to privacy and mutual obligations in regard to neighbors, the German and Japanese patterns show some remarkable similarities. Hall has also observed that the heavy German furniture seems to fill a need for stability and at the same time ensure that social relationships will remain at an acceptable distance.

Finally, we might mention one element of contemporary life we have not considered in the previous descriptions: the use of the telephone. Professor Mary Badami has noted that where homes in Germany have telephones, the use of the phone seems to conform to the general pattern described here.[5] Older Germans are especially prone to follow an elaborate but informal etiquette of phone usage: the morning is a good time to call a private house; calls should not be made around noon (since meals would be interrupted), calls should not be made through the early afternoon (people might be napping); late afternoon is acceptable, but not the evening meal time; a brief after-supper time segment is acceptable, if not too late—calls should not intrude on the bedtime hours.

CONCLUDING COMMENTS

Apparent in several of these descriptions of homes is a parallel between a strong central authority in the home and a set of norms which seem to help shape and regulate family life. Formality, a sharp distinction between guest and family member, and a related concern for properly impressing the guest; role behavior according to sex and age, and the corresponding use of particular rooms of the home; and throughout a sharply defined hierarchy within the home: These aspects seem so consistent in the previous descriptions of home that it is clearly the American "social-centered home" that stands out in sharp contrast. Such comparisons, for whatever they are worth, should not be twisted into preferential distinctions between "traditional" and "modern," or "stable" and "dissolving" kinds of family structures, however. In any case, our descriptions are intentionally brief and incomplete, for purposes of illustration and comparison.

Perhaps what is of greatest value has not been the description of any one composite home or even the more obvious similarities and differences when comparing these; rather it may have been the approach itself—seeing the home as a microcosm of society, the place where each person first learns how to communicate within the norms of his culture. We should each think back to our own homes and recall as best we can where, when, how, and with whom we first learned to communicate. Increasingly now, and not only in the United States, an individual's memories are of more than a single home. And that is significant, too.

NOTES

1. A recent expression of this appeared in a letter to *Time* (Sept. 24, 1973), from Shigeo Tahara of Osaka, Japan. He wrote that there was a marked difference between Americans and Japanese in the face of rising meat prices in each country. "Americans are protecting cows and shops with firearms and are experiencing violence and burglary. Here in Japan, prices are skyrocketing faster than in the U.S., but people are still quiet. Meat-eating people seem to get hot more easily than vegetarians. Meat seems to give people an irresistible urge for action."

2. Charles Reich, *The Greening of America,* pp. 235-239, Random House, New York, 1970.

3. Leland Roloff, personal correspondence; we express appreciation to Dr. Goodwin for this concept, though interpretations and application here are original.

4. These observations were provided by Mary Badami and Caroline Yousef.

5. Personal correspondence.

PROXEMICS IN A CROSS-CULTURAL CONTEXT: GERMANS, ENGLISH, AND FRENCH

Edward T. Hall

Excerpt from *The Hidden Dimension* by Edward T. Hall. Copyright © 1966 by Edward T. Hall. Used by permission of Doubleday and Company, Inc. Reprinted by permission of the author's agent, Lurton Blassingame.

The Germans, the English, the Americans, and the French share significant portions of each other's cultures, but at many points their cultures clash. Consequently, the misunderstandings that arise are all the more serious because sophisticated Americans and Europeans take pride in correctly interpreting each other's behavior. Cultural differences which are out of awareness are, as a consequence, usually chalked up to ineptness, boorishness, or lack of interest on the part of the other person.

THE GERMANS

Whenever people from different countries come into repeated contact they begin to generalize about each other's behavior. The Germans and the German Swiss are no exception. Most of the intellectual and professional people I have talked to from these two countries eventually get around to commenting on American use of time and space. Both the Germans and the German Swiss have made consistent observations about how Americans structure time very tightly and are sticklers for schedules. They also note that Americans don't leave any free time for themselves (a point which has been made by Sebastian de Grazia in *Of Time, Work, and Leisure*).

Since neither the Germans nor the Swiss (particularly the German Swiss) could be regarded as completely casual about time, I have made it a point to question them further about their view of the American approach to time. They will say that Europeans will schedule fewer events in the same time than Americans do and they usually add that Europeans feel less "pressed" for time than Americans. Certainly, Europeans allow more time for virtually everything involving important human relationships. Many of my European subjects observed that in Europe human relationships are important whereas in the United States the schedule is important. Several of my subjects then took the next logical step and connected the handling of time with attitudes toward space, which Americans treat with incredible casualness. According to European standards, Americans use space in a wasteful way and seldom plan adequately for public needs. In fact, it would seem that Americans feel that people have no needs associated with space at all. By overemphasizing the schedule, Americans tend to underemphasize individual space needs. I should mention at this point that all Europeans are not this perceptive. Many of them go no further than to say that in the United States they themselves feel pressured by time and they often complain that our cities lack variety. Nevertheless, given these observations made by Europeans, one would expect that the Germans would be more upset by violations of spatial mores than the Americans.

Germans and Intrusions   I shall never forget my first experience with German proxemic patterns, which occurred when I was an undergraduate. My manners, my status, and my ego were attacked and crushed by a German in an instance where thirty years' residence in this country and an excellent command of English had not attenuated German definitions of what constitutes an intrusion. In order to understand the various issues that were at stake, it is necessary to refer back to two basic American patterns that are taken for granted in this country and which Americans therefore tend to treat as universal.

First, in the United States there is a commonly accepted, invisible boundary around any two or three people in conversation which separates them from others. Distance alone serves to isolate any such group and to endow it with a protective wall of privacy. Normally, voices are kept low to avoid intruding on others and if voices are heard, people will act as though they had not heard. In this way, privacy is granted whether it is actually present or not. The second pattern is somewhat more subtle and has to do with the exact point at which a person is experienced as actually having crossed a boundary and entered a room. Talking through a screen door while standing outside a house is not considered by most Americans as being inside the house or room in any sense of the word. If one is standing on the threshold holding the door open and talking to someone inside, it is still defined informally and experienced as being *outside*. If one is in an office building and just "pokes his head in the door" of an office he's still outside the office. Just holding on to the doorjamb when one's body is inside the room still means a person has one foot "on base" as it were so that he is not quite inside the other fellow's territory. None of these American spatial definitions is valid in northern Germany. In every instance where the American would consider himself *outside* he has already entered the German's territory and by definition would become involved with him. The following experience brought the conflict between these two patterns into focus.

It was a warm spring day of the type one finds only in the high, clean, clear air of Colorado, the kind of day that makes you glad you are alive. I was standing on the doorstep of a converted carriage house talking to a young woman who lived in an apartment upstairs. The first floor had been made into an artist's studio. The arrangement, however, was peculiar because the same entrance served both tenants. The occupants of the apartment used a small entryway and walked along one wall of the studio to reach the stairs to the apartment. You might say that they had an "easement" through the artist's territory. As I stood talking on the doorstep, I glanced to the left and noticed that some fifty to sixty feet away, inside the studio, the Prussian artist and two of his friends were also in conversation. He was facing so that if he glanced to one side he could just see me. I had noted his presence, but not wanting to appear presumptuous or to interrupt his conversation, I unconsciously applied the American rule and assumed that the two activities—my quiet conversation and his conversation—were not involved with each other. As I was soon to learn, this was a mistake, because in less time than it takes to tell, the artist had detached himself from his friends, crossed the intervening space, pushed my friend aside, and with eyes flashing, started shouting at me. By what right had I entered his studio without greeting him? Who had given me permission?

I felt bullied and humiliated, and even after almost thirty years, I can still feel my anger. Later study has given me greater understanding of the German pattern and I have learned that in the German's eyes I really had been intolerably rude. I was already "inside" the building and I intruded when I could *see* inside. For the German, there is no such thing as being inside the room without being inside the zone of intrusion, particularly if one looks at the other party, no matter how far away.

Recently, I obtained an independent check on how Germans feel about visual intrusion while investigating what people look at when they are in intimate, personal, social, and public situations. In the course of my research, I instructed subjects to photograph separately both a man and a woman in each of the above contexts. One of my assistants, who also happened to be German, photographed his subjects out of focus at public distance because, as he said, "You are not really supposed to look at other people at public distances *because it's intruding.*" This may explain the informal custom behind the German laws against photographing strangers in public without their permission.

The "Private Sphere"   Germans sense their own space as an extension of the ego. One sees a clue to this feeling in the term "Lebensraum," which is impossible to translate because it summarizes so much. Hitler used it as an effective psychological lever to move the Germans to conquest.

In contrast to the Arab, as we shall see later, the German's ego is extraordinarily exposed, and he will go to almost any length to preserve his "private sphere." This was observed during World War II when American soldiers were offered opportunities to observe German prisoners under a variety of circumstances. In one instance in the Midwest, German PWs were housed four to a small hut. As soon as materials were available, each prisoner built a partition so that he could have *his own space.* In a less favorable setting in Germany when the *Wehrmacht* was collapsing, it was necessary to use open stockades because German prisoners were arriving faster than they could be accommodated. In this situation each soldier who could find the materials built his own tiny dwelling unit, sometimes no larger than a foxhole. It puzzled the Americans that the Germans did not pool their efforts and their scarce materials to create a larger, more efficient space, particularly in view of the very cold spring nights. Since that time I have observed frequent instances of the use of architectural extensions of this need to screen the ego. German houses with balconies are arranged so that there is visual privacy. Yards tend to be well fenced; but fenced or not, they are sacred.

The American view that space should be shared is particularly troublesome to the German. I cannot document the account of the early days of World War II occupation when Berlin was in ruins but the following situation was reported by an observer and it has the nightmarish quality that is often associated with inadvertent cross-cultural blunders. In Berlin at that time the housing shortage was indescribably acute. To provide relief, occupation authorities in the American zone ordered those Berliners who still had kitchens and baths intact to share them with their neighbors. The order finally had to be rescinded when the already overstressed Germans started killing each other over the shared facilities.

Public and private buildings in Germany often have double doors for soundproofing, as do many hotel rooms. In addition, the door is taken very seriously by Germans. Those Germans who come to America feel that our doors are flimsy and light. The meanings of the open door and the closed door are quite different in the two countries. In offices, Americans keep doors open; Germans keep doors closed. In Germany, the closed door does not mean that the man behind it wants to be alone or undisturbed, or that he is doing something he doesn't want someone else to see. It's simply that Germans think that open doors are sloppy and disorderly. To close the door preserves the integrity of the room and provides a protective boundary between people. Otherwise, they get too involved with each other. One of my German subjects commented, "If our family hadn't had doors, we would have had to change our way of life. Without doors we would have had many, many more fights. . . . When you can't talk, you retreat behind a door. . . . If there hadn't been doors, I would always have been within reach of my mother."

Whenever a German warms up to the subject of American enclosed space, he can be counted on to comment on the noise that is transmitted through walls and doors. To many Germans, our doors epitomize American life. They are thin and cheap; they seldom fit; and they lack the substantial quality of German doors. When they close they don't sound and feel solid. The click of the lock is indistinct; it rattles and indeed it may even be absent.

The open-door policy of American business and the closed-door patterns of German business culture cause clashes in the branches and subsidiaries of American firms in Germany. The point seems to be quite simple, yet failure to grasp it has caused considerable friction and misunderstanding between American and German managers overseas. I was once called in to advise a firm that has operations all over the world. One of the first questions asked was, "How do you get the Germans to keep their doors open?" In this company the open doors were making the Germans feel exposed and gave the whole operation an unusually relaxed and unbusinesslike air. Closed doors, on the other hand, gave the Americans the feeling that there was a conspiratorial air about the place and that they were being left out. The point is that whether the door is open or shut, it is not going to mean the same thing in the two countries.

Order in Space   The orderliness and hierarchical quality of German culture are communicated in their handling of space. Germans want to know where they stand and object strenuously to people crashing queues or people who "get out of line" or who do not obey signs such as "Keep out," or "Authorized personnel only." Some of the German attitudes toward ourselves are traceable to our informal attitudes toward boundaries and to authority in general.

However, German anxiety due to American violations of order is nothing compared to that engendered in Germans by the Poles, who see no harm in a little disorder. To them lines and queues stand for regimentation and blind authority. I once saw a Pole crash a cafeteria line just "to stir up those sheep."

Germans get very technical about intrusion distance, as I mentioned earlier. When I once asked my students to describe the distance at which a third party would intrude on two people who were talking, there were no answers from the Americans. Each student knew that he could tell when he was being intruded on but he couldn't define intrusion or tell how he knew when it had occurred. However, a German and an Italian who had worked in Germany were both members of my class and they answered without any hesitation. Both stated that a third party would intrude on two people if he came within seven feet!

Many Americans feel that Germans are overly rigid in their behavior, unbending and formal. Some of this impression is created by differences in the handling of chairs while seated. The American doesn't seem to mind if people hitch their chairs up to adjust the distance to the situation—those that do mind would not think of saying anything, for to comment on the manners of others would be impolite. In Germany, however, it is a violation of the mores to change the position of your chair. An added deterrent for those who don't know better is the weight of most German furniture. Even the great architect Mies van der Rohe, who often rebelled against German tradition in his buildings, made his handsome chairs so heavy that anyone but a strong man would have difficulty in adjusting his seating position. To a German, light furniture is anathema, not only because it seems flimsy but because people move it and thereby destroy the order of things, including intrusions on the "private sphere." In one instance reported to me, a German newspaper editor who had moved to the United States had his visitor's chair bolted to the floor "at the proper distance" because he couldn't tolerate the American habit of adjusting the chair to the situation.

THE ENGLISH

It has been said that the English and the Americans are two great people separated by one language. The differences for which language gets blamed may not be due so much to words as to communications on other levels beginning with English intonation (which sounds affected to many Americans) and continuing to ego-linked ways of handling time, space, and materials. If there ever were two cultures in which differences of the proxemic details are marked it is in the educated (public school) English and the middle-class Americans. One of the basic reasons for this wide disparity is that in the United States we use space as a way of classifying people and activities, whereas in England it is the social system that determines who you are. In the United States, your address is an important cue to status (this applies not only to one's home but to the business address as well). The Joneses from Brooklyn and Miami are not as "in" as the Joneses from Newport and Palm Beach. Greenwich and Cape Cod are worlds apart from Newark and Miami. Businesses located on Madison and Park Avenues have more tone than those on Seventh and Eighth Avenues. A corner office is more prestigious than one next to the elevator or at the end of a long hall. The Englishman, however, is born and brought up in a social system. He is still Lord—no matter where you find him, even if it is behind the counter in a fishmonger's stall. In addition to class distinctions, there are differences between the English and ourselves in how space is allotted.

The middle-class American growing up in the United States feels he has a right to have his own room, or at least part of a room. My American subjects, when asked to draw an ideal room or office, invariably drew it for themselves and no one else. When asked to draw their present room or office, they drew only their part of a shared room and then drew a line down the middle. Both male and female subjects identified the kitchen and the master bedroom as belonging to the mother or the wife, whereas Father's territory was a study or a den, if one was available; otherwise, it was "the shop," "the basement," or sometimes only a workbench or the garage. American women who want to be alone can go to the bedroom and close the door. The closed door is the sign meaning "Do not disturb" or "I'm angry." An American is available if his door is open at home or at his office. He is expected not to shut himself off but to maintain himself in a state of constant readiness to answer the demands of others. Closed doors are for conferences, private conversations, and business, work that requires concentration, study, resting, sleeping, dressing, and sex.

The middle- and upper-class Englishman, on the other hand, is brought up in a nursery shared with brothers and sisters. The oldest occupies a room by himself which he vacates when he leaves for boarding school, possibly even at the age of nine or ten. The difference between a room of one's own and early conditioning to shared space, while seeming inconsequential, has an important effect on the Englishman's attitude toward his own space. He may never have a permanent "room of his own" and seldom expects one or feels he is entitled to one. Even Members of Parliament have no offices and often conduct their business on the terrace overlooking the Thames. As a consequence, the English are puzzled by the American need for a secure place in which to work, an office. Americans working in England may become annoyed if they are not provided with what they consider appropriate enclosed work space. In regard to the need for walls as a screen for the ego, this places the Americans somewhere between the Germans and the English.

The contrasting English and American patterns have some remarkable implications, particularly if we assume that man, like other animals, has a built-in need to shut himself off from others from time to time. An English student in one of my seminars typified what happens when hidden patterns clash. He was quite obviously experiencing strain in his relationships with Americans. Nothing seemed to go right and it was quite clear from his remarks that we did not know how to behave. An analysis of his complaints showed that a major source of irritation was that no American seemed to be able to pick up the subtle clues that there were times when he didn't want his thoughts intruded on. As he stated it, "I'm walking around the apartment and it seems that whenever I want to be alone my roommate starts talking to me. Pretty soon he's asking 'What's the matter?' and wants to know if I'm angry. By then I am angry and say something."

It took some time but finally we were able to identify most of the contrasting features of the American and British problems that were in conflict in this case. When the American wants to be alone he goes into a room and shuts the door—he depends on architectual features for screening. For an American to refuse to talk to someone else present in the same room, to give them the "silent treatment," is the ultimate form of rejection and a sure sign of great displeasure. The English, on the other hand, lacking rooms of their own since childhood, never developed the practice of using space as a refuge from others. They have in effect internalized a set of barriers, which they erect and which others are supposed to recognize. Therefore, the more the Englishman shuts himself off when he is with an American the more likely the American is to break in to assure himself that all is well. Tension lasts until the two get to know each other. The important point is that the spatial and architectural needs of each are not the same at all.

Using the Telephone   English internalized privacy mechanisms and the American privacy screen result in very different customs regarding the telephone. There is no wall or door against the telephone. Since it is impossible to tell from the ring who is on the other end of the line, or how urgent his business is, people feel compelled to answer the phone. As one would anticipate, the English when they feel the need to be with their thoughts treat the phone as an intrusion by someone who doesn't know any better. Since it is impossible to tell how preoccupied the other party will be, they hesitate to use the phone; instead, they write notes. To phone is to be "pushy" and rude. A letter or telegram may be slower, but it is much less disrupting. Phones are for actual business and emergencies.

I used this system myself for several years when I lived in Santa Fe, New Mexico, during the depression. I dispensed with a phone because it cost money. Besides, I cherished the quiet of my tiny mountainside retreat and didn't want to be disturbed. This idiosyncrasy on my part produced a shocked reaction in others. People really didn't know what to do with me. You could see the consternation on their faces when, in answer to the question, "How do I get in touch with you?" I would reply, "Write me a post card. I come to the post office every day."

Having provided most of our middle-class citizens with private rooms and escape from the city to the suburbs, we have then proceeded to penetrate their most private spaces in their home with a most public device, the telephone. Anyone can reach us at any time. We are, in fact, so available that elaborate devices have to be devised so that busy people can function. The greatest skill and tact must be exercised in the message-screening process so that others will not be offended. So far our technology has not kept up with the needs of people to be alone with either their families or their thoughts. The problem stems from the fact that it is impossible to tell from the phone's ring who is calling and how urgent his business is. Some people have unlisted phones, but then that makes it hard on friends who come to town who want to get in touch with them. The government solution is to have special phones for important people (traditionally red). The red line bypasses secretaries, coffee breaks, busy signals, and teen-agers, and is connected to White House, State Department, and Pentagon switchboards.

Neighbors   Americans living in England are remarkably consistent in their reactions to the English. Most of them are hurt and puzzled because they were brought up on American neighboring patterns and don't interpret the English ones correctly. In England propinquity means nothing. The fact that you live next door to a family does not entitle you to visit, borrow from, or socialize with them, or your children to play with theirs. Accurate figures on the number of Americans who adjust well to the English are difficult to obtain. The basic attitude of the English toward the Americans is tinged by our ex-colonial status. This attitude is much more in awareness and therefore more likely to be expressed than the unspoken right of the Englishman to maintain his privacy against the world. To the best of my knowledge, those who have tried to relate to the English purely on the basis of propinquity seldom if ever succeed. They may get to know and even like their neighbors, but it won't be because they live next door, because English relationships are patterned not according to space but according to social status.

Whose Room Is the Bedroom?   In upper middle-class English homes, it is the man, not the woman, who has the privacy of the bedroom, presumably as protection from children who haven't yet internalized the English patterns of privacy. The man, not the woman, has a dressing room; the man also has a study which affords privacy. The Englishman is fastidious about his clothes and expects to spend a great deal of time and attention in their purchase. In contrast, English women approach the buying of clothes in a manner reminiscent of the American male.

Talking Loud and Soft   Proper spacing between people is maintained in many ways. Loudness of the voice is one of the mechanisms which also varies from culture to culture. In England and in Europe generally, Americans are continually accused of loud talking, which is a function of two forms of vocal control: (a) loudness, and (b) modulation for direction. Americans increase the volume as a function of distance, using several levels (whisper, normal voice, loud shout, etc.). In many situations, the more gregarious Americans do not care if they can be overheard. In fact, it is part of their openness showing that we have nothing to hide. The English do care, for to get along without private offices and not intrude they have developed skills in beaming the voice toward the person they are talking to, carefully adjusting it so that it just barely overrides the background noise and distance. For the English to be overheard is to intrude on others, a failure in manners and a sign of socially inferior behavior. However, because of the way they modulate their voices the English in an American setting may sound and look conspiratorial to Americans, which can result in their being branded as troublemakers.

Eye Behavior   A study of eye behavior reveals some interesting contrasts between the two cultures. Englishmen in this country have trouble not only when they want to be alone and shut themselves off but also when they want to interact. They never know for sure whether an American is listening. We, on the other hand, are equally unsure as to whether the English have understood us. Many of these ambiguities in communication center on differences in the use of the eyes. The

Englishman is taught to pay strict attention, to listen carefully, which he must do if he is polite and there are not protective walls to screen out sound. He doesn't bob his head or grunt to let you know he understands. He blinks his eyes to let you know that he has heard you. Americans, on the other hand, are taught not to stare. We look the other person straight in the eye without wavering only when we want to be particularly certain that we are getting through to him.

The gaze of the American directed toward his conversational partner often wanders from one eye to the other and even leaves the face for long periods. Proper English listening behavior includes immobilization of the eyes at social distance, so that whichever eye one looks at gives the appearance of looking straight at you. In order to accomplish this feat, the Englishman must be eight or more feet away. He is too close when the 12-degree horizontal span of the macula won't permit a steady gaze. At less than eight feet, one *must* look at either one eye or the other.

THE FRENCH

The French who live south and east of Paris belong generally to that complex of cultures which border the Mediterranean. Members of this group pack together more closely than do northern Europeans, English, and Americans. Mediterranean use of space can be seen in the crowded trains, buses, automobiles, sidewalk cafés, and in the homes of the people. The exceptions are, of course, in the châteaus and villas of the rich. Crowded living normally means high sensory involvement. Evidence of French emphasis on the senses appears not only in the way the French eat, entertain, talk, write, crowd together in cafés, but can even be seen in the way they make their maps. These maps are extraordinarily well thought out and so designed that the traveler can find the most detailed information. One can tell from using these maps that the French employ all their senses. These maps make it possible for you to get around and they also tell you where you can enjoy a view; where you'll find picturesque drives, and, in some instances, places to rest, refresh yourself, take a walk, and even eat a pleasant meal. They inform the traveler which senses he can expect to use and at what points in his journey.

Home and Family   One possible reason why the French love the outdoors is the rather crowded conditions under which many of them live. The French entertain at restaurants and cafés. The home is for the family and the outdoors for recreation and socializing. Yet all the homes I have visited, as well as everything I have been able to learn about

French homes, indicate that they are often quite crowded. The working class and the petite bourgeoisie are particularly crowded, which means that the French are sensually much involved with each other. The layout of their offices, homes, towns, cities, and countryside is such as to keep them involved.

In interpersonal encounters this involvement runs high; when a Frenchman talks to you, he really looks at you and there is no mistaking this fact. On the streets of Paris he looks at the women he sees very directly. American women returning to their own country after living in France often go through a period of sensory deprivation. Several have told me that because they have grown accustomed to being looked at, the American habit of *not* looking makes them feel as if they didn't exist.

Not only are the French sensually involved with each other, they have become accustomed to what are to us greatly stepped-up sensory inputs. The French automobile is designed in response to French needs. Its small size used to be attributed to a lower standard of living and higher costs of materials; and while there can be no doubt but that cost is a factor, it would be naïve to assume that it was the major factor. The automobile is just as much an expression of the culture as is the language and, therefore, has its characteristic niche in the cultural biotope. Changes in the car will reflect and be reflected in changes elsewhere. If the French drove American cars, they would be forced to give up many ways of dealing with space which they hold quite dear. The traffic along the Champs-Elysées and around the Arc de Triomphe is a cross between the New Jersey Turnpike on a sunny Sunday afternoon and the Indianapolis Speedway. With American-size autos, it would be mass suicide. Even the occasional "compact" American cars in the stream of Parisian traffic look like sharks among minnows. In the United States, the same cars look normal because everything else is in scale. In the foreign setting where they stand out, Detroit iron can be seen for what it is. The American behemoths give bulk to the ego and prevent overlapping of personal spheres inside the car so that each passenger is only marginally involved with the others. I do not mean by this that all Americans are alike and have been forced into the Detroit mold. But since Detroit won't produce what is wanted, many Americans prefer the smaller, more maneuverable European cars which fit their personalities and needs more closely. Nevertheless, if one simply looks at the styles of the French cars, one sees greater emphasis on individuality than in the United States. Compare the Peugeot, the Citroen, the Renault, and the Dauphine and the little 2 C.V. shoebox. It would take years and years of style changes to produce such differences in the United States.

French Use of Open Space   Because total space needs must be maintained in balance, the urban French have learned to make the most of the parks and the outdoors. To them, the city is something from which to derive satisfaction and so are the people in it. Reasonably clean air, sidewalks up to seventy feet wide, automobiles that will not dwarf humans as they pass on the boulevards make it possible to have outdoor cafés and open areas where people congregate and enjoy each other. Since the French savor and participate in the city itself—its varied sights, sounds, and smells; its wide sidewalks and avenues and parks—the need for insulating space in the automobile may be somewhat less than it is in the United States where humans are dwarfed by skyscrapers and the products of Detroit, virtually assaulted by filth and rubbish, and poisoned by smog and carbon dioxide.

The Star and the Grid   There are two major European systems for patterning space. One of these, "the radiating star" which occurs in France and Spain, is sociopetal. The other, the "grid," originated in Asia Minor, adopted by the Romans and carried to England at the time of Caesar, is sociofugal. The French-Spanish system connects all points and functions. In the French subway system, different lines repeatedly come together at places of interest like the Place de la Concorde, the Opéra, and the Madeleine. The grid system separates activities by stringing them out. Both systems have advantages, but a person familiar with one has difficulty using the other.

For example, a mistake in direction in the radiating center-point system becomes more serious the farther one travels. Any error, therefore, is roughly equivalent to taking off in the wrong direction. In the grid system, baseline errors are of the 90-degree or the 180-degree variety and are usually obvious enough to make themselves felt even by those with a poor sense of direction. If you are traveling in the right direction, even though you are one or two blocks off your course, the error is easily rectified at any time. Nevertheless, there are certain inherent advantages in the center-point system. Once one learns to use it, it is easier, for example, to locate objects or events in space by naming a point on a line. Thus it is possible, even in strange territory, to tell someone to meet you at the 50 KM mark on National Route 20 south of Paris; that is all the information he needs. In contrast, the grid system of coordinates involves at least two lines and a point to locate something in space (often many more lines and points, depending on how many turns one has to make). In the star system, it is also possible to integrate a number of different activities in centers in less space than with the grid system. Thus, residential, shopping, marketing, commercial, and recreation areas can both meet and be reached from central points.

It is incredible how many facets of French life the radiating star pattern touches. It is almost as though the whole culture were set up on a model in which power, influence, and control flowed in and out from a series of interlocking centers. There are sixteen major highways running into Paris, twelve into Caen (near Omaha Beach), twelve into Amiens, eleven for Le Mans, and ten for Rennes. Even the figures don't begin to convey the picture of what this arrangement really means, for France is a series of radiating networks that build up into larger and larger centers. Each small center has its own channel, as it were, to the next higher level. As a general rule, the roads between centers do not go through other towns, because each town is connected to others by its own roads. This is in contrast to the American pattern of stringing small towns out like beads on a necklace along the routes that connect principal centers.

In *The Silent Language* I have described how the man in charge of a French office can often be found in the middle—with his minions placed like satellites on strings radiating outward from him. I once had occasion to deal with such a "central figure" when the French member of a team of scientists under my direction wanted a raise because his desk was in the middle! Even De Gaulle based his international policy on France's central location. There are those, of course, who will say that the fact that the French school system also follows a highly centralized pattern couldn't possibly have any relationship to the layout of offices, subway systems, road networks, and, in fact, the entire nation, but I could not agree with them. Long experience with different patterns of culture has taught me that the basic threads tend to be woven throughout the entire fabric of a society.

The reason for the review of the three European cultures to which the middle class of the United States is most closely linked (historically and culturally) is as much as anything else a means of providing contrast to highlight some of our own implicit patterns. In this review it was shown that different use of the senses leads to very different needs regarding space no matter on what level one cares to consider it. Everything from an office to a town or city will reflect the sense modalities of its builders and occupants. In considering solutions to problems such as urban renewal and city sinks, it is essential to know how the populations involved perceive space and how they use their senses.

YOUR ACTIONS SPEAK LOUDER . . .

Melvin Schnapper

From *Peace Corps: The Volunteer,* June 1969, pp. 7-10. Reprinted by permission of the author.

A Peace Corps staff member is hurriedly called to a town in Ethiopia to deal with reports that one of the volunteers is treating Ethiopians like dogs. What could the volunteer be doing to communicate that?

A volunteer in Nigeria has great trouble getting any discipline in his class, and it is known that the students have no respect for him because he has shown no self-respect. How has he shown that?

Neither volunteer offended his hosts with words. But both of them were unaware of what they had communicated through their nonverbal behavior.

In the first case, the volunteer working at a health center would go into the waiting room and call for the next patient. She did this as she would in America—by pointing with her finger to the next patient and beckoning him to come. Acceptable in the States, but in Ethiopia her pointing gesture is for children and her beckoning signal is for dogs. In Ethiopia one points to a person by extending the arm and hand and beckons by holding the hand out, palm down, and closing it repeatedly.

In the second case, the volunteer insisted that students look him in the eye to show attentiveness, in a country where prolonged eye contact is considered disrespectful.

While the most innocent American-English gesture may have insulting, embarrassing, or at least confusing connotations in another culture, the converse is also true. If a South American were to bang on his table and hiss at the waiter for service in a New York restaurant, he would be fortunate if he were only thrown out. Americans usually feel that

Japanese students in the United States are obsequious because they bow all the time. Male African students in the States will be stared at for holding hands in public.

It seems easier to accept the arbitrariness of language—that dog is *chien* in French or *aja* in Yoruba—than the differences in the emotionally laden behavior of nonverbal communication, which in many ways is just as arbitrary as language.

We assume that our way of talking and gesturing is "natural" and that those who do things differently are somehow playing with nature. This assumption leads to a blindness about intercultural behavior. And the individual is likely to remain blind and unaware of what he is communicating nonverbally, because the hosts will seldom tell him that he has committed a social blunder. It is rude to tell people they are rude; thus the hosts grant the volunteer a "foreigner's license," allowing him to make mistakes of social etiquette, and he never knows until too late which ones prove disastrous.

An additional handicap is that the volunteer has not entered the new setting as a free agent, able to detect and adopt new ways of communicating without words. He is a prisoner of his own culture and interacts within his own framework. Yet the fact remains that for maximum understanding the American using the words of another language also must learn to use the tools of nonverbal communication of that culture.

Nonverbal communication—teaching it and measuring effect—is more difficult than formal language instruction. But now that language has achieved its proper recognition as being essential for volunteer success, the area of nonverbal behavior should be introduced to Peace Corps training in a systematic way, giving the trainees actual experiences, awareness, sensitivity. Indeed, it is the rise in volunteer linguistic fluency which now makes nonverbal fluency even more critical. A linguistically fluent volunteer may tend to offend even more than those who don't speak as well if he shows ignorance about interface etiquette; the national may perceive this disparity between linguistic and nonlinguistic performance as a disregard for the more subtle aspects of intercultural communication. Because nonverbal cues reflect emotional states, both volunteer and host national might not be able to articulate what's going on.

While some Peace Corps staff, in Washington as well as overseas, have recognized how proficiency in nonverbal communication would help erase unnecessary strain between volunteers and host nationals, others dismiss its importance, feeling that volunteers will simply "pick it up" or that it can be dealt with as a list of "do's and don't's.." Occasionally a language coordinator or cross-cultural studies coordinator recognizes its possibilities; but overall, nonverbal communication has been dealt with in a very haphazard way. That nonverbal interaction is a part of every encounter between a volunteer and a host national should be enough of a statement about its importance.

For all the discussion about this area and its treatment in *The Silent Language* and *The Hidden Dimension* by Edward Hall and for all the scattered, anecdotal "war stories," there has not been a refined method for training or sensitizing volunteers to nonverbal behavior. Because no one knows all the answers about it, practically everyone has hesitated to approach this as a training activity. In the rest of this article, I would like to discuss the method with which I have worked and which I feel has implications for both language and cross-cultural studies. I work for Volunteer Training Specialists, Inc., which has contracts for Peace Corps training at Baker, La. There I have worked with groups bound for Swaziland and Somalia, and at the Peace Corps' Virgin Islands Training Center I have been a consultant to trainee groups headed for six other African nations.

While it would be difficult to map out all the nonverbal details for every language that Peace Corps teaches, one can hope to make volunteers aware of the existence and emotional importance of nonverbal channels. I have identified five such channels: kinesic, proxemic, chronemic, oculesic, and haptic.

Kinesics—movement of the body (head, arms, legs, etc.). The initial example from the health center in Ethiopia was a problem caused by a kinesic sign being used which had different meaning cross-culturally. Another example, the American gesture of slitting one's throat implying "I've had it" or "I'm in trouble," conveys quite a different message in Swaziland. It means "I love you."

Americans make no distinction between gesturing for silence to an adult or to a child. An American will put one finger to his lips for both, while an Ethiopian will use only one finger to his child and four fingers for an adult. To use only one finger for an adult is disrespectful. On the other hand, Ethiopians make no distinction in gesturing to indicate emphatic negation. They shake their index finger from side to side to an adult as well as to a child, whereas this gesture is used only for children by Americans. Thus, if the volunteer is not conscious of the meaning of such behavior, he not only will offend his hosts but he will be offended by them.

Drawing in the cheeks and holding the arms rigidly by the side of the body means "thin" in Amharic. Diet-conscious Americans feel complimented if they are told that they are slim and so may naturally assume that to tell an Ethiopian friend this is also complimentary. Yet in Ethiopia and a number of other countries, this is taken pejoratively, as it is thought better to be heavy-set, indicating health and status and enough wealth to ensure the two.

Proxemics—the use of interpersonal space. South Americans, Greeks, and others find comfort in standing, sitting, or talking to people at a distance which Americans find intolerably close. We give their unusual closeness the social interpretation of aggressiveness and intimacy, causing us to have feelings of hostility, discomfort, or intimidation. If we back away to our greater distance of comfort, we are perceived as being cold, unfriendly, and distrustful. Somalis would see us as we see South Americans, since their interface distance is greater still than ours.

Chronemics—the timing of verbal exchanges during conversation. As Americans, we expect our partner to respond to our statement immediately. In some other cultures, people time their exchanges to leave silence between each statement. For Americans this silence is unsettling. To us it may mean that the person is shy, inattentive, bored, or nervous. It causes us to repeat, paraphrase, talk louder, and "correct" our speech to accommodate our partner. In the intercultural situation, it might be best for the volunteer to tolerate the silence and wait for a response.

Oculesics—eye-to-eye contact or avoidance. Americans are dependent upon eye contact as a sign of listening behavior. We do not feel that there is human contact without eye contact. In many countries there are elaborate patterns of eye avoidance which we regard as inappropriate.

Haptics—the tactile form of communication. Where, how, and how often people can touch each other while conversing are culturally defined patterns. We need not go beyond the borders of our own country to see groups (Italians and black Americans, for example) which touch each other more often than Anglo-Americans do. Overseas, Americans often feel crowded and pushed around by people who have much higher toleration for public physical contact and even need it as part of their communication process. A volunteer may feel embarrassed when a host national friend continues to hold his hand long after the formal greetings are over.

These five channels of nonverbal communication exist in every culture. The patterns and forms are completely arbitrary, and it is arguable as to what is universal and what is culturally defined.

With trainees, my objective has been to make them conscious of nonverbal communication, construct situations which will result in emotional responses (something impossible from reading in a book that you may expect to be bear-hugged and kissed on both cheeks), and encourage them to continue the practice of this behavior until it becomes a natural and accepted part of their repertoire of communication skills.

Part of the technique has been to divide a group of trainees in half, give directions to one half so that when they are paired up with a member of the other half, the nondirected partner will have feelings of discomfort about his partner's "strange" behavior.

As a sample exercise on proxemic behavior (use of space), the trainees are divided into two groups. In separate locations both are led into discussions of topics like "why they applied for the Peace Corps," "anticipated difficulties overseas," and similar topics in which trainees are interested. After awhile, one group is given a set of instructions. They are told that when they rejoin the "uninformed" group and are matched with their partners, they are to establish a distance of comfort and then decrease it by one inch. At each signal from the group leader, they are to come one inch closer to the partner. These signals may be the group leader's moving from one spot in the room to another, or his stopping the group to find out what specifics they talked about and then asking them to continue. His questions always will be about the content of the conversation, not about the experiment in process. Eventually, when the distance has been shortened by six inches or more, the nondirected partners will experience discomfort and consciously or unconsciously will start moving back. It is easy at this point to explain to them that their directed partners were imitating the comfortable positions of South Americans and that if the undirected partners were to behave in the same way with a Latin, the Latin would think them unfriendly and cold. Conversely, in Somalia, it would be the American who would be perceived as aggressive by standing too close for Somali comfort.

The basic format of the above exercise has been used to sensitize trainees to many other behavior patterns which relate to nonverbal communication. The idea is to start out with an "informed" partner and a "control" partner and inform the one to alter his nonverbal behavior in a graduated manner to make his partner react. Both persons will have an emotional or visceral reaction, after which time they are ready to discuss what happened in an intellectual way. Emphasis is placed on the reciprocal nature of the discomfort and confusion.

These group sensitizing techniques are based on the principle that people will have an emotional reaction and will give social meaning to alterations of standard American patterns of nonverbal behavior. When someone blinks often, he is nervous. If he avoids our eyes, he's insecure, untrustworthy. If he doesn't nod his head in agreement or shake it in disagreement, he's not paying attention. And generally our interpretation is correct—if the other person is an American.

In addition to group exercises with a self-awareness emphasis, there are role-playing techniques in which nonverbal patterns of the target language culture group are emphasized. Trainees watch and interpret, after which there is a dialogue with the host national role-player. In this way the trainees discover where cues were misread and what the consequences might be for them.

These potential areas of discomfort for both the American and host national are further explored after the trainee and host national have engaged in a role-playing exercise with the host national critiquing the trainee's behavior. These are not done to imitate behavior, but to explore emotional reactions. The focus is on behavior of a certain culture and does not attempt to compensate for the differences between individuals in that culture.

The discussions which follow the exercises in part are an attempt to merge the traditionally separate components of language and cultural studies as usually presented in training programs. Another purpose is to give trainees a foundation of awareness and skill which will allow them during Peace Corps service to continue building up their personal inventory of language behaviors. Training for nonverbal communication serves as an excellent orientation for an immersion language program. A heightened awareness of nonverbal behavior will make the trainees less tempted to break out of the target language and diminish their overall frustration. It is not giving them a new tool for communication, but making use of one whose potential has been dormant.

And finally, the treatment of nonverbal communication introduces some activities and discussions which are both interesting and fun while engaging volunteers and language instructors in looking at how they perceive each other. Often trainees need a formal excuse to start asking real questions of the host nationals. This format gives them and host nationals a situation where the potentially explosive topic can be discussed dispassionately. Corollary activities involve movies, videotapes, and photographs of interface action and reaction.

The host nationals with whom I have worked at Baker, La., and the Virgin Islands have found this interesting. Once the atmosphere of mutual exploration has been established, host nationals delight in this area, for it gives them a chance to explore their own cultural patterns and those of the trainees. It also goes a long way toward clearing up misconceptions the host country national got while dealing with Americans and with the potential misconceptions of the volunteer.

To determine the heightened awareness of nonverbal behavior of volunteers who were "sensitized" as trainees, questionnaires are being prepared for groups in Ethiopia, Swaziland, Niger, Chad, and Somalia. Already these groups have given the nonverbal presentations a high rating on program evaluation forms.

Ultimately, I want to include these techniques in a handbook offering a variety of formats, emphases, and time allocations and showing how they can be adapted for the different needs of training programs. The group exercises, role-playing, and audiovisual aids will focus the trainee's efforts on answering the question: "How do I conduct myself when talking with a host national in his language?"

Of course, there is no guarantee that heightened awareness will change volunteer behavior. Indeed, there may be situations where he should not alter his behavior, depending on the status, personalities, and values in the social context. But the approach seeks to make volunteers aware of an area of interpersonal activity which for too long has been left to chance or to the assumption that a volunteer will be sensitive to it because he is surrounded by it.

ASIA IN AMERICAN TEXTBOOKS

The Asia Society

INTRODUCTION

This study distills the results of an intensive survey of how Asia is depicted in American school textbooks. Conducted by the Asia Society with support from The Ford Foundation, the study considered 306 social studies texts in use in the 50 states as of early 1975. The books came primarily from state and city adoption lists across the country, but since some states and localities do not mandate teaching about Asia, the list was supplemented by additional titles supplied by teachers who were using the books in their classrooms. In this way the Asia Society hoped to conduct as complete a survey as possible of those texts in actual use in American schools.

The books were read by over one hundred experts: scholars of Asian studies, elementary and secondary school teachers with Asian specialization and experience in teaching about Asia, and writers with a special concern about how Americans see Asians.

The study was not the first to analyze attitudes toward Asia in American textbooks, but what distinguishes it from its predecessors is its scope, believed to be the most extensive ever attempted, and even more important, its methodology.

To provide both a common frame of reference for the readers and a tool for quantifying the results, staff of the Society's Educational Resources/Asian Literature Program developed a highly detailed evaluation guide with the assistance of participants in a master's program in

Asian studies for teachers at New York University and revised and refined it several times in consultation with an advisory committee of outstanding leaders in the fields of education and Asian studies.

The questionnaire asked readers to respond to a number of very specific questions on the following elements:

- Accuracy and authenticity
- Underlying assumptions and approaches
- Attitudes toward Asian life and culture and the use of primary Asian sources such as literature, the fine arts, historical documents, case studies, and similar materials (referred to in the evaluation guide as humanistic/human interest materials)
- Style and tone
- Format and illustrations
- Attitudes toward women
- Qualifications of authors and consultants

Readers were asked to document their answers wherever possible by citations from the texts and to indicate how they would rate the books on an overall basis as suitable for classroom use.

Since 34 of the original 306 books turned out to be excerpts from larger units in the sample, the Society did not solicit complete answers on these duplications, although it did receive and tabulate data on the qualifications of authors and consultants for 302 texts—virtually the complete sample. In addition, because not every reviewer answered every question, the number of texts for which information is presented varies from question to question. Data compiled on approaches and underlying assumptions about Asia, for instance, reflected expert opinions on 263 texts; that on the treatment of Asian cultures and the use of primary Asian source materials was based on 260 texts. Every reviewer was asked to report on accuracy, and replies were tabulated for those reports from scholars, 97 in all.

The primary purpose of the study, however, was not to produce a precise numerical profile on the Asian content of American textbooks. It was not even to pinpoint good or bad textbooks, although this indeed was an important consideration. (By far the majority of the texts are a mixture of good and bad.) *Rather, the primary purpose of the survey was to catalog the variety of themes and source materials which can contribute to an understanding of Asia, and on the other hand, those which can distort Asian reality.* It is hoped that this identification will serve as a guide to publishers in the revision and production of new texts, to textbook adoption committees as they select the books that will be used in their schools, and to teachers as they teach about Asia in the classrooms.

It took two years to conduct the survey and compile a full report on the findings, copies of which are on file at both The Asia Society and The Ford Foundation and in limited circulation. In another sense, however, the study has been in the making for nearly 20 years, almost the entire lifespan of The Asia Society.

Founded in 1956 to deepen American understanding of Asia and stimulate thoughtful trans-Pacific intellectual exchange, the Society early undertook two important tasks. One was to produce guides for teachers to books, paperbacks, films, and other supplementary educational materials about Asia. The other was to search out Asian works of literature, find experts to translate them, provide editorial services to translators, encourage the publication of the works in books and literary magazines, and promote their dissemination through readings, conferences, radio programs, and other means.

A logical second step in both these long-term efforts would have been to develop Asian literature selections that might be used to supplement social studies courses on Asia in the elementary and secondary schools. It became apparent, however, that before the Society could create such materials, it must take thorough stock of the social studies texts themselves to find out what was being taught about Asia at each grade level. This report summarizes the findings.

THE ASIA-CENTERED APPROACH

Every textbook approaches Asia with a set of attitudes and assumptions, explicit or implicit, conscious or unconscious. The study also had its own basic point of view—one that it shares with many, if not most, cultural anthropologists: To understand a society one must assume that its cultural system is based upon a coherent set of values—in other words, that commonly held patterns of thought and ways of acting "make sense" to the members of the society. Conveying the reality of the society, then, becomes a matter of describing it in such terms that its people seem "normal" and "logical." Attitudes and actions that may appear to an outsider to be shortsighted, senseless, self-destructive, or even bizarre become rational when viewed from a vantage point within the society.

While this approach avoids the conclusion that the members of another society are strange or stupid, it does not lead to the conclusion that they are "just like us" either. But it does enable us to empathize with the people of that society, to imagine something of the way they feel, think, and look at the world.

One textbook, for instance, employs such an approach in explaining the morning rounds made by Buddhist monks in Thailand. It begins its account by stating that "one of the most common forms of giving is feeding the Buddhist monks, who live on the generosity of the community." The text helps the student to understand this activity as very different from begging in a Western society by going on to say that the monks *do not ask for a contribution, and they receive one in silence. It is rather the giver who states his thanks for the opportunity to gain merit through performing a good deed."* [1]

A textbook employing what we shall call "the Asia-centered approach" does not describe a Japanese home as lacking in the furniture and solid walls with which we are familiar, but tells students that homes in Japan are designed with a simplicity of furnishings and a flexibility of space so that each room can be used in many different ways.

Such a textbook does not recount 19th Century history merely in terms of the Chinese refusal to trade with Europeans or the morality of the opium trade. It also discusses the traditional Chinese tribute system of foreign relations and then describes what followed when *"Europeans rejected the Manchu system of foreign relations."* [2]

Attempting to get beyond the alien and exotic surface of another culture, one textbook employing an Asia-centered approach explains to children that Japanese people prepare and drink tea in a special way and then asks, *"How might you feel if you went to Japan and you were the only person not sitting on the floor to eat?"* Such a textbook helps children to lift their cultural blinders by asking, *"Why is this kind of behavior strange when you think about doing it in the United States, but not when you think about doing it in another country or in a Japanese restaurant?"* It reinforces the child's conclusion by pointing out, *"People have learned to do different things because they live in different places. These things don't seem strange when everyone else does them."* [3]

The Asia-centered approach appears in only 30 percent of the books in the study and predominates in only 18 percent.

THE PROGRESS-CENTERED APPROACH

Far more frequently than the Asia-centered approach, textbooks employ one or another of a cluster of value judgments that can be summarized under the heading of the progress-centered approach. In this view, which was that of 71 percent of the texts in the sample, change is good, necessary, and historically inevitable. "The story of man is one of progress," as one text puts it.

A reader found eight examples from one elementary book on India alone. Among them were the following: *"Its people are changing from old ways of living to new modern ways." "Rural India is changing, though slowly." "Some villagers are learning how to run dairies. They learn how to make the milk safe to drink. Many other villagers go to industrial training schools. They learn to use the machines in India's new factories. They stop being farmers. They begin to lead a new life." "All these things mean that the people of India have a good chance of keeping their freedom during the transition to an up-to-date way of life."* [4]

In *Social Change and History* (Oxford University Press, 1969) the sociologist Robert Nisbet has pointed out that Western thought, following the Greeks, once assumed that social systems are biological organizations that are born, grow to maturity, and die. Since the time of Augustine, the West has tended to believe that cultures and societies grow in a straight line and develop by stages into higher systems. The view that social change is purposeful is no longer confined to the West, however. On the contrary, many Asians now emphasize the importance of development for their own societies. The danger is that the criterion of progress can be applied in such a way that the enduring cultural values of a society—any society—are distorted or neglected. If this happens, tradition (because it is old) may be regarded as existing in quaint juxtaposition with the new rather than interacting with it:

"Rocket experts ride buses alongside Indian mystics. Sacred cows share the streets with automobiles. Indian industries produce tractors, yet millions of peasants still use wooden plows. The contrasts are endless." [5]

Other texts describe modernity as challenging, conflicting with, or contradicting tradition: *"Some of this will become clear as we examine conflicts between the new ways and old in the family, the position of women, and the social classes."* [6]

Some textbook writers find the interaction of past and present simply perplexing: *"Chiyo's youth had been a rather confusing combination of Japanese tradition and Western modernity."* [7]

In citing passages like these from the texts, some readers added that the dichotomy between tradition and change is based on superficial definitions of the two concepts. "Modernity," pointed out a reader of one text, "mentioned in connection with the strivings of Southeast Asian leaders here and there, is characterized implicitly as consisting of tall buildings, electricity, and air-conditioning. . . . The complexity of change is not really brought up at all."

One Way of Presenting Change that Recognizes Continuity   History would seem to indicate that in all societies change has taken place at all times. But in the process, past and present interact; cultural traditions are not destroyed, they are transformed.

The following example from a text assumes a constructive relationship between modernity and tradition: *"Maoism was deliberately invented to replace Confucianism, but in many ways it resembled what was displaced. Anything else would be strange, for Mao was educated in a traditional way until his twenties, when as a young college student he first met Lenin's ideas and began his career as a Marxist. Other Chinese Communist leaders, as well as many of the rank and file, have a similar personal history. Massive carryover from the Confucian past is, therefore, inescapable, even if doctrines have been officially and fundamentally changed."*[8]

Social Institutions as Impediments to Progress   When tradition and modernity are seen as antithetical, traditional social institutions, especially religious ones, become obstacles to the modernizing process, whether economic, social, or political. Readers found these examples, among others, in the texts: *"Religious beliefs and lack of education make progress slow."*[9] *"Thus industrialization and modern agricultural techniques were slow in coming to the Indian subcontinent—partly because of the firm hold tradition has on the way of life of the people."*[10]

The attitude that Asian social institutions are impediments to progress was found by readers in 63 texts. Most of the examples cited by readers centered on Hindu beliefs about caste and animals. The texts tend to regard caste as an obstacle to nationalism or democracy or as a cause of economic deprivation: *"India is a democracy. In a democracy, all men are created equal. The caste system does not fit in with the idea of a true democracy."*[11] *"This system has made life a hopeless nightmare of toil and unspeakable poverty for countless millions of India's people."*[12]

Following this line of thinking, teacher's guides and questions at the end of chapters in student texts frequently suggest that students compare the caste system with racial segregation in the United States.

Many of these texts also lament the Hindu willingness to take the lives of a variety of creatures ranging from cattle and monkeys to snakes and silkworms. A classic expression of the attitude of these texts toward Indian treatment of the cow, for instance, states: *"[Nehru] also had to fight ancient Hindu customs. These customs often hindered India's economic progress. One of these customs were the belief that the cow was a sacred animal. . . . Hindus do not eat beef, and the cattle served no useful purpose."*[13]

In answering questions on accuracy in the texts, scholars heavily criticized discussions of caste and cattle for their failure to reflect the great diversity of views about these elements of Indian culture. The scholars pointed out that these treatments of caste confuse it with class and neglect the fact that castes and their relationship "have been in constant flux" historically and that their underlying principles are "readily adaptable to modern conditions." As one reader argued, "a caste system makes for a division of labor, a high degree of interdependency (and) promotes solidarity by requiring exchanging and distribution of goods and other resources among households of different occupation, caste, and economic class."

How Might a Text Discuss Caste and the Cow?

An exception to the rule, one text was cited as expressing far more accurately the part which the cow plays in the Indian economy. The text included a poem by an Indian, R. K. Narayan:

"Living, I yield milk, butter and curd, to sustain mankind
My dung is as fuel used,
   Also to wash floor and wall;
Or burnt, becomes the sacred ash on forehead.
When dead, of my skin are sandals made,
Or the bellows at the blacksmith's furnace;
Of my bones are buttons made . . .
But of what use are you, O Man?"[14]

Two readers argued that a text might discuss caste more profitably by considering how it gives meaning and security to life. They suggested looking at the advantages and disadvantages of a society based on the Indian dharma (duty, seen as function of one's status level) rather than on competition.

The Importance of Economic Wealth and Technology

One of the results of seeing history in terms of "progress" is to place great emphasis on economic conditions and technological advancement. Textbooks tend to speak about nations and people in terms of their material wealth or poverty: *"Like its history and its people, the Japanese government is interesting, but easily the most interesting thing about Japan is its economy."*[15] *"The followers of Zoroaster, from ancient Persia, are called Parsees. Though there are only about 200,000 of them in India, they are important as businessmen."*[16]

The questionnaire did not ask readers to comment on the texts' specific attitudes toward technology, but some readers make a special point of describing a book's tendency to place great emphasis on, or faith in, technology. As evidence, they gave examples like these: *"Modern science, technology, and medicine can provide the means to improve the quality of life for the Indian people."*[17] *"Radio, television and jet airplanes are bringing the billions of people on earth closer together."*[18]

"You can see clearly now that the farmers of East Asia have lagged somewhat behind those in many other lands. But they are not standing still. Here and there, men are learning about new crops and new ways of caring for the old, familiar crops. A few new machines are coming into use. For example, the picture above shows a new way of lifting water to irrigate a rice field. This is Thailand. . . . From such simple beginnings, a new kind of farming and a new way of life may take shape, in time, in East Asia."[19]

"Americans use more machines than any other people in the world. These are found in office buildings, factories, homes, and many other places. With these tools and machines, Americans make many good things for people. Think for a moment of the machines and tools in your home and school. In your home there may be a can opener, a toaster, and a refrigerator."[20]

Readers did not indicate that they thought it was wrong to emphasize the importance of improving the quality of life in Asia. But they reported that the books in which they found these and similar examples showed no awareness that technology can be a mixed blessing, bringing problems as well as advantages.

THE WESTERN-CENTERED APPROACH

Many of the preceding quotations from the texts not only suggest that the proper perspective from which to view a society is how far along it has come on the road to "progress." They also assume that in Asia "progress" by definition must follow the path it has historically taken in the West. The basically ethnocentric character of this point of view has been analyzed in *The Modernity of Tradition* by sociologists Lloyd I. and Susanne Hoeber-Rudolph. They argue that "The myths and realities of Western experience set limits to the social scientific imagination, and modernity becomes what we imagine ourselves to be." This approach is one of a closely related cluster of Western-centered attitudes that occur in 76 percent of the texts and form the exclusive approach of 56 percent of them.

It could be argued that some Asians would share a belief in Western technological, political, economic, or social superiority. Nevertheless it is one thing for an Asian to hold this belief; it is quite another for it to be the only point of view presented to American school students by textbook authors.

"Catching up with the West"   Most frequently (in 99 out of 263 texts) Western ethnocentrism takes the form of portraying Asia as "catching up with the West": *"Once Europe developed machines and mastered the use of power to run these machines, the West forged ahead rapidly. Now, belatedly, the countries of the Orient are trying to catch up."* [21]

"In the twentieth century, the peoples of Asia and Africa have come alive. They have adopted the nationalistic creeds, the democratic ideals, and the modern science of the West, and they have demanded freedom from imperial rule."[22]

"Western civilization developed in Europe among men of the Caucasoid race. This fact tended to give Caucasoids a belief in their own superiority, because they had better ships, weapons, and technology than the non-Caucasoid peoples they conquered. But Western civilization is a cultural factor, not something biological. It can be learned, and is being learned, by people of every race. Western civilization is becoming world civilization. The races of man are competing or, better, cooperating more and more on a basis of equality."[23]

Confusing Westernization with Modernization   In some books (28 in the sample) a Western orientation is reflected in a failure to distinguish "Westernization" from "modernization." In such examples "modernization," "Westernization," and even "industrialization" are used interchangeably, as if they were synonyms. Referring to a photograph in a student text, the teacher's guide, for instance, suggests that the attention of the students be called *"to the fact that the father in the Japanese family is wearing traditional dress, while the other members of the family are dressed in modern clothes."*[24] The reader who cited this example pointed out that "the 'modern' clothes referred to are Western clothes." He added that the kimono worn by the father in the photograph "is no closer to Japanese clothes of a few centuries ago than the Western clothes worn by other family members are to Western clothes a few centuries ago." Both are modern adaptations.

Other readers did not find an explicit identification of "Westernization" with "modernization" but argued that it was often implied, as in a text which said that the Indian government believed that: *"India's enormous problems of illiteracy, poverty, and a very low standard of living could only be resolved by following the currents of industrialization and modernization, courses already travelled by the Western democracies."*[25]

Readers point out that such treatments fail to take into account that Western ideas are actually adapted by Asians, not slavishly copied; that Asians have also borrowed from Asians, and that this has occurred to a far greater extent over a much longer period of time (witness the seminal impact of Chinese and Indian civilizations on most of the rest of Asia); and that Asians have also influenced the West. While texts describe 19th Century Japan as alternately "modernizing" or "Westernizing," for instance, they fail to note that at the same time a passion for "Japonaiserie" was sweeping the arts of Europe.

A Perspective on Japanese Imitation   One reader offered a helpful perspective from which to view Japan, the Asian nation most frequently described as imitating others. "The question of whether or not Japanese culture is all an 'imitation' of China or the West is a tough one to deal with," he said. "It depends on what one means by imitation, and particularly on what value one ascribes to it. At worse, imitation is parrot-like mimicry; at best, it's a truly creative adaptation and eventual assimilation of the high achievements of another.

"The European peoples are so diverse, and they fade off so delicately, in time and geography, into the vast reaches of Asia and the Near and Middle East, that the whole issue of 'imitation' seems never to arise. This is so because mutual influences have been so continuous that they've been almost invisible; and the notion arises that the 'Western' culture is and always has been essentially homogeneous too, and so is all of Asia on into Europe and across the Bering Straits.

"In the meantime, though, Japan is a long way out in the ocean, and whenever she opens herself to foreign influence, she gets caught red-handed stealing goodies from somebody else's island. Of course, the tycoons on the other island are very magnanimous about it, and the more so since they've forgotten what clever imitators they once were themselves; or still are."

Praising and Describing by Western Standards   A very effective method of introducing new material to students is to build on situations with which they are already familiar. Unfortunately, if applied to the study of other societies, this otherwise excellent pedagogical device can easily slide over into ethnocentrism: *"Japanese children study much the same things American children do. English is also taught. Japanese boys and girls even enjoy many of the same sports Americans do, such as baseball, tennis and swimming."*[26] *"Ice cream is a favorite in the United States and is becoming a favorite around the world."* (caption for photograph of Japanese boy with ice cream and baseball glove)[27]

Readers argued that comparisons like these and others they found in the texts assumed American technological, political, economic, sartorial, athletic, or even culinary standards as goals to be met. Some examples can be downright condescending: *"Japanese ocean liners are operated with great efficiency. Their ships which carry passengers to the Orient are quite as comfortable and safe as those of any other nation."* [28]

What readers objected to in these well-intentioned comparisons was the assumption that Asian societies are acceptable to the extent that they are reflections of our own.

Emphasis on Asian Problems—Neglect of Asian Strengths   Although textbooks sometimes use Western yardsticks in an attempt to promote a positive (if sometimes condescending and superficial) portrait of Asia, they more often use these standards to project a picture of technological, economic, political, and social "underdevelopment." Readers were asked by the evaluation guide to note whether the differences between Asian and Western nations were explained in such a way that there is an emphasis on what the Asian societies do not have and whether there was an overemphasis on the poverty of a country or area. The range of examples they offered in return was very great. Some show the very subtle form which Western ethnocentrism can take:

"There was no bread or meat, no milk or fruit, no toast or jelly—just plain oatmeal-like porridge." [29] (From a book on the "emerging" nations)

"Farm families, like Slamet's, do not use knives, forks, or spoons, as you do." [30] (From a book on Indonesia)

By far the majority of the examples, however, depict Asia as a place of unrelieved misery, with insufficient food, flimsy houses, little electricity, a low income level, a short life span, poor health care, few machines, low literacy rates, too many people, and inflexible social and political institutions. Here are some typical examples of what the readers found in 89 out of 263 books:

"In Africa and Asia, millions of people live in small huts that have less protection and less comfort than the huts of Europe in the early Middle Ages. These people do not have any of the conveniences made possible by electricity and gas." [31]

"Most (Indonesian) villagers have no electricity in their homes so they have no radios or television sets for entertainment. They have no books or magazines to read either." [32]

These descriptions are not necessarily inaccurate. But by assuming that the social and material aspects of United States culture are universal norms of the good life, texts describe Asian societies from the perspective of what they *do not* have. The readers' chief quarrel was that this viewpoint offers a very one-sided look at Asian countries. Many of Asia's "huts," for instance, exist in places of year-round warm climate—unlike medieval Europe. In a typical village in Java, where almost half of Indonesia's people live, poeple might watch dramatic presentations of the *Mahabharata,* the *Ramayana,* or indigenous Javanese epics that last 12 hours at a time, and in many a village every male can play some instrument of the *gamelan* orchestra. Similarly, the following textbook description of regimentation in China gives no hint of the satisfactions that Chinese living in the system may find for themselves:

"In 1958, Mao launched 'The Great Leap Forward.' This was probably the most extreme example of communization in history. China's hundreds of millions of peasants were gathered together on huge farms called communes. They were organized into brigades to work in the fields, ate together in community dining halls, and slept in large dormitories. Before and after work, they were required to attend Communist lectures and drill in the militia. Each commune also had to establish and operate small steel furnaces or other small industries. City people were subjected to similar treatment. Many were sent out to work in the communes or were drafted for labor on huge public work projects."[33]

Perhaps of all the countries, textbook treatment of India most reveals negative attitudes. The stench of rotting garbage and the pall of disease and death hang over many of the passages excerpted from texts by the readers. The following example sums up the grim image that is often evoked: *"Death in India comes in so many more ways: A playful nip from a rabid puppy, a burning fever, a gnawing belly, a leprous hand. . . . Perhaps in no other country is it so easy to talk about life and death, about God and eternal salvation, as it is in India."*[34]

Since textbooks depict India's economic and health conditions with so harsh a brush, it was perhaps all too likely that they would make incorrect or negative inferences about the role of the caste system and the multiplicity of languages in India: *"The village people live in 'another world.' Many of them have barely heard of Gandhi or Nehru. Many of them are sick and cannot read or write. So many different languages are spoken that Indians have a difficult time communicating with one another. Many are terribly poor. The caste system still divides the people, though it has been outlawed by the new government."*[35]

One-sidedness and inaccuracy-by-omission are also at the heart of a textbook discussion of technology and transportation in India: *"Most Indians living in village India find machinery difficult to control or understand. Machines are a mystery. The automobile is a constant source of wonder to Indian peasants. Westerners who ride in cars almost from birth on learn very quickly that in order to stay on a truck as it turns a corner, one must lean into the turn. . . . Many villagers in India so rarely ride in vehicles that they fail to correct for this. . . . In learning to drive an auto, they find it difficult to go around curves smoothly. At 35 to 60 miles per hour, they are constantly overturning autos, trucks, and buses because they find themselves going off the road and jerking the wheel in order to frantically make the last-second adjustments necessary to stay on the road.*" Having set forth the "problem," the textbook offered the following "solution": "*Time and practice, of course, solve this problem. Americans started with slow-moving Model-T Fords and, as a nation, over the years built and became adept at driving cars traveling at sixty to eighty mile-an-hour speeds on modern four-lane freeways. Indians are being thrust into the automobile age without a corresponding Model-T phase.*"[36]

Stated the reader who found this example, "The implication is that Indians are completely unable to handle technology. It is not mentioned that India is the sixth largest industrial power. Furthermore, Indians are able to keep automobiles running which would be on the scrap heap elsewhere."

Charges of one-sidedness as well as inaccuracy were also leveled by readers against treatments of 19th Century Japan and China, which are often portrayed as stagnant until contact with the West.

Readers particularly objected to the inaccurate treatments they found of the People's Republic of China. The following example is typical of the out-of-date economic information they discovered in many textbook discussions of China: "*The beggars at left illustrate the hunger of China's people. Given all these conditions, disease spreads quickly. The Communist government has been unable to solve these problems that have long plagued the nation.*"[37]

"*Communes are a failure . . . there is good reason to believe that the average Chinese is not getting enough food to keep healthy, and in many cases even enough food to keep alive.*"[38] (This same text, which was published in 1974, also said that China was "poor in petroleum.")

While some texts do report economic progress made by the People's Republic of China, they frequently describe it grudgingly: "*The communist Chinese have tried to combine these small farms into large agricultural cooperatives, with modern machinery and methods. So far, however, these methods have not been entirely successful. But progress has been made, and agricultural production in China has increased.*"[39]

Economic desperation is seen by the texts as the rationale for acceptance of political restrictions, which are sometimes described as having been achieved through tricks and deceptions rather than motivated by social goals: "*Everyone would live happily ever after. While these were mainly empty promises, they found sympathetic ears in a country where poverty and war had destroyed all other hope. . . . The* newly 'liberated' peasants were organized into 'mutual aid teams.' The peasants were lured by promises of what they longed for."[40]

Using Different Yardsticks   The eradication of poverty, hunger, disease, and social injustice are worldwide goals. No reader quarreled with discussion of these problems where they exist provided the texts did not concentrate on them to the exclusion of the positive side of Asian life. But readers did object to the assumption of American social or economic standards behind the discussions of Asian deprivations: *"If you were a Brahmin, could you go to a movie with a Kshatriya? Think of some Americans who started life as farm boys or poor city boys, and became presidents of the United States. . . . Could this happen in India under the caste system?"*[41]

"The (Chinese) government has not shown a great effort to improve the living standard of the individual."[42]

Charging "gross unfairness," the reader who cited the second of these passages said, "I am afraid that the author means Western, American standards of living when he uses that term." Similar examples were found in other texts which emphasized the absence of cars in China without regard for the fact that two cars for every family is not the national goal of the Chinese themselves.

Readers argued that using standards such as life span or number of cars can produce a favorable picture of the United States and a dismal one of many countries in Asia. However, concentration on the problems of our society, such as pollution and high consumption of irreplaceable sources of energy, could easily reverse the image. Indeed it is ironic that these standards should be used to derogate Asia just when we are beginning to wonder whether they are fully valid for us. Reports from readers, questioning whether it is right to continue to glorify the use of the car and electricity, pointed up how texts lag behind recent public opinion.

Readers also discovered that the picture of Asia set forth in the texts was sometimes even more unflattering by comparison with that of the West because Europe or America had been painted in unrealistically rosy tints: *"At a time when Europe was rapidly entering the modern age and new nations were rising, Japan was still living under feudalism."*[43]

Remarked the reader, "This attitude is taken for granted by a lot of people and by a great many Japanese indeed. Nonetheless, I think it's unfair. Japan in, say, 1800 seems to have been a good deal more lively and 'progressive' (if this is what one wants) than is generally supposed; and Europe and America were a good deal more grubby than we care to remember."

How Might a Text Discuss a Technologically Less Developed Society in a Sympathetic Way?   It is possible to compare our way of life with that of technologically less advanced societies in a way that does not make them (or us) sound inferior. It is even possible to show that very positive values exist in such societies. One textbook does this so well that we quote it at length:

"The standard of living in rural Southeast Asia, from our point of view, might seem only slightly above subsistence level. We would find it difficult to live without running water, refrigerators, package foods, and the host of conveniences surrounding us. The typical one or two room dwellings made of bamboo and palm leaves would strike us as interesting to visit but impossible to live in. The privacy valued by most Americans is not part of the Southeast Asian peasant's life. Life is simple and, consequently, needs are not so great. The competitive drive which so dominates our urban, industrialized society is largely lacking in the peasant society of Southeast Asia. It is interesting that even most of the games played by young people are non-competitive in nature.

"Due to the relatively small size and interdependent nature of the village, rural life tends to be typified by harmonious community relations. They include a democratic election of village offices, communal plowing and land ownership, and various forms of mutual aid. Nearly an entire village participated in the dedication of a new house in a small village in Northern Thailand recently. Hunters went into a jungle and shot a wild boar which they contributed to a village feast. Most of the members of the village came to pay a visit to the owner of the house to wish him well and sample some of the special treats he had prepared. It was an occasion largely foreign to our experience, but one with which our early forefathers had more in common. In fact, it was not totally unlike an Amish barnraising in our own country today."

"Again, in another place, the same text explains the differences between life with machines and life surrounded by nature without making either seem less satisfying from a human point of view:

"Many of us in America have grown up in a highly controlled environment. Modern machines have eased the burden of physical labor; lighting and heating systems enable us to alter the pattern of hot to cold, light to darkness; and modern modes of transportation and communication have vastly reduced conceptions of time and space. Our industrialized, highly mechanized world view greatly conditions our behavior and attitudes. . . . While modernity is beginning to change life in many parts of rural Southeast Asia, these societies are still largely traditional. The forces of nature which determine the successful rice harvest are to be placated rather than controlled, and the major values of the human

community are still centered about the family and religion. The most important celebrations revolve around the agricultural calendar, significant occurrences in family life such as weddings and funerals, and the major religious events of Buddhism, Islam, or Hinduism."[44]

Europeans and Americans in Asia   Some textbooks not only describe Asia from a Western point of view but also magnify the historic role of Americans and Europeans. Readers reported that 48 books in the sample either discuss Asia primarily in terms of its contact with the West, so that it is seen as merely a stage on which some of the drama of Western history unfolds, or give a disproportionate amount of attention to the West by comparison with Asia. So-called "world" history books are particularly susceptible to this flaw. Two-thirds of the world's people live in Asia. Yet the average amount of text devoted to it in the 42 "world" histories in the survey is 15.6 percent.

But most frequently the glorification of Europe and America takes the form of showing Westerners as helpers in Asia, bringing technology, government, and security to the area. The colonial period, the occupation of Japan after World War II, and the assistance rendered to Asia through AID, the Peace Corps, and our military establishment are usual topics for textbook writers who, in the judgment of the evaluators, discuss only the Western contributions to Asian life and fail to mention any Asia initiatives and strengths at all.

"During the many years the British occupied India, new ideas and ways were introduced. The British contributions to India were railroads, schools, and a European form of government. Under British rule, the people of India also learned a little about manufacturing."[45]

"The occupation authorities instituted many significant changes in Japanese life. Japan was given a democratic constitution, guaranteeing the people the right to participate in their government. Women were given the vote.... Schoolbooks were rewritten to teach Japanese children the ways of democracy. The Japanese people have taken enthusiastically to their new form of government, and to the new freedom in their personal lives."[46]

"With Western help, American surplus food, and improved transportation, the devastating famines of a few decades ago are currently being thwarted...."[47]

"Red China is using its growing power throughout the region.... If they (nations trying for democratic forms of government) fail, much of the Far East will be closed to the people of the free world. American soldiers and arms have been sent to Southeast Asia to help keep South Vietnam free of communism."[48]

None of the readers argued that Western contacts with Asia be ignored or that humanitarian motives are not also operating along with those of self-interest in our postwar activities in Asia. They do believe, however, that a more balanced view would lessen the impression of Asia the weak and America the powerful.

Textbooks might achieve balance in their description of the Western presence in Asia by considering Asian experiences under colonialism and United States military and economic aid in the period following World War II. The books might discuss Asian initiatives toward development as well as Western ones.

Why Learn about Asia?   The emphasis on Asian weaknesses and deficiencies in the majority of American texts might lead one to suspect that in the eyes of many textbook writers, a discussion of Asia is merely a device to teach students, by comparison, the blessings of the American way of life. Such indeed was the explanation given by one teacher's guide that explained its objective as enabling the pupil *"to appreciate the basic American values which make the United States distinct from other nations."*[49]

The readers had no quarrel with this purpose as a valid educational goal for American schoolchildren. They merely questioned whether it should be carried out in the context of teaching about other societies. Must the United States be praised at the expense of other peoples?

Readers also found explicit references in 33 of the books to another argument for studying Asia, that of American self-interest: *"If we are wise, we shall realize that nothing important can happen in any part of the world (even Asia) without in some way affecting us. It will make a difference to us whether Asia has peace.*

"We may not care to get mixed up in the problems of government in India or Southeast Asia, but it will be to our interest that those who do have responsibility for those things shall be our friends, and that the native people of those distant lands shall be able to live peacefully and happily with as democratic a government as they are able to manage."[50]

"First, by helping the less-developed nations raise their standards of living, we are creating future customers for American goods and those of our European allies. Second, most of this country's leaders believe that people who are well fed and well clothed are more capable of resisting the influence of communism."[51]

It may be true that some part of Asia is vital to our security. It is undoubtedly true that a peaceful and prosperous Asia is a better customer for American business. It is also undoubtedly true that the world is becoming increasingly interdependent. All these points may make excellent arguments for selling technical and military assistance programs in Asia to Congress and the American taxpayer. But readers argued that quotations like those cited above present Asia in a Western-centered, rather than Asia-centered, context.

ASIA AS INSCRUTABLE OR EXOTIC

The progress-oriented and Western-centered approaches are not the only ones which fail to present Asian reality fully. Regarding Asia as inscrutable—once a common attitude among Westerners—also fails dramatically the first criterion for interpreting a society: to reveal it as it is to its members. One teacher's guide suggested that Asia might be depicted initially as strange to stimulate student interest. But, as the reader commented, "the goal should be to demystify Asia."

Presenting Asia as exotic also fails to reflect the full humanity of its people by making them seem alien and "other than" us. In a textbook on the Philippines, for instance, one ethnic group, the Moros, is described solely in terms of its colorful dress. In an anthropology text for younger children, the student's first introduction to any Asians is to a group of headhunters: *"India, where the Nagas live, is in Asia. Asia is the largest of all the continents. About half of the world's people live in Asia."*

Breathtakingly juxtaposing a familiar situation (having neighbors) with the fearfully different, the textbook then asks the student: *"How would you like to have headhunters for neighbors?"* [52] It goes on, in a description of a Naga village, to suggest that the child would be scared silly by the sight of human skulls hanging all over the place.

Another text emphasizes the strangeness and exoticism of Hindu religious practices (and errs in the use of *Brahma,* the name of an individual Hindu deity, instead of the correct, *Brahman,* meaning the universal spirit):

"They worshiped thousands of gods and offered bloody sacrifices to them. They became fatalistic about life, passively accepting the evils about them. Fanatical holy men achieved fame by half-starving themselves or by performing incredible feats like lying for years on a bed of nails. In such ways they hoped to free their souls from the burden of flesh and to become one with Brahma." [53]

Readers reported, however, that textbooks only relatively rarely spoke of Asia as inscrutable or exotic.

Scrutinizing the "Inscrutable"   Mysticism is one of the aspects of certain Asian cultures most bewildering to Westerners. It is possible, however, to present it in such a way that it becomes approachable. The following discussion from a text shows how this might be accomplished:

"Though we may find it hard to take mysticism and asceticism seriously, more than half the human race has done so. Indian transcendental ideas spread to China and Southeast Asia, and influenced Christianity as well. Such a career requires us to adjust our usual habits of thought and ask ourselves what we would do and how we might behave if it really were true that reality lay behind the world of sense. How do you know that it does not? How do you know that the Indian mystics were not on the right track after all, and that it is we moderns who are chasing after illusions? Many people in our time have asked themselves this question. Many people in every age of the past, from the time when such ideas first clearly came to be formulated, have been fascinated by these questions. It would be absurd to scoff and pay no attention, or refuse to take seriously ideas that sustained one of the world's greatest and most successful civilizations." [54]

ECLECTICISM

The fact that many Asians are progress-oriented while retaining many of their own cultural values suggests that there are times when a text might profitably adopt a multivalued approach to Asia. Even a Western-centered point of view might be used, provided that it is carefully labeled as such and presented as one of several that can be taken toward Asia. Obviously, one of the others should be Asia-centered. If a text employs more than one perspective consciously, we shall call its approach "eclectic." While many, if not most, of the texts unconsciously—and thus, uncritically—adopted several basic approaches, only 14 out of the 263 titles were truly eclectic in this sense. The core of the method is described in the following excerpt from a reader's report:

"In Volume I, the (Indian) culture seems quite rational. Given Hindu assumptions, the whole system seems to make so much sense that many students are quite attracted to the model. But then in Volume II, especially during the section on 'development,' students begin to question the assumptions of Volume I. They see that there is a plurality of value systems at work in India and many of the values are difficult to reconcile to each other. How does one digest dharma, karma, and caste together with egalitarianism, social revolution, and technological progress?"

Teachers sometimes use the technique of "values clarification" as a way of introducing questions of value into the classroom without inculcating any specific set of values. As a reader pointed out, however, the danger is that with such an approach, another culture is not studied for its own sake but is used as a tool of student self-discovery. "If a student is asked to clarify his or her attitudes toward the question of violence (e.g., was peasant violence during the Chinese Revolution justified)," he argued, "the student will naturally appeal to the value base of his own culture in clarifying this question. The point here is not that confronting such a question may not be a useful thing to do (which it is) but whether confronting it tells you anything significant about Chinese values (which it doesn't.)"

How "Values-Clarification" Can be Eclectic   One reader reported that a text did indeed present an Asian culture as rational within its own context by providing exercises in which the students were asked to examine the feelings of the people within the culture before making a cross-cultural comparison. For instance, it asked them to compare the meaning of "a good life" as the Japanese parents in the text saw it with how the young people saw it. Only then were the students to compare their own view with that of the young Japanese.

TALKING ABOUT ASIANS
AND THE ASIAN EXPERIENCE

To overcome the barriers in the way of understanding another society, a text should avoid focusing exclusively on "important" people such as heads of state (or at least the public, political side of such people), or upon "typical" people such as "farmers" or "city dwellers." It should make the effort to relate such abstractions as problems, forces, events, and movements to individual people and the concrete reality of their everyday lives. It should let the people speak for themselves—and allow students to think for themselves without becoming involved in judgments about what is good and bad in the lives they are studying. That texts must center on peoples and their cultures was a fundamental point of view behind the evaluation study.

With such an approach, for instance, a textbook on Japan shows how (in the words of one reader) "at a TV factory, the employees sing a company song at the start of each work day . . . how many students, even in grade school, attend special afternoon classes to prepare for college entrance examinations . . . and how religion, music, and calligraphy play some small part in the lives of the people."

In discussing the Korean war, another book deals with questions of foreign policy and the conduct of war, but relates all of these issues to real individuals. In addition to revealing the personalities and philosophies of the military and civilian leaders of the age, it provides a movingly real account of the plight of the ordinary foot soldier and even the noncombatant.

A text encourages understanding of what is being attempted in the People's Republic of China by quoting three statements from Mao Tse-tung: "Of all the things in the world ... people are the most precious." "Our duty is to hold ourselves responsible to the people." "Anyone should be allowed to speak out, so long as he means to be helpful."[55]

Literature, art, music, dance, drama, philosophy, religion, and other primary expressions of the human experience provide excellent devices to present a people and their culture vividly and concretely, as do such materials as journalistic pieces, letters to the editor, historical and political documents, case studies, and photographs of people.

Readers were asked to rate books on how Asian life was discussed and to what extent actual Asian sources were included. Of the 260 texts for which responses were received on this topic (termed "humanistic/human interest approach and content" in the evaluation guide), readers found that only 43 were centered on people and their culture; only 23 books actually included primary sources. Far more frequently, readers found the books to be negative or inadequate in their treatment of Asian peoples and their cultures.

NEGATIVE AND ETHNOCENTRIC TREATMENT OF ASIAN CULTURAL ACHIEVEMENTS

Considering the strong emphasis on change and progress in American textbooks and the insistence of many that tradition and modernity are incompatible, it is not surprising that textbooks often treat Asian cultures negatively, regarding them as hindrances to progress or as primitive trappings that will become outmoded when change has taken place. One reader characterized a book on India as suggesting that pride in its cultural achievements is "preventing India from changing rapidly enough to keep its people from starving."

The readers found many examples in the texts in which Asian art forms are referred to as "strange" or as lacking what ours have. One textbook, for instance, describes Indian and East Asian music in the following terms:

"Hindu music is confined largely to popular songs and to accompaniments for the famous temple dances. Drums, cymbals, wooden flutes, and many stringed instruments have been used for centuries. Because it lacks harmony and relies solely on melodies that are so different from our own, Hindu music, like that of most East Asian countries, seems strange to Western ears."[56]

Many students would probably never experience Indian music or other Asian art forms as strange unless prompted to do so. On the contrary, there is strong evidence that art forms of other cultures are particularly accessible to children, especially younger ones. While some older students might find Asian art forms unfamiliar (a preferable word), there is no reason that this has to be the lasting effect. But when the first and only impression of some aspect of an Asian culture is one of "strangeness," why should anyone want to explore it further?

Other ethnocentric and in effect negative treatments of Asian art forms are to be found in textbook characterizations of Japanese plays as moving *"too slowly for Westerners"*[57] or of Afghan singing as *"a monotonous groan with a kind of growl quality."*[58]

Ironically, textbooks also adopt the opposite outlook. They describe Asian artists and art forms in terms of ours: *"Kalidasa, who lived in the 400's A.D., has been called the Indian Shakespeare. He wrote three plays, the most famous of which is* Sakuntala. *The story, a romantic one, concerns. . . ."*[59]

"As with Christian churches during the Renaissance, wealthy Buddhist monasteries employed numerous painters and sculptors. They have left us with many figures of Buddha, usually carved but also shown in fine fresco paintings such as those in the Ajanta caves. In style the paintings somewhat resemble the work of early Italian Renaissance artists."[60]

"Asoka's services to Buddhism compare to Constantine's to Christianity."[61]

If sensitively done, these comparisons might have potential for a positive initial introduction to a new art form, but the textbooks from which the readers took these examples go no further than the Western-oriented references. The problem with these facile analogies—beyond their superficiality—is that they fail to relate Asian arts and thinkers, and their achievements, to their own cultures and thus fail to say anything very meaningful about them. Like all descriptions of Asia in Western terms, they are essentially ethnocentric in character.

FAILURE TO PROVIDE ASIAN SOURCES

Some texts signal their awareness of the need to use Asian sources in teaching about Asia but fail to include such sources or explain how to go about finding them. Teacher's guides suggest that students prepare a Japanese tea ceremony or write *haiku,* for instance, but fail to provide instructions on how to go about these activities. More seriously, however, some texts use Western sources instead of Asian ones. Probably the most widespread example is the inclusion of works by Pearl Buck and Rudyard Kipling in the Chinese and Indian literature sections of some textbooks. But the "Pearl Buck-Rudyard Kipling syndrome" has many symptoms. One takes the form of presenting a Western author as if he or she represented an Asian point of view. Other symptoms are the dependence, exclusively or primarily, on Western authors or documents and the failure to list Asian authors in bibliographies. Readers' comments leave no doubt as to the distortions such treatment can create:

" 'Shooting an Elephant' is authentic Orwell, not authentic Burma. It tells how he felt about the Burmese and how he thought the Burmese felt toward him."

"The author . . . has a tendency to quote from Western writers when characterizing India; e.g., there are a number of quotations from Mark Twain and one from H. G. Wells. I would like more quotations from Indian writers and ordinary people to make India come alive."

"It's interesting that many novels are suggested out of Western literature. These include: *A Tale of Two Cities, Drums along the Mowhawk, Hornblower and the Hotspur, Celia Garth, The Three Musketeers,* and *A Bell for Adano.* In spite of the fact that there are many excellent Asian novels available in English translation, nothing comparable is suggested, unless you count *Anna and the King of Siam,* which is offensive to most Thai people."

"Where outside commentators are quoted—in the teacher's guide—only Americans are doing the commenting; e.g., J. Anthony Lukas and C. L. Sulzberger of *The New York Times.* Political cartoons in the text come from the United States, England, and the Netherlands, not from Indian newspapers."

How Might Asians' Voices be used in the Texts?

One reader praised the artistic, philosophical, and literary selections he found in a book on Confucian China as serving not only to "establish the existence of artistic activity in China," but also to "elucidate and make real the other subjects, such as historical events and social structure, being discussed."

In another book on China, proverbs were cited frequently throughout. The enthusiastic reader pointed out that they were "always pertinent, always shedding new light on the subject under discussion or bringing some difficult conglomeration of facts and events into a comprehensible pattern."

Traveler's Tales

To impart a vivid dimension to a discussion of life in an Asian country, textbooks sometimes employ what might be called "the traveler's tale." The problem with eyewitness accounts by foreign visitors, however, is that the authors are more concerned with their own impressions than with trying to convey the Asian experience:

"I had to assume the lotus position by tucking my feet under myself and sitting calmly. The session lasted only 15 minutes, but it was difficult to concentrate on nothingness. . . . At the time I did not realize enough about true Zen to have the experience of satori." [62]

Remarked the reader who found this example, "From the standpoint of an American first visiting Japan, the author's reactions are pretty standard and quite authentic. But they are also quite out of place in a textbook on Japan."

The essence of entertaining travel writing is to convey a sense of the distance one has come from the familiar. One tends to exploit the potential for amusement or excitement in the unfamiliarity of the surroundings. First-time impressions are very different from those experienced by someone who has grown up in a culture.

In addition to presenting an inaccurate view of a culture, the use of "travelers' tales" usually precludes the utilization of actual Asian accounts.

Westernization of Asian Sources   By retelling Asian myths, legends, folktales, or history, textbooks also in effect Westernize Asian sources. If sensitively and authentically done, a retelling can be effective, especially if the vocabulary and writing style would otherwise be too advanced for the textbook's grade level. All too often, however, texts present retellings as actual Asian sources; fail to provide identification, so that it is impossible to know whether the story is authentically Asian; rewrite history in a condescending manner; or change the concept and story line. In a description of Commodore Perry's arrival in Japan, for instance, one textbook does not draw upon actual Japanese accounts in translation. Instead it presents the following fictionalized, Westernized version:

"On July 7, 1853, the crews of some Japanese fishing boats in Tokyo Bay saw a strange sight. Into the mouth of the bay steamed a squadron of warships flying a foreign flag. The Japanese fishermen were speechless with amazement, for they had never seen a vessel propelled by steam." [63]

The Japanese myth of creation in its accepted version has been available in English translation for over 75 years and readily accessible in a standard anthology for more than 10 years, yet two recent textbooks, in remarkably similar versions, retell the myth, transforming its male and female deities Izanami and Izanagi, into a single unnamed masculine figure reminiscent of Neptune or Jupiter; turn "the floating bridge of heaven" on which they stand in the original version into a rainbow;

eliminate the delightful dialogue between the two deities; and portray them as producing not "countries," as in the authentic version, but merely the islands of Japan. Yet both textbook versions are accompanied by a Japanese painting from the Museum of Fine Arts in Boston which depicts both Izanami and Izanagi thrusting down "the jewel spear of Heaven" into the waters to produce the first island, Ono-goro-jima. One wonders whether students ever notice the inconsistency and what they think about it.

THE USE OF CASE STUDIES

Textbooks often advocate case studies of an individual, a family, or a village as an effective way of presenting social studies concretely. In fact, case studies are frequently the only attempt a textbook will make to focus on a people and their culture. Out of the sample of 260 texts, readers reported that case studies appeared in 75. Unfortunately, in only 8 of these was an Asian-centered approach dominant and only 3 scored "dominant" on the use of actual Asian sources.

Far more frequently textbook case studies are inventions, replete with "fanciful misinformation," as one reader put it. They are filled with situations, dialogue, and attitudes that either have been made up outright or seem to have been very loosely constructed from scholarly evidence and presented as fact.

One textbook contains an account of a civil service examination in Confucian China. The character is named Cheng She Kit, which the reader characterized as "a hodgepodge of Mandarin and Cantonese," and the text describes in detail how Cheng *"cut a piece from the stick of ink,"*[64] mixed it with the water on his palette, and then proceeded to take his examination, writing out each passage as it was read by the examiner, and then writing an explanation for it. Commented the reader, "It is wholly inaccurate, from the way Chinese ink is used to the way the examinations were conducted, as any one who has read a single book on China might know."

Readers also faulted the case studies for the general lifelessness and robot-like character of their people. In effect, they appeared reminiscent of the Dick and Jane robots the American schoolchild frequently meets when first learning to read. ("See, Jane, see. Run, Dick, run.") Such characters talk and question in a cardboard way and live in families typically consisting of a brother and sister heroine, "Mother," "Father," and "Little Brother." Such characters, if they do not utterly bore the students, can give the false impression that case-study characters are typical of people in the country.

Asia through Western Eyes   Although it is possible to present authentic Asian data but color it with a Western point of view, readers suspected that many case studies were invented because they seemed to reveal more about the ways in which Americans see Asians than about how Asians see themselves. One book, for instance, tells the story of Sachin, an Indian untouchable, who goes to the city, makes good with top grades and a well-paying job, and then returns to his village wearing a Western suit and shiny new shoes, only to be rejected and left standing in the dust by the caste-conscious people of his village. The reader commented that "going out with a few girls" is "nice and American" but not the way things are usually done in India. But the reader found it plainly incredible that the people where Sachin worked would not be aware—or at least curious—about his caste, and that Sachin himself would not know what to expect of the villagers when he returned home. The tenor of the story is far more that of a Horatio Alger plot gone sour than that of an actual Indian experience.

Another book uses the device of boy and girl twins to introduce village life in Thailand. But the reader argued that had the writer really been familiar with Thailand, she would have introduced a brother and sister with one or two years' difference in age, so that she could have presented the Thai social relations of status and reciprocity, in which, in the case of family members, the younger automatically owes obedience to the older and the older has a natural obligation to protect the younger.

Still another book on Pakistan talks about a youth's preference for tight jeans and his hope for "good grades," and has a Pakistani bride saying "I do."

Many of the case studies fail as genuine projections of the Asian experience because they are used exclusively or primarily to convey an aura of backwardness, deprivation, and material poverty. In short, the studies portray Asians from the standpoint of how far they have come along the road of Western progress. The following example from a textbook on Japan illustrates the bias that often occurs when a village, a family, or an individual is described in terms of possessions familiar to Americans that it may or may not have: *"All the Nakamuras sleep in one bedroom divided by a screen. The road to the house is not paved. There is a growing list of appliances in the Nakamura home—an electric refrigerator, stove, toaster, and color television. Yet the bathroom is far from modern. The toilet is primitive, and there is no shower."*[65]

Ethnocentrism in the form of explicit comparisons with the United States also enters into some of the progress-oriented case studies. One book makes the point with pictures: A woman in an American laundromat is pictured alongside a painting of Indian women doing their washing in a stream. Another book compares the situation of a Japanese farmer with what can only be described as that of an upper middle class American: *"Sekine . . . owns only 1.5 acres of land–hardly more than a 'backyard' in American terms, but an average-size farm in overcrowded Japan."*[66]

The insistence on "learning new ways" and the condescension of the "white man's burden" combine in another typical "case study" to suggest a strong ethnocentric flavor and the overwhelming likelihood that the "study" is actually the figment of a textbook writer's mind. The book describes how an American girl and her businessman father are seeing Bangkok's canals by boat and run into a Thai youth with the improbable (for a man) name of Siri. Unlike most Thais, who won't talk politics with strangers, Siri speaks of *"the threat of Communist China"* and says that the Thais *"have little defense against the huge army of China."*[67] Reports the reader, "The American, acting in an almost patronizing and certainly 'let me, the American, help you' manner, tells Siri that he and his group of men can get him a scholarship to learn modern ways so that Thailand will have educated leaders."

The progress-centered case study as seen through American eyes with a cast of unreal people, is vividly illustrated by two characters which appear most frequently in textbook discussions of India. One, whom we'll call "Toothless Ram," is pathetically backward and poverty-stricken. The following excerpts from different texts show him in two typical appearances: *"Ram is a toothless little man who lives in a small village in India. He is a poor tenant farmer. He cannot read or write, but he is no different in this respect from millions of others. At 42, he looks and feels like an old man. He and his wife had seven children, but only three, two sons and a daughter, are still alive. Both of his sons are married and live with him. He is worried because his daughter is not yet married."*[68]

"Arun cannot read or write. . . . For the past few years he has had a bad cough in his chest. He went to the village doctor and paid him three rupees or 42 cents for treatment. The doctor rubbed his chest with a large red stone and told him the coughing would stop. It never did, but Arun has not been back to the doctor because he does not want to spend more money."[69]

"Enlightened Ram," on the other hand, is the mirror opposite of "Toothless Ram." He is in favor of progress, modernity, and Western ways. He is impatient with his countrymen who cling to old ways and are slow to change: *"Ram is a farmer who is now living in a small village near Bombay. One of the government advisers came to discuss the new* method of rice growing. . . . *Even his own father warned him against changing his ways. 'Take whatever God gives you,' he said. 'Don't ask for too much.'* "

However, he agrees to try the new agricultural methods, and: "*Many years later, Ram looked back on the changes he had made. He had learned to use fertilizer. He was now borrowing tools from the village's new cooperative. He was buying good seed. He was using a new plow and sickle that were better than the ones his father and grandfather used. All of this puzzled Ram's father. He remarked, 'You are getting everything—good seed, fine fertilizer, and good tools—as if a spirit is bringing all these to you.'* "[70]

Sometimes the issue is not one of technology but of social customs: "*This was the home Krishna was expected to return to. But after six years of being away, he was no longer sure that he was suited to live under the rules of the family. For some time he had run his own life, and he thought it would be hard to take orders from the older members of the family. He wanted to choose his own career and his own wife. This was not acceptable to his grandfather's way of life.*"[71]

While there might be some Indians who resemble "Toothless Ram" or "Enlightened Ram," in the textbooks both Rams are caricatures.

OTHER DIMENSIONS OF ADEQUACY AND ACCURACY IN THE TEXTS

Treating an Asian topic superficially and imposing a Western framework on it are essentially forms of inaccuracy. Scholar-readers also found inaccuracies in fact, such as "The practice of suttee was common through Asia" and "Bengal is a province"; in the use and definition of foreign terms, such as *Hinayana* instead of the correct *Theravada* Buddhism and *hara-kiri* instead of the preferred *seppuku*; and in the identification of illustrations and photographs.

The unattractiveness of some formats is another dimension of the inadequacy of many texts. Exactly 50 percent of the 168 readers who replied to a question on whether the format was initially appealing to the eye said that the poverty of the design of the book did not invite children to read onward.

Illustrations tend to perpetuate stereotypes and cliches about Asia. The inevitable pictures of the Taj Mahal, of beggars, and of cows in the streets abound in books on India, while Japan is represented with the usual delicate women in kimonos, the tea ceremony, gardens, and shrines, as well as overcrowded subways, student riots, and traffic jams in Tokyo. "There seems to be no middle ground," remarked a reader. In general, illustrations and photographs give no indication also of the ethnic diversity of many Asian nations.

There were also instances of sexism in the stereotyping of women's roles and the neglect of women as characters in the case studies.

The tone of the terminology used reinforces many of the Western ethnocentrisms apparent in the texts. One book says that *"to a remarkable extent the Japanese citizen can say what he thinks, read what he wishes, and write what he believes."*[72] Why should this be remarkable unless one assumes that Asian countries in general should model their behavior on American patterns? Another text likens colonial countries to *"problem children"* in a hurry to grow up. But the most prevalent offenders are such terms as *"underdeveloped,"* *"backward,"* *"primitive,"* *"tradition-bound,"* *"superstitious,"* *"old-fashioned,"* *"static,"* *"unchanging,"* *"have-nots,"* and *"new nations"* as applied to the countries of Asia. Continued use of cold war language, even in very recent texts, is revealed by such habitual phrases as *"Communist China"* or *"Red China,"* instead of the relatively value-free and correct designation, The People's Republic of China, and by such rubrics as *"Communist challenge"* or *"the ruthless imperialism"* of China.

Readers also took exception to the number of instances in which Asia was referred to Europocentrically as the *"Far East"* or *"the Orient,"* a term whose root meaning is "the East." Sometimes Asian and African societies are lumped together under the designation *"non-Western."* Terminology like this encourages American (or European) students to develop a belief in the centrality of their own culture.

Still another dimension of ethnocentrism, readers reported, is revealed in the use of such condescending terms as *"the friendly, fun-loving Filipinos"* and *"the happy, gentle Thais,"* which suggest a childlike nature in need of guidance, if not domination.

Expert knowledge is no insurance that Western biases will not creep into the formulation of American textbooks on Asia, nor does all Asian experience qualify an author to take on the responsibility of interpreting an Asian culture to American students. Nevertheless it is noteworthy that of 302 texts on which replies were tabulated to questions concerning the qualifications of authors and consultants, only 24 percent listed authors and consultants credited with Asian expertise. Fewer than one percent of the membership of the Association for Asian Studies, the leading professional organization in the field, were involved in the production of any of the texts. Moreover, of those few experts who did participate in the formation of the texts, only a fraction were specialists in the humanities.

Overall Ratings   Basing their judgments on the variety of factors set forth in the evaluation guide, readers were asked to give overall ratings of the books they reviewed. Out of 261 books for which these evaluations were received, 63 were designated either as "excellent, should be highly recommended" or "can be used, but has some problems." Reports from readers indicated that 118 books should not be used without revision and an additional 80 were declared to be so inadequate that they should be replaced by new texts. On any given topic there appear to be at most 4 usable titles. Most of the material on Asia judged to be suitable is produced for the high school student. Of 16 elementary books given "suitable" ratings, only one series of basic texts received consistently good marks. Twelve books on the junior high level and 35 on the high school level were seen as usable by readers.

PLAN FOR ACTION

The Asia Society has concluded from the reports of the readers that the majority of textbooks in common use in American elementary and secondary schools do not come close to reflecting what thoughtful educators have long been recommending for teaching about other societies: a recognition of these societies' unique aspirations, lifestyles, systems of values, and modes of thinking.

More than 70 percent of the books emphasize the importance of progress, a yardstick which, if applied uncritically, can neglect or distort the persistent themes and continuities inherent in all cultures. The result in many texts is that Asian traditions are regarded as irrelevant to the present or thought of as obstacles to modernization.

Three-fourths of the texts approach Asia from a Western-centered point of view. They assume Westernization and modernization are one and the same and talk of Asia as "catching up" with the West. They describe it in terms of what it possesses—or lacks—by comparison with us. They discuss the material poverty of Asian nations without pointing out the satisfactions of life for Asian peoples.

The role of Americans and Europeans in Asian history is also magnified in the textbooks, and in world histories, a disproportionate amount of space is given to America and Europe.

An even larger percentage of the texts fail to discuss Asians as individuals, to depict the concrete reality of their everyday lives, and to include authentic Asian sources or at least bibliographies of these sources.

Inaccuracies of fact and definition are frequent, and illustrations and terminology perpetuate Western ethnocentrism, stereotyping, and condescending attitudes toward Asian peoples. Few Asian specialists are involved as authors or consultants in the preparation of the texts and of those who are, a very small proportion hold credentials in the humanities.

If the texts are characteristic of social studies curricula across the country, then serious questions should be raised about the effectiveness of the entire post-World War II movement for "international" education or "global" studies.

The Asia Society intends to disseminate the findings widely to the general public, teachers, publishers, writers, textbook selection committees, state education departments, teacher training programs, and government agencies. A list of outstanding texts was drawn up as a result of the evaluation survey, and is currently available to anyone requesting it.

Through the Association for Asian Studies and other professional organizations, the Society will work to enlist the concern and involvement of specialists in Asian studies, particularly in the humanistic disciplines, and assist them in the preparation and distribution of papers on frequently misrepresented topics, such as caste and cattle in India. It will also use the findings on the individual texts to assist publishers in the revision of texts and the preparation of new ones.

NOTES

1. *Thailand,* p. 41, Ginn, 1966.
2. *China,* p. 107, Houghton Mifflin, 1972.
3. *Communities We Build,* p. 51, Follett, 1973. Teacher's guide.
4. *The Indian Subcontinent,* pp. 1, 90, 93, 117, Allyn & Bacon, 1971.
5. *India: Focus on Change,* p. 1, Prentice-Hall, 1975.
6. *Global History of Man,* p. 444, Allyn & Bacon, 1974.
7. *Women of Asia,* p. 2, Cambridge, 1974.
8. *The Ecumene,* p. 744, Harper & Row, 1973.
9. *The Social Studies and Our World,* p. 325, Laidlaw, 1974.
10. *People in a Changing World,* p. B 105, Laidlaw, 1974.
11. *How People Live in India,* p. 80, Benefic, 1973.
12. *The Human Achievement,* p. 543, Silver Burdett, 1970.
13. *You and the World,* p. 300, Benefic, 1968.
14. *India,* p. 81, Prentice-Hall, 1975.
15. *Diversity of Ideas,* p. 94, Harper & Row, 1972.
16. *How People Live in India,* p. 49, Benefic, 1973.
17. *Exploring World Cultures,* pp. 178-179, Ginn, 1974.
18. *The Earth,* p. 5, Globe, 1971.
19. *A World View,* p. 133, Silver Burdett, 1968.
20. *Communities around the World,* pp. 35-36, Sadlier, 1971.
21. *The World Today,* p. 528, Webster McGraw-Hill, 1971.
22. *Living World History,* p. 201, Scott Foresman, 1974.
23. *Geography and World Affairs,* p. 30, Rand McNally, 1971.
24. *Living in Places Near and Far,* p. 104, Macmillan, 1969. Teacher's guide.

25. *Class and Caste in Village India,* p. 38, Addison-Wesley, 1969.

26. *Exploring a Changing World,* p. 474, Globe, 1968.

27. *Three Billion Neighbors,* p. 49, Ginn, 1965.

28. *Eastern Lands,* p. 402, Allyn & Bacon, 1968.

29. *Voices of Emerging Nations,* p. 14, Leswing, 1971.

30. *The Story of Indonesia,* p. 27, McCormick-Mathers, 1965.

31. *World Cultures Past and Present,* p. 315, Harper & Row, 1964.

32. *The Story of Indonesia,* p. 10, McCormick-Mathers, 1975.

33. *Past to Present,* p. 683, Macmillan, 1963.

34. *India: Today's World in Focus,* p. 38, Ginn, 1968.

35. *Exploring a Changing World,* p. 481, Globe, 1968.

36. *India: Focus on Change,* p. 63, Prentice-Hall, 1975.

37. *Eastern Lands,* p. 396, Allyn & Bacon, 1968.

38. *World Geography,* pp. 426, 429, Ginn, 1974.

39. *People in a Changing World,* p. A 71, Laidlaw, 1974.

40. *China: Development by Force,* pp. 20, 27, Scott Foresman, 1964.

41. *The Indian Subcontinent,* p. 62, Allyn & Bacon, 1971.

42. *China,* p. 72, Oxford, 1972.

43. *The Story of Japan,* p. 44, McCormick-Mathers, 1970.

44. *The Third World: Southeast Asia,* pp. 23, 19, Pendulum, 1973.

45. *The World around Us,* p. 136, Harcourt Brace Jovanovich, 1965.

46. *The World Today,* p. 585, Webster McGraw-Hill, 1971.

47. *Inside World Politics,* p. 231, Allyn & Bacon, 1974.

48. *Exploring the Non-Western World,* p. 227, Globe, 1971.

49. *Communities around the World,* p. 8, Sadlier, 1971. Teacher's guide.

50. *Eastern Lands,* p. 363, Allyn & Bacon, 1968.

51. *World Geography Today,* p. 540, Holt, Rinehart and Winston, 1971.

52. *Inquiring about Cultures,* pp. 80-81, Holt, Rinehart and Winston, 1972.

53. *Past to Present,* p. 51, Macmillan, 1963. Teacher's edition.

54. *The Ecumene,* p. 132, Harper & Row, 1973.

55. *The Social Sciences: Concepts and Values,* p. 317, Harcourt Brace Jovanovich, 1975.

56. *The Human Achievement,* p. 553, Silver Burdett, 1970.

57. *Exploring World Cultures,* p. 376, Ginn, 1974.

58. *The Story of Afghanistan,* p. 39, McCormick-Mathers, 1965.

59. *Men and Nations,* p. 171, Harcourt Brace Jovanovich, 1971.

60. *Record of Mankind,* p. 223, D.C. Heath, 1970.

61. *A Global History of Man,* p. 472, Allyn & Bacon, 1974.

62. *Japan and Korea,* p. 91, Oxford, 1972.

63. *East Asia,* p. 113, Silver Burdett, 1970.

64. *The Story of China,* p. 50, McCormick-Mathers, 1968.

65. *China-Japan-Korea,* p. 196, Cambridge, 1971.

66. *Japan,* p. 53, Scott Foresman, 1971.

67. *Your World and Mine,* p. 388, Ginn, 1969.

68. *Exploring a Changing World,* p. 681, Globe, 1968. Teacher's guide.

69. *Exploring the Non-Western World,* p. 316, Globe, 1971.

70. *People and Cultures,* p. 278, Noble and Noble, 1974.

71. *South Asia: People in Change,* p. 29, Addison-Wesley, 1975.

72. *Japan, Ally in the Far East,* p. 27, Laidlaw, 1967.

BODY RITUAL AMONG THE NACIREMA

Horace M. Miner

Reproduced by permission of the American Anthropological Association from the
American Anthropologist, 58 (3), 1956.

The anthropologist has become so familiar with the diversity of ways in which different peoples behave in similar situations that he is not apt to be surprised by even the most exotic customs. In fact, if all of the logically possible combinations of behavior have not been found somewhere in the world, he is apt to suspect that they must be present in some yet undescribed tribe. The point has, in fact, been expressed with respect to clan organization by Murdock (1949:71). In this light, the magical beliefs and practices of the Nacirema present such unusual aspects that it seems desirable to describe them as an example of the extremes to which human behavior can go.

Professor Linton first brought the ritual of the Nacirema to the attention of anthropologists twenty years ago (1936:326), but the culture of this people is still very poorly understood. They are a North American group living in the territory between the Canadian Cree, the Yaqui and Tarahumare of Mexico, and the Carib and Arawak of the Antilles. Little is known of their origin, although tradition states that they came from the east. According to Nacirema mythology, their nation was originated by a culture hero, Notgnihsaw, who is otherwise known for two great feats of strength—the throwing of a piece of wampum across the river Pa-To-Mac and the chopping down of a cherry tree in which the Spirit of Truth resided.

Nacirema culture is characterized by a highly developed market economy which has evolved in a rich natural habitat. While much of the people's time is devoted to economic pursuits, a large part of the fruits of these labors and a considerable portion of the day are spent in ritual activity. The focus of this activity is the human body, the appearance and health of which loom as a dominant concern in the ethos of the people. While such a concern is certainly not unusual, its ceremonial aspects and associated philosophy are unique.

The fundamental belief underlying the whole system appears to be that the human body is ugly and that its natural tendency is to debility and disease. Incarcerated in such a body, man's only hope is to avert these characteristics through the use of the powerful influences of ritual and ceremony. Every household has one or more shrines devoted to this purpose. The more powerful individuals in the society have several shrines in their houses and, in fact, the opulence of a house is often referred to in terms of the number of such ritual centers it possesses. Most houses are of wattle and daub construction, but the shrine rooms of the more wealthy are walled with stone. Poorer families imitate the rich by applying pottery plaques to their shrine walls.

While each family has at least one such shrine, the rituals associated with it are not family ceremonies but are private and secret. The rites are normally only discussed with children, and then only during the period when they are being initiated into these mysteries. I was able, however, to establish sufficient rapport with the natives to examine these shrines and to have the rituals described to me.

The focal point of the shrine is a box or chest which is built into the wall. In this chest are kept the many charms and magical potions without which no native believes he could live. These preparations are secured from a variety of specialized practitioners. The most powerful of these are the medicine men, whose assistance must be rewarded with substantial gifts. However, the medicine men do not provide the curative potions for their clients, but decide what the ingredients should be and then write them down in an ancient and secret language. This writing is understood only by the medicine men and by the herbalists who, for another gift, provide the required charm.

The charm is not disposed of after it has served its purpose, but is placed in the charm-box of the household shrine. As these magical materials are specific for certain ills, and the real or imagined maladies of the people are many, the charm-box is usually full to overflowing. The magical packets are so numerous that people forget what their purposes were and fear to use them again. While the natives are very vague on this point, we can only assume that the idea in retaining all the old magical materials is that their presence in the charm-box, before which the body rituals are conducted, will in some way protect the worshipper.

Beneath the charm-box is a small font. Each day every member of the family, in succession, enters the shrine room, bows his head before the charm-box, mingles different sorts of holy water in the font, and proceeds with a brief rite of ablution. The holy waters are secured from the Water Temple of the community, where the priests conduct elaborate ceremonies to make the liquid ritually pure.

In the hierarchy of magical practitioners, and below the medicine men in prestige, are specialists whose designation is best translated "holy-mouth-men." The Nacirema have an almost pathological horror of and fascination with the mouth, the condition of which is believed to have a supernatural influence on all social relationships. Were it not for the rituals of the mouth, they believe that their teeth would fall out, their gums bleed, their jaws shrink, their friends desert them, and their lovers reject them. They also believe that a strong relationship exists between oral and moral characteristics. For example, there is a ritual ablution of the mouth for children which is supposed to improve their moral fiber.

The daily body ritual performed by everyone includes a mouth-rite. Despire the fact that these people are so punctilious about care of the mouth, this rite involves a practice which strikes the uninitiated stranger as revolting. It was reported to me that the ritual consists of inserting a small bundle of hog hairs into the mouth, along with certain magical powders, and then moving the bundle in a highly formalized series of gestures.

In addition to the private mouth-rite, the people seek out a holy-mouth-man once or twice a year. These practitioners have an impressive set of paraphernalia, consisting of a variety of augers, awls, probes, and prods. The use of these objects in the exorcism of the evils of the mouth involves almost unbelievable ritual torture of the client. The holy-mouth-man opens the client's mouth and, using the above mentioned tools, enlarges any holes which decay may have created in the teeth. Magical materials are put into these holes. If there are no naturally occurring holes in the teeth, large sections of one or more teeth are gouged out so that the supernatural substance can be applied. In the client's view, the purpose of these ministrations is to arrest decay and to draw friends. The extremely sacred and traditional character of the rite is evident in the fact that the natives return to the holy-mouth-men year after year, despite the fact that their teeth continue to decay.

It is to be hoped that, when a thorough study of the Nacirema is made, there will be careful inquiry into the personality structure of these people. One has but to watch the gleam in the eye of a holy-mouth-man, as he jabs an awl into an exposed nerve, to suspect that a certain amount of sadism is involved. If this can be established, a very interesting pattern emerges, for most of the population shows definite masochistic tendencies. It was to these that Professor Linton referred in discussing a distinctive part of the daily body ritual which is performed only by men. This part of the rite involves scraping and lacerating the surface of the face with a sharp instrument. Special women's rites are performed only four times during each lunar month, but what they lack in frequency is made up in barbarity. As part of this ceremony, women bake their heads in small ovens for about an hour. The theoretically interesting point is that what seems to be a preponderantly masochistic people have developed sadistic specialists.

The medicine men have an imposing temple, or *latipso,* in every community of any size. The more elaborate ceremonies required to treat very sick patients can only be performed at this temple. These ceremonies involve not only the thaumaturge but a permanent group of vestal maidens who move sedately about the temple chambers in distinctive costume and headdress.

The *latipso* ceremonies are so harsh that it is phenomenal that a fair proportion of the really sick natives who enter the temple ever recover. Small children whose indoctrination is still incomplete have been known to resist attempts to take them to the temple because "that is where you go to die." Despite this fact, sick adults are not only willing but eager to undergo the protracted ritual purification, if they can afford to do so. No matter how ill the supplicant or how grave the emergency, the guardians of many temples will not admit a client if he cannot give a rich gift to the custodian. Even after one has gained admission and survived the ceremonies, the guardians will not permit the neophyte to leave until he makes still another gift.

The supplicant entering the temple is first stripped of all his or her clothes. In everyday life the Nacirema avoids exposure of his body and its natural functions. Bathing and excretory acts are performed only in the secrecy of the household shrine, where they are ritualized as part of the body-rites. Psychological shock results from the fact that body secrecy is suddenly lost upon entry into the *latipso.* A man, whose own wife has never seen him in an excretory act, suddenly finds himself naked and assisted by a vestal maiden while he performs his natural functions into a sacred vessel. This sort of ceremonial treatment is necessitated by the fact that the excreta are used by a diviner to ascertain the course and nature of the client's sickness. Female clients, on the other hand, find their naked bodies are subjected to the scrutiny, manipulation, and prodding of the medicine men.

Few supplicants in the temple are well enough to do anything but lie on their hard beds. The daily ceremonies, like the rites of the holy-mouth-men, involve discomfort and torture. With ritual precision, the vestals awaken their miserable charges each dawn and roll them about on their beds of pain while performing ablutions, in the formal movements of which the maidens are highly trained. At other times they insert magic wands in the supplicant's mouth or force him to eat substances which are supposed to be healing. From time to time the medicine men come to their clients and jab magically treated needles into their flesh. The fact that these temple ceremonies may not cure, and may even kill the neophyte, in no way decreases the people's faith in the medicine men.

There remains one other kind of practitioner, known as a "listener." This witch-doctor has the power to exorcise the devils that lodge in the heads of people who have been bewitched. The Nacirema believe that parents bewitch their own children. Mothers are particularly suspected of putting a curse on children while teaching them the secret body rituals. The counter-magic of the witch-doctor is unusual in its lack of ritual. The patient simply tells the "listener" all his troubles and fears, beginning with the earliest difficulties he can remember. The memory displayed by the Nacirema in these exorcism sessions is truly remarkable. It is not uncommon for the patient to bemoan the rejection he felt upon being weaned as a babe, and a few individuals even see their troubles going back to the traumatic effects of their own birth.

In conclusion, mention must be made of certain practices which have their base in native aesthetics but which depend upon the pervasive aversion to the natural body and its functions. There are ritual fasts to make fat people thin and ceremonial feasts to make thin people fat. Still other rites are used to make women's breasts larger if they are small, and smaller if they are large. General dissatisfaction with breast shape is symbolized in the fact that the ideal form is virtually outside the range of human variation. A few women afflicted with almost inhuman hyper-mammary development are so idolized that they make a handsome living by simply going from village to village and permitting the natives to stare at them for a fee.

Reference has already been made to the fact that excretory functions are ritualized, routinized, and relegated to secrecy. Natural reproductive functions are similarly distorted. Intercourse is taboo as a topic and scheduled as an act. Efforts are made to avoid pregnancy by the use of magical materials or by limiting intercourse to certain phases of the moon. Conception is actually very infrequent. When pregnant, women dress so as to hide their condition. Parturition takes place in secret, without friends or relatives to assist, and the majority of women do not nurse their infants.

Our review of the ritual life of the Nacirema has certainly shown them to be a magic-ridden people. It is hard to understand how they have managed to exist so long under the burdens which they have imposed upon themselves. But even such exotic customs as these take on real meaning when they are viewed with the insight provided by Malinowski when he wrote (1948:70):

> Looking from far and above, from our high places of safety in the developed civilization, it is easy to see all the crudity and irrelevance of magic. But without its power and guidance early man could not have mastered his practical difficulties as he has done, nor could man have advanced to the higher stages of civilization.

REFERENCES CITED

Ralph Linton, *The Study of Man,* D. Appleton-Century Co., New York, 1936.

Bronislaw Malinowski, *Magic, Science, and Religion,* The Free Press, Glencoe, 1948.

George P. Murdock, *Social Structure,* The Macmillan Co., New York, 1949.

AN AMERICAN RESEARCHER IN PARIS:
INTERVIEWING FRENCHMEN

Daniel Lerner

When a Frenchman answers the telephone, he says: *"j'écoute"* (I am *listening*). In this way he takes up a position of defense against the unknown interlocutor at the other end of the line. To the greeting on the street, *Comment va?* (How goes?), one is likely to receive the ironic reply, *On se défend* (One defends oneself). In this slightly mocking fashion, with their special gift for self-conscious clarity, the French take note of a profound trait of their national character. The defensiveness of this posture startles an American used to the open style of saying "hello! " to every anonymous telephone ring and "fine! " to every casual "Hi? "

Defensive remarks greeted me when I arrived in September 1954 to start interviewing Frenchmen of the "elite classes," as part of a larger sociological study. What could one learn from such interviews? Besides, how could it be done? There was universal doubt about the value and the feasibility of the enterprise. The French, I was told, would never talk to a stranger with no other claim to their confidence than that of being an interviewer. Two years later, we had in fact managed to complete over fifteen hundred long interviews with Frenchmen of very high standing. Respondents included, in round figures, five hundred top businessmen, three hundred political leaders (including all but two of the postwar prime ministers and foreign ministers), a hundred high civil servants representing *les grand corps de l'Etat,* a hundred senior military men, a hundred clerical and lay spokesmen of the church, and a hundred officials of labor, farmer, and other pressure groups.

The trick was to get them started; but, once started, how they talked! The average length of the fifteen hundred interviews was over two hours, and a substantial number of them ran toward eight hours. (The same interview schedule, in England, averaged a bit over one hour and the questions were fully answered.) Frequently the interviewer was requested to return, after a single session lasting two or three hours, by respondents eager to have their full say in an interview that resembled an interior dialogue uttered aloud. The essential is that, once engaged, the Frenchman talked volubly. But, to engage him, one had to scale the defensive wall—as the French put it, *franchir le mur.*

"LES FORMULES DE POLITESSE"

Our first approaches to interviewing were modest, tentative, apologetic. Trial-and-error, hit-and-miss (what the French love to call *"L'empirisme anglo-saxon"*) finally produced a workable formula. To each prospective respondent, the interviewer explained that his Institute had undertaken a study of attitudes among the elite. As Frenchmen do not respond readily to questionnaires, he continued, we were seeking the counsel of specially qualified persons. "Would you be so kind as to review with us the questionnaire we propose to use and give us the benefit of your criticisms? In responding yourself, you could explain which questions a Frenchman would be likely to resist and why; which questions would draw ambiguous or evasive responses that could not be properly interpreted; and which questions could be altered in such a way as to require reflective rather than merely stereotyped answers."

By casting the interviewee in the role of expert consultant, we gave him the opportunity to indulge in a favorite indoor sport—generalizing about Frenchmen. This exercise suggested procedures that were, in fact, used in subsequent interviewing. More important, it provided us with a comprehensive set of French images of the French. How Frenchmen see each other—this became the starting-point of our inquiry on how they see the world around them.

Their comments clarified, for example, the psycho-cultural role of French conventions of courtesy. The highly elaborated set of *formules de politesse* is an elegant way of maintaining proper distance between individuals. By comparison with the American desire for quick intimacy, for promptly reaching a first-name basis, there is a general appreciation in France of the reserved person. This is the mark of a person *bien élevé,* raised with a proper sense of right conduct. A rule that governs personal relations in France is: *"Il faut garder ses distances"* (One must keep his distance). It is generally believed that a person is likely to suffer if, *par manque de réserve* (lack of personal reserve), he exposes himself to the will and way of others. French distance-maintaining mechanisms make it easier to ritualize all sorts of relationships that elsewhere are met by improvisations.

There is an established code of behavior in most matters of daily routine. French gastronomy is a case. *La cuisine française* is widely recognized as a high order of artistic achievement, but its ritual characteristics are less widely noted. Frenchmen tend to be rigid in all matters associated with feeding. There is practically no variation in *les heures de repas* (eating hours) of any region. There is little deviation as to which type of wine goes with which food, and few venture from established rules in order to "try something different." Even the conception of a well-composed meal (*repas bien composé*) is a distinctly Gallic idea with certain fixed features. A young French writer, returning from a summer vacation in the United States, where he was outraged by many native practices, gives priority to the utter shock (*bouleversement*) he suffered from the American habit of nonscheduled snacks—*"les repas pris à n'importe quelle heure et n'importe comment"* (meals taken no matter when and how).

The case is more dramatic with respect to Chinese cuisine, which many non-French gastronomes regard as the only serious rival to the French if not its superior. But the notion of eating according to another logic than the linear progression from the spicy appetizer (*pour ouvrir l'appétit*) through fish, flesh, salad, cheese, fruit, sweet, coffee, seems to Frenchmen curious and *invraisemblable* (improbable). The Chinese logic, if anything more complex and refined, of arranging taste sensations in cyclical fashion appears to them as being merely comic: *"Figurez-vous, ils vous servent un entremêt, tout d'un coup, après quelques poissons variés et puis ils terminent le repas avec la soupe! C'est drôle, hein?"* (Imagine, they serve you a sweet, suddenly, after a variety of fish dishes, and then they end the meal with soup. Droll, eh?)

"LE REFUS DE S'ENGAGER"

The French desire for an environment arranged in a stable fashion, with familiar routines defined by recognizable limits, manifests itself also on questions of public consequence. Typical expressions of distaste for innovation are *"Pas de surprise! "* (no surprises) and *"Pas d'aventure! "*

(no adventures). This systematic French distrust of whatever is new and strange underlies a variety of otherwise inexplicable phenomena.

Take the notorious case of French politics. During many years, the government suffered from a sustained incapacity to act decisively. Characteristically, the French themselves quickly found *le mot juste* (the correct term) to describe this situation: *l'immobilisme*. Political immobility became pervasive when France was confronted by a new and strange set of demands. The major test was the European Defense Community, which asked nothing less than that Frenchmen henceforth conceive their political identity in terms of being Europeans. There were better reasons for hesitation than many foreigners recognize. But to prolong the issue over four years before they finally rejected an idea they had themselves created was peculiarly characteristic of French politics. Perhaps its sublime expression was the declaration of M. Antoine Pinay, former prime minister and minister of foreign affairs: *"Je suis autant que personne partisan du mouvement, mais j'entends qu'il ne débouche pas sur l'aventure."* (As much as anyone I favor action, but I don't intend action to expose us to adventure.)[1]

France has become a land in which "surprise" and "adventure" are pejorative words. Every approach from "the outside" must be regarded with suspicion by a person in his right mind. The prudent posture, when confronted by any new and strange proposition, is defense: *"On veut m'avoir"* (they want to do me out of something). The safest way to defend one's self, naturally, is a refusal to participate at all (*"je ne marche pas"*), thereby avoiding the risk of *l'aventure*. And the danger of adventure, among people whose defensive shell often protects a wistful interior, is that one would be disappointed. It seems especially important to avoid *déception* (the peculiar French word for disappointment). The famous French skepticism is, at bottom, a defensive measure for avoiding future deprivation by maintaining deliberately low expectations.

Underlying this view of political action is a more general ontological perspective that has been worked into the French sensibility. Frenchmen commonly perceive the environment as more detached and remote from themselves than do, say, Anglo-Americans. The external world possesses for them rather definite characteristics, including a capacity for action which is independent of the will of particular human beings. Ordinary French conversation produces an array of phrases which expresses this idea. One speaks often, for example, of *"la force des choses"* (the power of circumstances), a notion rarely heard in America—where it is regarded as defeatist rather than realist—and hardly more often in Britain. Another way of referring to the external world as possessing a reality independent of human effort is the phrase *"les choses sont ce qu'elles sont."* ("Things are as they are" implies for a Frenchman that it is useless to try to change them.)[2]

This perspective tends to disengage the individual from great public issues. Politics becomes a random series of events about which one can do little. The Anglo-American idea that policy is a sequence of decisions by which one seeks to alter events before they become the *données* (data) of the next public crisis—this idea seems to very many Frenchmen pretentious and rather tiresome. The young express this sentiment by making *je-m'en-foutisme* (privatization) into an ideology; their elders are content with the celebrated Gallic shrug whereby passive indifference connotes superior intelligence. Either way, this attenuates political life by a widespread *refus de s'engager* (refusal to get involved), which limits personal interaction with *la chose publique.*

A consequence of the *refus de s'engager* is the relative scarcity of voluntary organizations in France as compared with the massive American proliferation of channels whereby individuals engage themselves in public enterprise. The absence of active civic participation is evident in all social classes in France. There are very few "clubs" of the sort developed by the upper social groups in Britain. Among the middle class there are few parallels of Rotary, Kiwanis, and Lions. Certainly, such institutions as the Parent-Teachers' Association, the League of Women Voters, and the Association of University Women play only a feeble role among a people whose women remain firmly rooted in their primordial sexual role. Among the working class only the labor union has made any headway. Still, it hardly touches the French worker in his daily life—offering him neither educational opportunities, recreational facilities, consumers' cooperatives, nor social diversions. All classes of Britons are likely to be shocked by the absence of an effective Society for the Prevention of Cruelty to Animals. The participant life languishes because the Frenchman is repelled by "groupism": he guards his inner privacy, the mastery of his individuality (*maîtrise de soi*), by a resolute *méfiance* (distrust) toward others.

This is part of the fixed self-image of Frenchmen as *réalistes,* which finds varied expression in the phrases used to praise one's compatriots. The French are "hard-headed" (*réfractaires*); they do not get taken in (*pas d'illusions*). Or, as one of our "consultants" phrased it, *"les français n'aiment pas se raconter des histoires"* (the French do not like to kid themselves). Realism is associated intimately with another self-ascribed trait: skepticism. A person who holds optimistic views on practically any subject is sure to suffer a hard blow (*prendre un coup dur*). In popular parlance the man who buys the Brooklyn Bridge is a "soft fruit" (*une poire*). He gets universal derision with little of the underlying sympathy Americans retain for the "sucker." For the Frenchman, *une vache à lait* (milk cow) is strictly *un pauvre type* (boob) and *"tant pis pour lui!"* (too bad for him!). After all, *"il faut savoir se défendre! "* (one must know how to defend oneself!).

And so *la chose publique* yields pride of place to the austere demands of privatization. By rejecting involvements in the public arena, *le soi* (the self) guards its privileged status as a *territoire sacré*. The flow of public discourse in France profoundly respects the sanctity of the ego. Even in technical psychology, the vocabulary used for describing the "self-system" and its manifold operations is underdeveloped. Privacy among Frenchmen is less the product of mutual respect than a code of self-defense.

"IN THE SOUP"

Once the restraints of privacy have been loosened, an interviewer must deal with the special French conventions of cognition. The metaphysics which endows the external world with active attributes of its own also creates new problems of question-formulation for a foreigner accustomed to more empirical habits of thought. In our earliest interviews I was baffled by the recurrent request from respondents to state "precisely" various questions that seemed to me already precise. It required much conversation and reflection before I realized that, for the French, precision has a quite different and special meaning, a literally Cartesian meaning. What makes questions "precise" for Frenchmen is their capacity to frame the object of reference in a specific context (*bien délimité, dans un cadre qui lui est propre*). The object of reference, to be clear, must be perceived as discrete—with external boundaries sharply defined (*"circonscrire l'objet"* in the conventional vocabulary of French philosophy).

French insistence upon a discrete, disengaged object of reference underscores their revulsion against relationships without clearly perceived boundaries. The language abounds in pejorative expressions to express this horror of inadequate distance between subject and object. Such phrases as *dans le jus, dans le sirop, dans la soupe,* convey vividly the image that fluidity (*des idées floues*) is the enemy of clarity because liquids exhibit no boundaries. Other expressions of distaste for "fuzziness" are *dans le cirage, dans la vaseline, dans le coton* (wax, vaseline, cotton wadding), where the soft and shapeless mass without defined margins represents the antonym of clarity and precision.

The limits which such a posture impose upon the interview are illustrated by a respondent who served us as "consultant." Director of an important national research organization, with long experience in survey work, this man seemed perfect for our purpose. Indeed, he gave us many practical suggestions for question-wording, which helped us to avoid the vague and achieve the "precise." At first, different questions scattered through our interview schedule, however, made this man throw up his hands in utter contempt and despair. "You will never get any Frenchman to answer questions like these," he declared, without explaining why. These were the questions:

1. If you were *président du conseil* (prime minister), what would be the main lines of your policy?

2. If you had to live in another country, which one would you choose?

3. If you had your life to live over again, what sort of life would you want?

4. Who are the most enviable people in the world? Why?

5. What functions do you think you could fill in a Communist France?

What these questions have in common—reflection suggested and experience confirmed—is that they ask the interviewee to imagine himself in a situation other than his real one (i.e., they are "role-playing" questions). Such an idea is regarded as frivolous, not worth the attention of Frenchmen, who are, after all, *"des gens sérieux"* (sober people). These questions were bound to provoke resistance among people who consider as their strongest traits realism, skepticism, and mistrust. And indeed they did, many interviewees regarding them as merely silly: *"de la blague!" "de la fantaisie pure!"* (a bad joke! pure fantasy!).

An instructive study could be made of the diverse ways in which people of different nations respond to role-playing questions of this sort. Our British interviewees, for instance, responded to precisely these questions with only minor incident. In general, such questions are handled with greater facility by people who are habituated to ready ego-involvement with the new and strange. Such people, having a less rigid conception of themselves and their proper conduct in the world, show a more supple capacity for rearranging their self-image upon short notice. A clear difference in the capacity to empathize, to play roles, emerged from interviews conducted in the Middle East several years ago. There it was possible to identify the Traditionalists by their total incapacity to answer such questions as "What would you do if you were president of Egypt?" By contrast, the Moderns seemed to experience no difficulty whatsoever when asked what they would do as editor of a newspaper, or as leader of their country, or if they had to live in another country.

There is a vast psychic difference between the illiterate and untutored traditionalism of the Middle Eastern peasant and the traditionalism which prevails among the contemporary elite of France. The Frenchman has acquired his traditionalism as an intellectual discipline and as part of an explicit psychic code. He is taught from childhood an articulate conception of *le bonheur* and a system of appropriate behavior designed to maximize his satisfactions. Whereas the Arab peasant usually has no sense of possible alternatives to his traditional ways but simply "does what comes naturally," the Frenchman has a very sophisticated rationale for his conduct. He not only is quite aware of other ways of behaving but can, and usually does, tell you with the greatest clarity why his way is better than any other.

The personality associated with traditionalism takes a quite different turn, then, among the French. It explains why Frenchmen often accuse Americans, who used to think of themselves as the world's greatest individualists, of a *manque d'individualisme.* For contemporary Americans, individualism implies nonconformity; expressing oneself means doing something just a little differently from the other fellow. For Frenchmen, individualism lives quite comfortably with a massive conformism. Their underlying principle is not to do some things a little differently, but rather not to do very many things at all. In French eyes the American loses individuality by identifying himself too readily with other persons, by associating himself too intensely with public causes, and by joining too many organizations. The Frenchman guards his individuality by maintaining *le soi* inviolate from the impingements of the public arena.

POLITICS AND POLICE

We gained *entrée,* in due course, to spokesmen of those social groups which constitute the political Center and Right—businessmen, high civil servants, military leaders, even chiefs of the non-Communist trade unions. But we made little headway on the Left, a sector of the political continuum which is inadequately interpreted even in France and which reaches far beyond the Communist Party and fellow-travelers.

There exists in France a pervasive political sentiment called *gauchisme.* It is a sentiment because it entails no specific judgments on specific issues but expresses rather a diffuse general hostility to the powers-that-be and things-as-they-are. One approximation of a psychological definition of this sentiment was sketched by Albert Camus in *L'homme révolté,* with reference to "the alienated intellectual." The special importance of *gauchisme* in France is its sociological diffusion. Types of Frenchmen have been affected by chronic oppositionism who, in other countries, are conservative or have no clearly defined political sentiment at all (e.g., army officers, civil servants, rich businessmen). A systematic sociology of the diffusion of *gauchisme* in France would do much to explain the French incapacity to act decisively on critical public issues during the last two decades.

It was among these *gauchisants* that our inquiry encountered the most widespread suspicion and resistance. We had decided, early in the game, that complete candor on the sponsorship of our study was essential. Our interviewers had been instructed to respond, when questioned, that the inquiry was jointly sponsored by French and American universities and that an American professor was a member of the scientific committee directing the study. The impact of this disclosure upon French *gauchisants* was strong enough to draw caustic remarks, to limit responsiveness, and, in some cases, to distort substance. Some *gauchisant* respondents framed their remarks primarily to cause anguish to the American professor—a performance more frequent among those who took their *gauchisme* rather lightly.

More committed Leftists not only refused to answer at all, but in some cases went further. We were reported to the weekly journal *L'Express,* a leading mouthpiece of *gauchisme,* and for most of a week were haunted by a young reporter determined to denounce and expose our enterprise. Several hours of explaining carefully our interview schedule, our sampling procedure, and our modes of analysis failed to persuade the sleuth that it would be impossible for us to derive information useful to the police, French or American. It was perfectly clear to the reporter that there must be some hidden trick; once I was an American, the enterprise was necessarily a maneuver of the Right and, *ipso facto,* despicable.

The extreme *gauchisant* went even further. In two regions we were denounced to the departmental *préfet.* Our interviewers there reported that, unless we could clear matters with the *préfet,* their usefulness would be at an end. In Paris we were subjected to two visits by agents of the DST (*Défense de la Sécurité du Territoire,* the French FBI). These persons scrutinized very carefully our intentions, procedures, and, most particularly, our affiliations in France. We were able to surmount those inquiries, only because our commmittee of sponsors (*comité de patronage*) was composed of Frenchmen of impeccable standing.

LES ANGLAIS: A PROJECTIVE TEST

We learned from these interviews, among other things, that how the French see other nations is now a function of how they see themselves. This sector of French sentiment has a special piquancy with respect to the British. With no other people do the French lead as complex and many-layered a psychic life as with their neighbors across the Channel. For penetration of the French fantasy world, *les Anglais* make a splendid projective test.

We can deal better with current French judgments of others when we recall André Siegfried's theorem that French culture had been "completed" by the 18th Century. Indeed, one can usefully classify Frenchmen today in terms of their reckoning with the marvelous XVIII*ème*. There are those who are still for it (and sometimes in it); those who flaunt the XIX*ème's* reaction against it—the *bons esprits* who, in the phrase of Marcel Aymé, "still assign a high revolutionary coefficient to masturbation"; those who have reacted against XIX*ème's* reaction against it (the, so to speak, anti-anti-XVIII*èmes*). Here and there, one encounters someone who is in and of the XX*ème*. In some ways he seems hardly French any more!

These historic levels reverberated, like geologic layers in a tremor, when our interviewers asked Frenchmen how they felt about *les Anglais*. The ancient orders—military and clerical—emitted the sonorous peals of classic Anglophobia. No happenings *circa* A.D. 1960 dim, for the true Gallic Anglophobe, the vivacious souvenirs of Jeanne d'Arc and Waterloo. Compiègne still symbolizes *perfide Albion* and not a few among our respondents still used, as a summary expression, some variant of the ancient formula *"l'argent anglais et les poitrines françaises."* (Military alliance between the two countries is said to consist of "English money and French lives.")

Recent events not only fail to alter this undertow of Anglophobia, but are themselves transformed by its force. Thus, one 70-year-old retired cavalry colonel attributes current French ills mainly to British design— the interbellum failures of French policy; the defeat of 1940 "caused" by British evacuation at Dunkerque; the undermining of European unity by British nonparticipation in EDC; even the tragedy at Dien Bien Phu (where British desire to safeguard Burma, he alleges, prevented U.S. use of the napalm bombs that would have gained the French victory). Doubtless he is today explaining why the sad situation in Algeria is due to the British. Enveloped in his antique reverie, this Old Soldier—who interlards trenchant critiques of others with such dicta as *"L'Etat doit être fondé*

sur la fidelité, la discipline et l'honneur! "—still considers the principal
obstacle to French glory to be *les Anglais.*

The classic Anglophobia, while still vibrant in the subsoil of French
emotion, no longer is a prescriptive item in the national doctrine to
which every Frenchman good and true must subscribe. The evidence of
our interviews suggests, indeed, that Anglophobia of all types has
declined in frequency and intensity. A perfectly upright Frenchman can
nowadays ignore the old chestnut of British perfidy and say: *"Les
Anglais ont une grande loyauté dans l'exécution des contrats particu-
liers."* (The English are honorable in the performance of private
commitments.) This revision of diehard dogma occurs mainly among
people who have scaled down ancient French pretensions to an
appropriate up-to-date level of national aspiration. The relationship, in a
word, is this: as appraisals of French power decline so evaluations of
British virtue rise.

Frenchmen are certainly not enamoured of their other principal
allies—Americans and Germans. By contrast, *les Anglais* come to seem
utterly admirable to many Frenchmen. Interesting variations occur when
the Anglo-French relationship is cross-tabulated with French sentiments
toward these others. It is rare, for example, that one should look with
equal favor upon both Germans and Englishmen. To look with equal
disfavor upon both is less rare and forms the basic syndrome of French
xenophobia, since these are still the two most salient national entities in
the conventional French image of the world. To the Germanophile—and
he constitutes a species of Frenchman more numerous than is ordinarily
supposed—the English usually figure as rivalrous and even diabolical, the
principal component of disarray in a world that might otherwise be
molded into an orderly image of heart's desire. Such a person is much
more likely than most of his compatriots to reveal a highly authoritarian
set of preferences, including, if he is a relentless ideologue, the peculiarly
French variety of matter-of-fact racism. He is likely, on current issues, to
despise the Arabs (for whom his main adjectives are *sale, bête,* and
brutal) and to blame French decline in North Africa upon British lack of
imperial backbone in dealing with the colonial peoples.

Conversely, the Germanophobe—when he is not comprehensively
xenophobic—is more likely to tend toward Anglophilia. For him *les
Anglais,* at least, have the virtue of sharing his antipathy for the Germans
(by contrast with the Americans, say, whose idolatry of productivity and
efficiency supposedly blind them to more fundamental traits of human
character). Depending upon the intensity of his Germanophobia, such a
Frenchman's Anglophilia may carry him to extreme postures of

filiopietism toward *les Anglais*. If there is intense anxiety in his feeling against Germany—and paranoid symptoms are not infrequent among such respondents—then his attitude toward the English is likely to exhibit the ambivalent adoration usually reserved for Big Brother.

These extremist syndromes of Germanophilia-cum-Anglophobia and Germanophobia-cum-Anglophilia are most clearly defined, of course, at the limits of the French spectrum of attitudes. While they surely resonate in the breasts of many ordinary Frenchmen, they are most revealing as expressions of political psychopathology in a nation whose historic self-imagery makes a poor fit to the current reality of forced choices presented, largely, by its partners.

"PRIVATE FACES IN PUBLIC PLACES"

More subtle, in this context, are the discriminations which Frenchmen make between their major pair of partners—the English and the Americans. For a majority of Frenchmen the direction of sentiment is unilateral: they "like" both or "dislike" both with approximately equal vigor. But two substantial clusters of deviant cases appear among our respondents. One group dislikes the English and likes the Americans. These appear to be largely the same authoritarian types who like the Germans. They are also relatively more discontented with *"l'état actuel des choses"* in France. They find in common among the Germans and Americans the admirable traits of diligence, organization, efficiency. These traits satisfy a compulsive craving for orderliness—traits whose absence they deplore in France and whose failure to triumph in the world they attribute to the wily and unpredictable *Britanniques* (the epithet which usually replaces *les Anglais* in this context).

The other deviant group dislikes the Americans and likes the English. The underlying sentiment here appears to stem from a sense of shared greatness gone, a wistful affection for the lifeways evolved during the centuries when Frenchmen and Englishmen disputed between themselves for supremacy in the familiar arena of Europe (and the game overseas was merely an extension of the continental play). These older lifeways are felt to be a more suitable *règle de jeu* than the stark code, known as the Cold War, which defines right conduct for the powerful primitives (U.S./U.S.S.R.) now disputing mastery of the great globe itself.

This preoccupation with the aesthetic surface of life starts from a net affirmation of W. H. Auden's dictum that

> private faces in public places
> are nicer and wiser
> than public faces in private places.

It expresses itself in the frequent selection, for special admiration, of personal deportment among the English as compared with the Americans or the Russians—since the two giants are usually perceived by such respondents as more alike than different. The preference for a private style of life is manifested also in their evaluation of public behavior. There is a wistful conviction, among these Frenchmen, that the English have somehow managed better than others to adapt their admirable traditions to *la force des choses* in the world today.

The tensions generated by the current need to reconstrue one's Self in terms of Others imposes a new set of demands upon French culture and personality. In meeting these demands, the French pay a heavy psychic cost. It may be, as some have averred, only the *rentier's* horrified and belated discovery that his vested values have declined and he has been living off capital. But current French psychopathology as the outcome of a XVIII*ème* culture that was too "complete" may aid diagnosis without advancing therapy. Granted that France no longer is what it was, its future will be shaped by the modes that prevail among Frenchmen of perceiving what it is. For the classic self-image no longer works. Gone are the days when Frenchmen could see their civilization as a perfect whole (*un tout*), and rank all other peoples simply by the direction and degree of their deviation from this perfect model. Nowadays, Frenchmen are obliged to judge themselves afresh when they judge others. This is a far more complex psychocultural task.

SOME NOTES ON METHOD

Interviewing Frenchmen thus involves a number of special problems derived from the national character, reinforced by behavioral codes and social institutions, and made acute by current political conditions. Making initial contact is complicated by the distance-maintaining mechanisms embedded in the French code of courtesy. The *formules de politesse* serve as index and agent of French distrust of the strange, their identification of security with privacy. Most refusals were based squarely upon the feeling that such an interview was an unwarranted intrusion into their personal affairs. Few said simply "No! " Rather more evaded a flat refusal by having their secretaries phone to postpone the rendezvous indefinitely as a less rude rejection. But, of those who explained instead of evading their refusal, many said: "This is not my concern! " "My opinions would not interest you! " "I do not know your Institute! " "Could you have Monsieur X [a member of our committee known to him] phone me to explain your purpose and introduce you?" To scale the defensive wall was not at all, among Frenchmen, a routine matter.

Once received, however, the interviewer figured as a person rather than a faceless machine for recording a one-way flow of short answers. Quite often, before granting a rendezvous, the interviewee specified that, if this was merely *"un Gallup"* (i.e., Yes-No contact poll), he was not interested. He would, however, be willing to *discuss* some of the important questions that concerned us. In such discussions the interviewer figured as a respected specialist. His own opinions on the questions, and on the respondent's expressed views, were often solicited. This was partly a gesture of courtesy but mainly an expression of the profound preference for the dialogue in French discourse.

The impact of the interviewer as a person was especially dramatic among Leftists, who are perhaps more richly endowed with the manipulative inclinations of the propagandist. Quite often a *gauchisant* who began by refusing an interview sponsored by "the Americans," and berating the French interviewer for using his talents under such auspices, would be drawn into heated discussion of the specific questions. After several hours of such dialogue, which furnished some extremely rich data, he might conclude by inviting the interviewer to have a drink—over which, if a relentless ideologue, he might advise the interviewer to quit this job and take more respectable employment.

The insistence upon a highly participant interviewer—one who relieved the respondent's anxieties about "exposing" himself to a strange person—gradually reshaped the basic format of our interview. In the early phase, a particularly gifted and versatile member of the interviewing team had tried out a variety of roles, ranging, as he put it, from the *lampiste* ("poor slob") to the *gavroche* ("dead-end kid"). His experiments indicated that the preferred role was that of the competent specialist, who, maintaining a posture of self-respect, exhibited the expectation that he would accord and receive respect from others. It was less effective, for example, to say, "Please answer my questions or I will lose my job," than to say, "I am obliged to ask you a number of questions, but you are obliged to answer only those that interest you." The latter formula seemed to define the relationship between subject and object—the distance between interviewer and interviewee—in a manner liberating to respondents worried about "engaging" themselves in a strange situation that might lead to *déception.*

As we moved from pretesting into the main phase of interviewing, the highly structured questionnaire with which we began became a minimally directive dialogue in the format of a free-flowing conversation. This transformation of the schedule reduced the utility of precoding and other mechanical devices for assuring uniform reporting. Instead, we used more personal procedures for testing interviewer reliability—mainly, brief daily meetings between the research director and each interviewer, and a weekly three-hour meeting attended by all interviewers. At each session detailed discussion of the new interviews gradually produced clarity and consensus on the permissible range of variation in wording questions and recording responses.

The consistency developed thereby was demonstrated in the subsequent coding phase, when extremely high rates of speed and reliability were obtained by the former interviewers acting as coders. While lacking the elegant simplicity of objective procedures, the method of continuous personal consultation among interviewers solved empirically some thorny problems of open-ended interviewing in a sample survey. These problems are threefold: (1) Since respondents are not obliged to choose one precisely worded answer (precoded) to a precisely worded question, strict comparability of responses is reduced. (2) As comparability is reduced, so the analytic code must be expanded to take account of all significant variations in the responses. (3) As the code is expanded, so reliability among coders tends to be reduced (since increases of choices normally increase chances of errors).

Daily review of each interview between the interviewer and research director, supplemented by weekly reviews of the full week's work among all interviewers, enabled us to solve problems of comparability as they arose. The interviewers presented every significant variation of question and response that occurred in their conversations. Each variation was thrashed out until a clear agreement on its interpretation (coding) was understood and accepted by all interviewers. Naturally, such a crude empirical procedure depends greatly upon the quality and quantity of the personnel. It is the research director's taxing job to review each interview, detect significant variations, and arbitrate differences of interpretation among interviewers. The interviewers must be few in number, high in quality, and steadfast in performance.

Our team consisted of six "hard core" interviewers, who stayed with the project from start to end. Only a few others were taken on, at peak periods or for special purposes, and each of these worked directly alongside a member of the "hard core." In a larger team, the demands of continuous intercommunication might easily become excessive. Each interviewer must be intelligent enough to recognize the essential matter in each of his responses, to detect the significant variations among them, to discriminate the comparable and noncomparable components exhibited by the verbal variations. Finally, the interviewers must be steadfast, since the method hinges on establishing very high consensus (virtual unanimity) among the team. Comparability can be steadily increased only as the interviewers reach clear and common understandings on how to deal with varied responses. Hence, any defection from the "hard core" increases the time and cost of obtaining comparable responses and reliable codes—since the whole team marks time while any new member is brought into the consensus.

Even under favorable circumstances, as in the present study, the method lacks the satisfying certifications conferred by more objective procedures. It is impossible to determine precisely how many significant variations of response have been undetected or misinterpreted (consensus can be formed on an erroneous interpretation). Yet the "hard core" of this team was able to obtain reliability scores averaging around .90 in coding each other's interview records at high speed during the final stages of the project. This indicates that the method *can* gain the richer data obtained in open-ended interviews without paying the excessive costs of ambiguity, noncomparability, and unreliability in their analysis.

The initial conditions of our study imposed the method upon us by the unassailable argument of *faute de mieux*. Our exploratory pretest showed that highly structured, fully precoded interviews would get us nowhere—or, at least, nowhere we wanted to go. They would save us time, money, and uncertainty, but they would not produce the data we wanted. Since these initial conditions involved nothing less than French culture and personality, as characterized in the preceding pages, they were not amenable to rapid rearrangement for the purposes of our study. Having to do the best we could, we did. The method evolved merits consideration by scholars concerned with studying personality cross-culturally.

A postscript on the sequel may be worth noting. Our interviewing program, begun in 1954, was executed in periodic "waves" over the next five years. By the spring of 1959, when we reinterviewed a panel of 100 French respondents who had been interrogated one or more times in preceding years, we felt able to use a structured, precoded questionnaire in a contact-poll type of interview. On this "wave" we encountered less rejection or evasion of our questions—fewer "don't knows" and "no opinions"—than in any preceding year. This fact raises important questions. Had these particular respondents become habituated to interviews by their previous experience with us—either accepting more readily invasion of their privacy by interviewers or ceasing to regard our interviewers as strangers? Or had some transformation of French behavioral conventions—manifestations of the deeper characteristics of traditional French culture and personality—occurred in the short space of five years? Neither hunch carries *prima facie* conviction with it. Our analysis, at present, indicates that a satisfactory account of the data will have to contain elements of both explanations. Whatever the new psychocultural mixture in France, it is clearly not the mixture as before. But this is a different story to be told on another occasion.

NOTES

1. A detailed case study of EDC is presented in Daniel Lerner and Raymond Aron, 1956, *La Querelle de la CED* (Armand Colin, Paris). The American title is *France Defeats EDC* (Praeger, New York, 1957).

2. Professor Laurence Wylie's excellent study *Village in the Vaucluse* (1957) shows how this metaphysic is built into French perspectives from their earliest school years: "Children are not encouraged to formulate principles independently on the basis of an examination of concrete cases. They are given the impression that principles exist autonomously. They are always there: immutable and constant. One can only learn to recognize them, and accept them. The same is true of concrete facts and circumstances. They exist, real and inalterable. Nothing can be done to change them. One has only to recognize and accept them." (p. 73)

BIBLIOGRAPHY

D. Lerner and R. Aron. *La Querelle de la CED,* Armand Colin, Paris, 1956. The American title is *France Defeats EDC,* Praeger, New York, 1957.

L. Wylie. *Village in the Vaucluse,* Harvard University Press, Cambridge, 1957.

THE GUEST'S GENERAL ROLE IN THE FAMILY

Raymond L. Gorden

It is quite obvious from the talks with the students and Peace Corps trainees that to be "a member of the family" is a very good thing in the minds of the American guests. Yet when we begin to see the meaning of "member of the family" in terms of specific behaviors and motivations, we find considerable ambivalence both in the North American guest and in the Colombian host as to whether they want the American to be "a member of the family." The high value placed upon this phrase by both guest and host seems to be based upon a mutual desire of each to be sociably acceptable to the other and to be viewed as accepting by the other.

THE AMERICANS' AMBIVALENCE[1]

The Americans' ambivalence seemed to be a conflict between a desire for emancipation from the older generation (or a desire for independence) and the desire for some special support, help, and advice needed while in the foreign environment. In short, there was a strong tendency for the American guest to accept such restrictions, advice, or supervision only when it gave him the support he felt he needed. When he did not feel the need, he tended to reject the aspects of his role in the family that were restrictive, made demands, or involved obligations. He was more interested in the aspects that entitled him to considerations, services, rights, and privileges.

This was not only because he was basically human but also because the mechanisms of social control that generally operate within our own society to get us to accept obligations as well as rights do not operate immediately upon the sojourner in the host culture. The degree to which a person accepts both the obligations and the rights connected with his role is an index of his integration into a particular group of culture.

Seventy-six percent of the students said they felt like members of the Colombian family, yet 35 percent of that group said that it was quite difficult for them to exchange ideas with their family. Of course, this in itself is not a clear contradiction, since some of them may find it difficult to exchange ideas with their own families in the United States. However, it is highly doubtful that they could feel like real members of the family when only 12 percent said that they did take the initiative in discussions with the family. Even though 77 percent said that the family did respond when they took the initiative, still 60 percent preferred to spend most of their free time with Americans. This particular group of 49 American students lived with Colombian families, took courses from Colombians in Spanish, and might have felt a need to reduce the pressure of the constant speaking of Spanish by seeking out their American friends in their free time. Of course, this is not totally consistent with wanting to be a member of the Colombian family.

The height of this ambivalence between wanting to be independent and needing some help is shown when we compare the fact that 70 percent said they preferred to meet people on their own initiative and 35 percent said they felt that the host family should open more social doors for them. Forty-seven percent said they think that CEUCA, the sponsoring American organization, should open more social doors for them. Thus there is evidence that they were not completely satisfied with the amount of social interaction they have been able to have with Colombians, and yet they did like to feel that they were capable of independently making the social contacts they wanted.

One of the most important locks on the social doors the American guest would like to open he often places there himself. This is the general image of social unacceptability projected by some of the Americans: The guests "acted like they felt superior to Colombians"; they were "generally thoughtless of others"; they did not "dress appropriately for the occasion"; they gave the impression that "they did not care about their reputation among the Colombians"; they "did not bathe frequently"; some of them "smelled bad at times"; and "they do not greet people properly."

Most of the negative images projected by the American guests were products of their own behavior patterns in a context of ignorance of the foreign cultural patterns, yet the interviews with the Americans showed that only rarely did a guest say there was any connection between his own behavior and the closed social doors. Those who thought that the sponsoring American organization should do more to help them socially usually thought that they merely needed help in making the initial contact with a certain kind of Colombian. The doubtful assumption seemed to be that they would know how to take advantage of the opportunity.

Whatever may be the forces of mutual attraction, it seems that there are also forces of mutual repulsion that derive their strength from the simple basic fact that tension and anxiety generated in cross-cultural interaction can be reduced by simply separating the actors, temporarily stopping the interaction. If this is true, the American guest's ambivalence about accepting the role of full-fledged family member is understandable, and the general direction of the solution is to learn how to interact with members of the foreign culture without producing anxiety and tension.

Basically, the American guest's ambivalence is generated by the conflict between his desire to be *independent* of the older generation, especially of his own parents; yet he is more *dependent* because he is in a foreign culture.

Other types of ambivalences develop when the American discovers that the price of being "a member of the family" is more than he would like to pay as he begins gradually to perceive the *obligations* of a family member of his own age. The *gringas,* particularly, may feel that the restrictions and supervision to which they are subjected as a member of the family make them long for dormitory life again.

The Colombian hosts also have ambivalences regarding the American guest's role in the household.

THE COLOMBIANS' AMBIVALENCE

The Colombian hosts, like the guests, also tended to be ambivalent about the proper role of the American living in their home. We have already seen that they think that a principal motivation for taking *norteameri-cano* guests is "to earn extra money," yet 87 percent of the señoras said that the American should be treated "like a member of the family" and none said they should be treated "like a guest who pays." Logically, since paying is important and since treating them "like a member of the family" also seems to be important, we would expect a fairly large portion of the señoras to have chosen the fourth response, "like a mixture of these." Yet only 9 percent chose this response in spite of the fact that the Americans were usually treated like some combination of a family member, special guest, and boarder.

This apparent contradiction is resolved to some extent when we analyze the spontaneous remarks of the señoras explaining why they preferred to treat the Americans as members of the family. First, it was clear that most of the señoras prided themselves in being good hostesses who can make anyone in the home feel comfortable. Seventy-four percent of the señoras volunteered the idea that the American should be treated like a member of the family so that he would feel more comfortable. Another 14 percent volunteered that it would also make the family more comfortable. The remaining 11 percent said that if they treated the American like a member of the family, he would in turn treat their own children in the same way.

Being a "member of the family" means not only that the person should be comfortable (in the Colombian way, of course) but also that he should assume certain responsibilities of a family member of the same age and sex. The señoras felt that the American should make his own bed neatly, keep his room orderly, leave the bathroom tidy, hang his towel out in the sun to dry, come to meals (lunch and dinner) on time, etc. There are additional responsibilities such as giving gifts on certain occasions, greeting and introducing people, paying one's way, and helping with household chores on special occasions.

Just as some of the American guests hope to carve out a role for themselves which has all the advantages and none of the disadvantages of the role of family member, some of the señoras also would like to have all the advantages of a family member who can "take the place of the son or daughter" but who has other advantages one's own son or daughter would not provide.

A large majority of the señoras preferred a North American to a Colombian guest if both paid the same amount. This may seem strange, since a Colombian could actually play the role of "member of the family" much more accurately than could the North Americans. Their reasons included the cross-cultural contact benefits (e.g., learning English) and that the North American would be less bother to the señora than a Colombian.

It was not easy for some of the señoras to articulate *why* or *how* the North American would be less bother. "More trustworthy" included a variety of statements such as "more honest," "dependable in paying what he owes," or "more sincere." "Easier to handle" meant that they thought the American guest was more docile because he felt insecure in the foreign setting and would need help and advice. "More respectful" meant both that North Americans were not so rebellious toward the older generation in general, but more often it meant that the North American male would be more respectful toward the señora, and the female would be more respectful toward the señor than would be a Colombian university student. "Less demanding" in some cases meant that the Colombian guest paying the same amount would demand more special services than an American. "More independent" often meant that the North American was more capable of getting around on his own initiative and would not be so dependent upon the family for his social life. This is in contrast to "too independent," which referred to a person who was not attached to the family and who did not have a warm relationship with the señora. "Males less fresh" usually meant that they viewed the Colombian male as more amorously aggressive, which might constitute a problem for the señora.

Many of the señoras felt that the *gringas* needed less supervision than would a Colombian girl of the same age, which is consistent with the idea of "less bother." To measure the extent of this belief among the host señoras we later asked whether they felt that the *colombiana* or the *gringa* guest would require the most supervision. Forty-one percent felt that the *gringa* should be supervised less strictly than the Colombian daughter; 4 percent felt they should have *more* strict supervision; 55 percent felt that the *gringa* should have the same amount of supervision.

MISCOMMUNICATION ABOUT THE GUESTS' ROLE IN THE HOUSEHOLD

The American guest did not know precisely how to play the role of either "guest" or "member of the family." He did not know how a member of a Colombian family would be treated. Some felt that they were being treated like a special guest rather than a member of the family *because* orange juice and coffee were brought to their bedroom at breakfast time. In several of the homes this is a practice, particularly for the señora or daughters in the home. Other Americans felt that since the Colombians were polite in their greetings and forms of address, they were not treating the American like a member of the family when in fact they were.

The American guests' underestimate of the number of señoras who *think* the American should be treated as a guest could be a reflection of the señora's own ambivalence or of a discrepancy between her idea of how they *should* be treated and how she actually treated them.

> They treat me sort of like a family member but more like a guest because they always make sure I get the best food and often do special favors that the other kids wouldn't get.

They expected me to help around the house like a member of the family, yet if I broke something they made me pay. Also, if you stay a few days longer into the vacation period they make you pay extra.

Miscalculation also results when the American guest tries to discover whether he is being treated like a member of the family with respect to a certain issue by observing how a Colombian family member is treated. In doing this he may fail to compare himself with a Colombian of the same age and sex. For example, "I am reprimanded if my room is disorderly although I clean it myself, change the bed and make the bed, while the kids in the house leave such things to the maid and are a hundred times more disorderly than I."

This sounds like evidence of discrimination, but in interviewing this host family it was discovered that "the kids" with whom the American college student was comparing himself were boys seven and nine years old.

In families where there are no members of the guest's age and sex, the guest cannot discover what is appropriate for himself by observing the others. The female guest cannot always assume that if the señora does a certain thing or has certain privileges or duties, the *gringa* should behave in the same way. Nor can the *gringo's* observations of the señor's behavior be a reliable guide, because parents and children occupy a different role and status in any household.

Even though a large minority of the señoras felt that the *gringa* should be less strictly supervised than a *colombiana,* a much larger portion (91 percent) of the American guests felt that the señora expected to exercise less supervision over the *gringa.* Usually the *gringa* was not aware that the señora was quite distraught because of the difficulty in exercising what she felt was adequate supervision. The American girl who tended to take her freedom and independence for granted often felt that she was bending over backward to meet the demands of the culture, but the señora was mainly aware of the shortcomings, particularly those that might damage her reputation.

We also saw a gap in communication in that only 7 percent of the señoras said that they had no preference for a Colombian versus an American guest if the amount paid were equal, but 36 percent of the guests thought their señora felt this way. There was an assumption among many of the Americans that the host families were being paid much more for board and room than could have been collected from a Colombian. In some cases this was because the student did not know how much the señora was paid but *assumed,* since he had paid into the Program the same board and room fee he would have paid on his home campus, this total amount was paid to the host family. He did not realize that a large portion of the cost of board and room in the foreign country went into locating and selecting the host families and in dealing with the developing problems of adjustment between host and guest.

Another possible reason for the American guests' reluctance to think that the señora would actually prefer an American if the pay were equal is that they found it more difficult than did the señoras to see reasons other than money for the señora's taking an American guest. For example, when the guests were asked why their señora might prefer an American, none of them had the idea that the señora would feel that the American would be less bother than a Colombian guest. All of the reasons they could give were in the cross-cultural experience category.

Another area of miscommunication was revealed in the fact that many guests did not realize the extent to which the host families would support their role as student. Some guests felt that there was a conflict between their role as student versus family member. The Americans reported in the interviews that their host family wanted them to skip classes for a day or two in order to take a long weekend trip with them, and they worried that the family would be insulted if they did not go. We asked the señoras, "If you were planning a trip over a long weekend and you invited your American guest to go with you, should he be willing to miss classes for two days if he really wanted to go? " Then the guests were asked to indicate how they thought their señoras would answer the question.

The guests greatly underestimated the proportion (79.5 percent versus 4.5 percent) of the señoras who felt the guests should not miss classes to go on a trip. A few of the señoras volunteered the comment that they should come on the trip because they should not stay in the house without the family there, particularly if the guest were a *gringa*. We cannot explain why more Americans did not realize how the señoras felt about interfering with their studies, nor do we know that their saying that the "studies come first" was not simply a polite excuse to leave the foreign guest behind. To take him might have caused overcrowding if they were driving, or the American might not have intended to pay his way to the extent expected by the host, or the Colombian family may have wanted some time away from the foreign guest they see every day. The student may also have been hopefully rationalizing his own desires to escape from his studies by saying that the family would be insulted if he put his studies above a long weekend trip with them.

FORMAL CUSTOMS OF COURTESY

The North American can easily give a Colombian the impression that he does not want to meet people or participate in social events because he does not observe the social rituals that are so important in Latin America. Even after the guests begin to sense the vital importance of these "superficial customs," he still may not know how to do them correctly.

The host-family señoras feel that they can separate the sheep from the goats among American guests by whether they make the proper polite responses such as greeting, introducing, and thanking people. None of the señoras interviewed took a neutral position on whether their particular American guest was polite in this respect. The señoras felt that the Americans' weakest point was in knowing how to greet people. To some hosts this meant that the guest did not know how or when to shake hands.

Shaking Hands   To the Colombians the Americans seemed to have some reluctance to shake hands.

> His customs were typically North American. Even in the way he greeted you. You know the Americans don't like this thing about shaking your hand.

> As an advisor to the North Americans as foreign students here in Colombia, I tell them that the only time they don't shake hands on greeting someone is when both hands are broken. It is difficult to impress them with the importance of this simple act.

Although there is a difference in the amount of handshaking that is customary in different regions of the United States,[2] in general the *bogotanos* tended to shake hands much more than the North Americans were accustomed to. The American at first had to force himself to shake hands with even 10 people when he arrived and left a dinner party, for example. The American college student's tendency to minimize the greeting rituals is even more emphasized when he is abroad where he feels unsure about the language and the accompanying actions. At first it takes considerable effort on the American's part even when he understands what the *bogotanos* expect. In time it becomes a habit and, when he returns to the United States, he catches himself extending his hand in many situations when it is not expected.

Here are some of the ways in which handshaking is different from the practice in most parts of the United States.

Shake hands more frequently. The probability that two North Americans will shake hands upon meeting depends upon (among other things) how recently they have seen each other. It is clear that the time lapse that requires the "reshaking" of hands is much shorter in Colombia than in the United States. For example, on entering the home of a friend or acquaintance it is expected that you shake hands even though you may have seen the person only a few minutes before.

Shake hands with more people. On entering a place where a social or business gathering is taking place you shake hands with each person, up to as many as 20 persons. In very large groups of 50 or more, it is customary to stop at each small group and shake hands with each person present.

Shake hands on more occasions. The North American is less inclined to shake hands when he leaves a group than when he arrives. Colombians shake hands as frequently upon leaving as when arriving.

Men do not wait for women to take initiative. When a man greets a woman, he does not wait for the woman to offer her hand because it is customary for women to shake hands on all the same occasions as would a man.

The woman-to-woman handshake is different. It is a custom for women to shake hands with women, particularly after the first time they have met, in a style different from the man-to-man or woman-to-man handshake. They frequently shake hands by simultaneously grasping each other's right forearm. If the North American girl first experiences this without any prior warning, she may be surprised.

> I went to this party at a relative's house where there were several Colombians I had met once before. The hostess shook hands with me like this [grasping forearm], and I thought maybe she was blind and had missed my hand or something.

> The first time I went to a party I was lucky because I had a chance to observe my señora welcoming guests to our home and noticed that she shook hands with the men one way and with the women another. Of course I didn't know how general this was, but then when I went to another house party I was on the lookout for it.

> For the first month or so I didn't realize that I wasn't shaking hands right, but I noticed a bit of fumbling confusion sometimes as our hands met. Then later I discovered that this was because I grabbed their hand before they could get past mine to clasp my arm like they do. I just never thought that they would shake hands with a man one way and with a woman another.

The man-to-man handshake is less vigorous. The American men also had a problem with the manner of shaking hands even though it is essentially the same act as in the United States. Many of the Americans were accustomed to a vigorous grasp and felt that many of the *bogotanos* had an insipid handshake: "You'd think some of these men are sick from the way they shake hands. It is like holding a dead fish. It's hard to believe that they mean it. They are certainly not very enthusiastic."

Similarly, some of the *bogotanos* interpreted the American's vigorous handshake as another expression of his feeling of superiority: "The Americans say that we are so concerned with *machismo,* in trying to prove our masculinity, but when they shake your hand they seem to be engaging in some kind of contest to prove that they are stronger."

In the eyes of some *bogotanos* both the American's reluctance to shake hands and his "aggressive" manner when he does so can contribute to that image, shared by many host families, that the American thinks he is superior to the *bogotano*. At the same time, the American can get the impression that the *bogotano* is not warmly enthusiastic about meeting him.

These differences in handshaking customs may not exhaust the whole range of differences,[3] but they include the most common cross-cultural dissonances encountered by the Americans and Colombians.

Thanking Colombians   A majority of the señoras thought that the North American guests knew "how to thank a person for a favor." Significantly, none took a neutral position on this issue. Again this shows the tendency for the host to put his guest clearly in either the positive or negative category with respect to his manners. We must, however, make a distinction between knowing how and actually doing it. If a Colombian thought his guest did know how but did not thank him properly for a favor, he concluded that the American did not appreciate the favors done for him. This interpretation is consistent with that fact that despite the majority who agreed that the American knows how, only half agreed that "they appreciate the favors they receive."

In the depth interviews with the señoras we found a few hints as to what was lacking in the American's attempt to thank them.

> ... and we took her on a picnic at Zipaquirá, went to the Salt Cathedral, took her to the market to take pictures, and then went to show her Villa de Leiva which is a long trip so we stayed overnight in Villa. When we got back home, all she said was "gracias"!

> He was interested in seeing some of the sights in Bogotá, so we went to Monserrate on the cable car, went through the museum of the Quinta de Bolívar, to the Cathedral, the Plaza de Bolívar, and the Plaza de la Constitución and even to the market which we never would go to, but he wanted to see it. We went to lunch at the Casa Vieja and returned home at about seven. When he got home, he just said "gracias" and that he was tired so went up to his room.

The key to the problem is expressed concisely in the phrase "all he said was 'gracias.' " This is enough if someone has just lent a person a match, but not adequate in the cases of larger favors. The following excerpts from the señoras' interviews give a strong stamp of approval to the guest who shows his appreciation more profusely.

> ... he wasn't a typical American in this way. He had very good manners. He was well brought up. For example, we invited him to the soccer game, then went swimming at the Club Militar and then to dinner at La Chesa. He was very appreciative. He said, *"Qué buena la excursión! Fue sumamente interesante para mí. Fue muy amable de su parte el haberme invitado. Es el*

dia más especial que he tenido aquí en Bogotá. Muchísimas gracias por todo."

He seemed to always appreciate little things we did for him. He was so different from the first student who would just say "gracias" in a very dry way.

It is not strange that the host does not teach the guest how to show his appreciation, because the role of host would preclude appearing to demand profuse thanks. If the guest does not do some equivalent favor for the host, he cannot learn by observing the example of the host's reaction to a favor. The breakdown in communication is facilitated by the señora's assumption that the guest knows how to express appreciation but does not feel any appreciation in a particular instance.

Greetings   The *bogotano's* feeling that the North Americans did not "greet people properly" was also related to the Americans' failure to say either "hello" or "goodbye." It was not necessary to ask the señoras specifically whether the American guest greeted people properly. It was clear that this was such an essential factor in their judgment of the American that in the depth interviews they would mention the greeting problem when they were asked questions such as: "What kind of a person was your last guest?" The responses most frequently given could be categorized into different dimensions of etiquette such as greeting people properly, thanking people, giving of gifts, and paying one's way.

Well, in general the American girls never say hello. I think it is only natural to greet people when you come into the house but they never do.

They never came to say hello and sometimes we were here. That bothered us.

Some of the Americans that came were very badly brought up in that they would not greet you.

Sometimes we would have parties and introduce them to my friends too. But later when you meet them again they do not even say hello to you. Maybe they don't remember us.

This last statement may involve much more than the simple reluctance to greet people. It may be due to a situation that typically confronts any foreigner who is new in the community. When he goes to any group function, he may be the only stranger to the group, while all the members are strangers to him. They have only one new face to remember while the foreigner has many. Nevertheless, there is considerable evidence that the American did tend to greet people less frequently and to be less formal or profuse when he did greet them.

The fact that the *bogotanos* appreciated those guests who did not "behave like typical Americans" can be seen in the following positive statements coming from the host señoras:

He was very polite and nice. He used to say hello and when he left the house he would say goodbye.

Ricardo would usually say hello and goodbye but some days he forgot it. That was very different from Russ who would even look for me to say goodbye. It was a big difference.

Whenever she would come in and there were people here, she would greet everyone and stay a little while before she went upstairs. She said goodbye in a very friendly way. All my friends liked her very much.

When there were people here she would come and would say hello as if she were a member of the family.

The majority of the señoras preferred that the American guest seek them out to greet them even in the routine daily return to the home. The proportion who preferred to bе sought out rises when the American returns after sightseeing on Saturday afternoon, and all the señoras felt the guest should greet them upon returning from a two-day absence. The señoras, as *dueñas* of the home, not only considered it polite, but also liked to know when the American was in the house just as they would like to know when one of their own children or their husband returned.

The Use of Adiós   The word *adiós* as a greeting was a source of mutual puzzlement between Colombians and North Americans. For example, the American was puzzled when he met a Colombian acquaintance on the street who simply said, "Adiós," and continued walking. The American in this case tended to think of *adiós* as being part of the leave-taking ritual, and therefore not to be used between two people as they approach each other on the street. In English the Americans would say, "Hello," "Hi," or "Good morning," and *adiós* seems to be inappropriate. Actually, the Colombian uses *adiós* in those situations where two people are going to pass each other without stopping, or if they do not wish to be detained. In effect it combined the idea of *hello* and *goodbye* in one word.

The Colombians, in turn, were puzzled by the North American's use of *adiós* as a parting formality. The American seemed to think of it as meaning simply *goodbye*; therefore, after he had spent the evening with a group he would say only, "Adiós," and leave. This was not enough. It was considered cold unless some phrase were added such as *mucho gusto de verte, que estés muy bien,* or *saludos en tu casa.* The incorrect interpretation of the use of *adiós* in these two situations was a source of mutual irritation.

Greeting Versus Leavetaking   The North American guests were sometimes confused by the use of *"Buenos días! " "Buenas tardes! "* and *"Buenas noches! "* to mean both hello and goodbye depending on the situation. A majority of the Americans seemed to think of these phrases as equivalent to "Good morning! " "Good afternoon! " and "Good evening! "[4] and therefore equal to a form of hello but not goodbye.

> When she said, *"buenos días"* I thought she had just arrived or that she thought I had just arrived. I felt that I had been talking to her in the group of Colombian students just before we went into the classroom, but when she said *"buenos días"* I was a bit confused because I thought I must be wrong in thinking she was the one I had just talked to. Later I realized that this was because I interpreted the *buenos días* to mean good morning in the sense of hello not goodbye.

> It took a while before I was sure that *buenos días* alone would not tell you whether they were saying hello or goodbye. It depends upon what else they say, if anything.

Inquiring About the Family   When greeting a married person who is not accompanied by the family, it is always polite to ask about the spouse and children. This is automatic with the *bogotanos* but takes practice for the North American.

Using Titles   In greetings, as in any form of direct address, it is customary to use the person's title. Never should we say, *"Buenos días, Martínez,"* or *"Buenas tardes, José."* It is much more polite to say *"Buenos días, señor Martínez,"* or *"Buenas tardes, don José."* The feminine equivalents of *señora* and *doña* are used in the same way. A specific degree such as *licenciado* can be used also.

In cases where someone has a professional status, the last name is often preceded by *doctor*. A student addressing a professor should always use the title *profesor* or *doctor* before the last name. *Doctor* is used much more generally than in the United States to refer to anyone with education or higher status. In Bogotá anyone with a college education may be addressed as *doctor*. To avoid confusion we must refer to a physician as *el médico* not *el doctor*. The lower class and the *campesinos* often address anyone in a higher socioeconomic class as *doctor*, which often surprises the American undergraduate student.

Of course, when using titles in indirect address the definite article is added, as in *la señora, el doctor*, but there is a very important exception to this rule in the case of *doña*. We should never refer to a woman as *la doña* which would mean "the madam" of a house of prostitution to some Colombians. This would severely shock a *bogotano* even though he knew it was not intentional on the part of the American. In some contexts it could appear to be quite intentional and would damage the American's image by lending credence to the idea, "Americans don't care about their reputation among Colombians."

The North American is often at a loss in addressing a nun or priest in Spanish. In general the priest should be *Padre* in direct address and *el padre* in indirect address parallel to the English *Reverend* and *the Reverend*. On some occasions the form *su reverencia* is also used. In addressing a nun the form *madre* or *hermana* is used depending on the nun's order and her position in the hierarchy. It is always safest to call her *madre* since this is the higher status. When possible the American should be alert to follow the lead of the Colombians in the particular situation. The Bishop is addressed as *su excelencia.*

Some of the Americans who were from Protestant or Jewish background found it very difficult and unnatural to use these forms of address which in their minds was like calling a stranger father, mother, or sister. Others felt that it implied some theological commitment on their part to Catholicism. Those who thought of it as simply a title to designate one's function in society did not find these titles difficult to use.

Introductions   It is a common practice for someone who is about to make an introduction to ask, *"¿Ustedes no se conocen?"* Then if one or both say, *"No tengo el gusto,"* one of three things might happen. The two may shake hands and give their names simultaneously. The person making the introduction may add, *"Quisiera presentar a mi amigo,"* or *"a mi primo,"* or *"a mi esposa,"* without giving the name, and the pair shake hands and give their own names simultaneously. The person making the introduction may give both names and they will shake hands. The first two forms are very common, but they make it very difficult for the American to hear the other person's name which is being given just as he gives his own name to the Colombian. Yet the system is often advantageous in that the introducer may not remember a person's name at the moment; so he can simply say, *"Quisiera presentar a mi estudiante,"* and then it is up to the two persons to give their own names, which allows the introducer to learn the person's full name. If the introducer uses the third form, he must not only be sure he has the correct name but must also remember to use the title with the article to indicate indirect address, *"Quisiera presentar al doctor García."*

Even though many of the American guests understood the correct forms of introductions, they were still considered aloof in situations that called for introducing themselves. For example, a guest would arrive home at 5:00 P.M. and find some strangers at the house in the living room. Since the señora was not with them at the moment, he might pass by them with a simple "Buenas tardes," as he headed for the stairway without stopping to introduce himself or giving the visitors a chance to introduce themselves. The *bogotano* hosts felt that the American guests failed to introduce themselves at times when it was considered appropriate. This was not due to the guest's general reluctance to introduce people, because a majority of the hosts felt the guest did very well in introducing his friends to the family.

Another aspect of the introduction situation that bothered some Colombians and gave the impression of the American's being aloof was what we might call the "hit-and-run" tendency. Instead of seeing the introduction as a prologue to a pleasant friendly chat, the American would immediately try to leave.

> for example, you would introduce him to your friends and he would say "hello" very kindly, but then he would immediately try to leave the situation.

> She came home that afternoon and I introduced her to some people in the living room and instead of sitting down and taking a moment, she just said, *"Con su permiso,"* and went upstairs to her room.

The lack of this knowledge could result in the American giving the impression that he is "aloof and superior" if he did not stay or that he was a "pushy intruder" if he did.

Using *tú* Versus *usted*   The English speaker often has difficulty in deciding between the use of the formal *usted* and the familiar *tú* forms of pronouns. Historically, he has lost his choice between *you* and *thou* and feels an added burden in making this decision when speaking Spanish. He has the linguistic problem of knowing both forms of pronouns and verb conjugations plus the more complex nonlinguistic problem of sensing when to use each.

He often arrives in Latin America with the idea that there is one simple consistent pattern for the use of these two forms. To the contrary, it is highly probable that this usage pattern varies from one region to another, from one social class to another, and according to other more subtle difference in the social situations in which the conversations take place.

The Americans were confused about the proper use of the familiar form. Some had obtained contradictory ideas from different Colombians they had asked for advice.

In general, *tú* was used when the señora addressed her husband, her children, and when her children addressed her. Most señoras used *usted* to address their maids. However, there is enough lack of unanimity to confuse the Americans. The señoras who chose the "other" category were almost all of two types—those who said they used both *tú* and *usted* depending on the occasion and those who used *su merced* instead of *tú*.

There is a possibility that the form used with children would depend upon their age. It was suggested by one respondent that with smaller children they used *usted* and for older ones *tú*. The exceptions to the general pattern are enough to shake the security of the American trying to learn the pattern.

The fact that most of the señoras used *tú* in addressing their children, and most of the children addressed their mothers in this way, would lead us to predict that these same señoras would expect their American guests to address them with *tú* since a large majority of them also expect the American to act "like a member of the family." To test this idea, which is very relevant to the American's role in the family, we asked the señoras about the conditions under which *tú* should be used between the guest and the host. We distinguished between the different sex combinations of host and guest and tried to determine how soon the *tú* relationship could be established. Then to determine the amount of guest-host communication on this point, we asked the American guests how they thought their particular señora would answer the questions.

In all four relationships the guests erred in the direction of assuming that they should never use *tú*. More of the Americans than the Colombians thought it was necessary to wait until after a certain relationship was established. Fewer Americans than Colombians felt that *tú* should be used from the beginning. The proportion of hosts choosing each category correlates mainly with whether the relationship is between persons of the same sex or opposite sexes. More say not to use *tú* when it is between opposite sexes.

When we ask whether the American guests were correct in perceiving the hosts' preference for *tú*, one clear pattern emerged. The American guests consistently underestimated the hosts' preference for using *tú* with their American guests. Fewer Americans expected *tú* to be used from the beginning, and more of them thought it should never be used than did the Colombians. This could be another factor supporting the Colombians' image of the "superior American" who does not want to be "a member of the family."

In some cases this unfortunate image was avoided when the señora took the initiative in directly instructing the guest.

> Three days after I was here I was told to address everybody as *tú* because we were a family.

> The señora said to me "You are a member of the family and you are not going to address us with *usted*!!"

> My family told me that I was a member of the family and was to address them as *tú*.

The lack of unanimity regarding the appropriate use of *tú* was also graphically demonstrated by the fact that of the four Colombian interviewers who interviewed most of the *señoras,* one always used the familiar form in the interview. When I asked her why she did this, she said, "in order to get their confidence." Other interviewers with the same educational background and socioeconomic status used the formal *usted* in all interviews.

In view of these inconsistencies, it is highly probable that there are not only regional and social class differences in the use of the familiar form, but also there may be a historical trend toward the use of only one of the forms or a breaking down of the rigid distinction between their use. In any event the simple one-sentence explanations of the use of the familiar form, still found in Spanish textbooks for English speakers, seems too simple to accurately reflect the realities in Bogotá.

Three salient results emerged from this exploratory study which are relevant to the central problem of communication barriers: There was no unanimity among these señoras regarding the appropriate use of the familiar form; the American guests often did not know when they were expected to use the familiar form and so failed to use it in situations where it was expected by the hosts; this failure was often interpreted by the Colombians as a symptom of the American's desire to remain aloof from the family.

If the Colombian did not directly suggest using *tú*, the American was often at a loss to know what to do. In some cases they were aware that the hosts had started using *tú* in addressing them, but they did not know whether this was a dependable sign that they should also begin to use *tú*. When one American tried to advise another on the problem, confusion would often result.

> My Colombian sister told me that in Bogotá *usted* is used more with close friends and *tú* with acquaintances and strangers.

> In my (Colombian) family, I would feel uncomfortable using *tú* with either the señor or the señora unless they asked me to. The girl should with the señor only if she completely trusts him and doesn't feel that it would embarrass the señora. They are starting to use *tú* much more with me but I won't with them until they ask me.

> Here in Bogotá, it seems to me that you only use *tú* with your boyfriend. Even within the family they use *usted* with each other.

> In Colombia *tú* is used less frequently than in Mexico. For example, even my (Colombian) twin brothers use the *usted* form. So I think it is better to treat it as a grammatical thing than as a personal reflection.

It is clear that a more thorough study should be made of the use of *tú* to determine the causes of this variation and search for dependable tactics for the American to use in specific situations to select the appropriate form of address.

NOTES

1. The data for this section are based on a questionnaire designed and administered by Miss Hermena W. Evans who was in charge of housing the CEUCA students with Colombian families in Bogotá.

2. For example, the New Englander is much less likely to shake hands than the Texan. The New Englander's pattern is more like that in England today, while the Texan's is more like that of the Mexican or Colombian.

3. The use of the *abrazo* and styles in between the standard handshake and the *abrazo* such as men grasping the other's upper arm or shoulder with the left hand while shaking with the right have not been discussed.

4. Some thought of "Good evening" as meaning hello and "Good night" as meaning goodbye.

CULTURE SHOCK AND THE
AMERICAN BUSINESSMAN OVERSEAS

Lawrence Stessin

Reprinted by permission of International Educational and Cultural Exchange, from
Exchange 9 (1), 1973.

The American businessman overseas often operates under demanding
conditions. He suffers the hardship of giving up cold martinis for warm
beer as one way to integrate into the English business community. He
must keep his mind on business during the rounds of Geisha houses as a
prelude to concluding a deal in Japan. And if he operates in Spain, he
must brace himself for the rigors of 11 P.M. dinners and negotiations that
continue into the small hours.

In an age of hangups, the American entrepreneur venturing into
overseas lands soon discovers his. It is what the anthropologists call the
"culture shock,"[1] a series of jolts that await even the wariest American
when he encounters the wide variety of customs, value systems,
attitudes, and work habits which make it difficult for him to move
comfortably in a foreign commercial environment.

Some adjust and survive; others retreat to the familiar atmosphere of a
service club in Hometown, U.S.A.

THE CULTURE GAP

American companies spend millions to immunize their about-to-go-
overseas personnel against culture shock. In some companies,[2] executives
pegged for foreign assignments are put through cross-cultural operations
courses. Almost every graduate business school with a curriculum in

international trade includes "Comparative Business Cultures" in its teaching and research disciplines. Donald Stone, former dean of the University of Pittsburgh's Graduate School of Public and International Affairs, remembers an experience he had which illustrates how subtle and intimately subversive the culture gap can be:

> In the Middle East, I was once with an American oil refinery which had installed an American-type canteen. The employees were shown how to queue up, extend their trays to the help behind the counters and have them fill their cups and plates with nourishing food. The management were perplexed when only a few workers responded. A visiting sociologist discovered the reason. The holding of a cup and a plate in outstretched manner was viewed by the natives as a symptom of begging. The management rearranged the serving line so that the food could be dispensed while the tray rested on a railing. Only then did the employees take advantage of the free lunches offered by the employer.

The executive assigned to ply his trade overseas must face an abrasive adjustment to what seems to him to be an exaggerated sensitivity of foreigners to certain forms of American etiquette. The practice of shaking hands to establish a cordial relationship with a stranger is part of the Western cultural repertory. It is a sign of warmth and friendship. Yet in India he meets a businessman who either won't shake hands or gives him a limp welcome that Americans associate with femininity.[3]

The stereotype of the American—hail fellow, well-met, cordial, friendly, outgoing, and gregarious—does not mesh with the discomfort he feels and often shows in his contacts with Latin Americans and Middle Easterners. There, people crowd close to him to talk, and in Latin America his host is likely to greet him with a warm abrazo, suggesting unfamiliar intimacy. Anyone who has ever attended a party or a reception in Latin America must surely have observed the self-consciousness of the uninitiated stateside visitor, who keeps backing away from his native host to whom it is natural to carry on a conversation separated by inches. Last year at a businessmen's club in Brazil, where many receptions are held for newly arrived U.S. executives, the railings on the terrace had to be reinforced because so many American businessmen fell into the garden as they backed away.

DIFFERING RELIGIOUS CUSTOMS

Culturally, the criterion for success in overseas assignments is the ability of the executive to dilute his American outlook and view alien ways as not being bad, but just different. In particular, religious beliefs and rituals and how they totally embrace the workaday lives of many peoples of the world create unforeseen problems for American management abroad. A U.S. company setting up a facility in the Arab countries must plan its productivity objectives in the face of over 20 religious holidays a year.[3] In Western countries religion and work are segregated, and to ask an employee to come in on a Sunday does not carry with it the same sacrilege it does when a Mohammedan or a Hindu is requested to put in worktime on one of his holy days.

In Germany one motor company faced a sticky religious situation when, a few years ago, it decided to import some 2000 Turkish workers to ease the firm's serious manpower shortages. It's been the experience of American companies that Turkish men make good factory employees. They train easily, take instructions well, and love to punch a time clock—this being a symbol of having outgrown the condition of peasantry from which most of them have been recruited. As everyone knows, the efficient production of an automobile depends on the continuity of the assembly line. A minute's stoppage is counted in many dollars lost. When the Turkish workers were put to the task of manning several hundred positions along a moving belt, the line began to go awry with stop-watch regularity—three times a day. Cars came off in disassemblement that would cross the eyes of a Ralph Nader. What happened? Came prayer time, the more devout Turkish employees forsook whatever it was they were doing, faced east, and gave a five-minute homage to Allah. And no amount of pleading from management could stay them from their appointed periods of devotion.

Here was a problem to be solved and the company solved it. It rescheduled the work of its religiously dedicated Turkish employees so that each man could take a "prayer break." He was allowed to leave his post and go to specially built prayer rooms with interiors simulating Turkish mosques. During the prayer breaks, relief squads of Italians and Germans filled in. The added manpower cost was minimal. Turkish employees willingly sacrificed the Western-oriented coffee break and lunch hour—it being proper for them to squeeze in a snack while giving thanks to their God.

AN OFT-REPEATED STORY

Every calling has its "hot stove league" where buffs meet and exchange experiences. One does not delve long into the life and times of the American businessman overseas without running into the story of the dislocated latrines.

It happened in a village which, until three years ago, was a journey into the unchangeable. Here a man lived and died in a hovel of mud, rocks, bone-dry timber, and rice straw under a cluster of poplar trees stripped bare by ravenous locusts. The village square was laid in uneven cobblestones and pockmarked by treacherous cesspools. Women wrapped their newborn infants in newspapers, and running water meant a canal flowing through the public streets—the gully reserved for drinking, washing, ablutions, and even worse. The industrial community—to use a gratuitous phrase—was a prison-like compound of crumbling shanties where a few rugs and some crude pottery were produced for the sidewalk market in the hope that some adventurous tourist would stumble by—and buy.

But apparently the village was not destined for an eternity of the mud and the crud of a feudal economy. American geologists, scratching the sun-dried earth, discovered a rich vein of copper deposits. Within a year the village was on its way to becoming a bubbling oasis. A consortium of American companies set up operations. Peasants from 50 nearby villages were recruited, hired, and trained, but the principal drawback to urbanization was a slow-moving government which tied up the installation of a transportation system to take workers to and from work. Many of the employees trod 8 to 10 miles to get to their jobs. The American companies took the initiative and planned a series of modest homes where the employees and their families could live near the mining sites without the hardship of crude commuting by foot and mule.

Back in America, bids were solicited from construction companies. In a short time plans were drawn and approved, and construction was started for 300 homes with architects and builders flown in for the project from the United States. The dwellings were built of concrete, and inside each one there was a kitchen, a bathroom, running water, and lights that turned on at the flick of a switch. When the compound was finished, the project was dedicated with elaborate ceremonies. American executives and local officials who came from a town a hundred miles away hailed the new homes as another forward step in the industrialization of the country. The country's leader, who had vowed to his people and to Allah that he would devote his life to modernizing his lands, sent his blessing. The workers were given a tour of the housing units and then asked to select the apartments they preferred. None applied. It was obvious that something about the houses bruised local sensibilities. It turned out that the latrines faced the wrong way. People had their backs facing east—Mecca—a sinful position for a good Moslem. The toilets were torn out and turned around.

Among the managerial imperatives of the big American companies establishing business bases overseas is to train and develop the nationals of the country to manage the enterprises. There are over 250,000 such foreign managers working for American firms,[4] and it's standard policy for many companies to bring some of these people to the United States for periods of orientation in modern management. Those selected for such training obviously relish the opportunity to observe and learn American skills from the "horse's mouth." Sometimes the foreign manager returns overly converted to the American way—like the English marketing man who came back to London after six months with his U.S. counterparts in the headquarters offices. He spouted the American jargon. He invited customers to his home and committed the social "gaff" of talking business at dinner. His "Americanization" annoyed his colleagues. One day when he came into his office, there on his desk was a sign: "YANKEE GO HOME!"

MANAGER LEARNS NEW SKILLS

There are cases where the cultural differences between Americans and foreigners are so marked that no amount of indoctrination will rub off on the native manager. Recently when I was in Tangiers, I was invited to tour one American company's plant by its local manager. He was most intelligent, urbane, and proud of his association with one of the elite in multicountry manufacturing. He had lived all his life in Morocco and was educated in its schools. He began his business career as a supervisor in a nearby factory and had been recruited to head up the company's Middle Eastern subsidiary. He talked most enthusiastically about his recent visit to the United States, where he was put through an intensive training course in the "5 M's" of management—how to handle Men, Money, Methods, Machinery, and Motivation. When the course was finished, he was asked if there was anything else in the way of training and development he felt he needed.

"I told them yes—all my life I had the desire to go to the Harvard School of Business. When I told this to the vice president, he granted my wish."

He left for Cambridge and was enrolled in the six-week "Advanced Management Development" course, which is the worldwide model of business training. As he was recounting his experience at Harvard, name-dropping the jargon of the managerial trade—"human relations," "the decision tree," "management by objectives," "the art of delegation"—I noticed a worker off in the distance reading a newspaper and leaving his machine unattended. This is a serious violation of company rules in any country, and I wondered what managerial skills this man would use to handle this situation. He was indeed up to the task. He stopped, caught the eye of a foreman nearby, and beckoned him to act. The supervisor tiptoed over and gave the employee a swift kick in the

---

Don't Bring Chrysanthemums!

The traumas that emerge from even the small deviations from conventional norms are quite likely to sound as if the American had wandered through the looking glass. Here's what some Americans had to say:

A banker: "The head of a company here does business in a strange way. Draw up a contract and he signs it right away. He reads the small print later at his convenience. He expects you to do the same."

A construction foreman: "How can you train these people? Tell a carpenter to cut a piece of wood and he *pulls* the saw. Now everybody knows that the only *right* way to cut a board is to *push* the saw.

A plant manager: "Now I've heard everything! I offered my assistant a raise and he turned it down. He said he would rather be allowed to come in a half-hour later every morning. It would give him more status."

A company president: "When you do business here, the chances are you will be invited for dinner to the businessman's house, which means that the deal has gone through. Be sure to bring flowers to the hostess. But for goodness sake, be careful what you bring. Not roses, because these are the flowers that a lover brings to his sweetheart. And not chrysanthemums— they're for funerals."

---

pants. The man jumped, dropped his paper, and unprotestingly took his position at the machine. My host nodded, pleased.

So I asked, "Is this what they taught you at the Harvard Business School?"

"Oh, yes," he replied, surprised at my question. "I used to kick the men myself, but since I went to Harvard, I now *delegate* the task to my foreman."

THE IMPATIENT AMERICAN

The trait that blurs the American image overseas is the impatience of the U.S. businessman. From Mark Twain's *Innocents Abroad* to *The Ugly American,* this equation has caused cultural trouble for the Yankee trader. His compulsion for action was caricatured by a commercial attaché who said: "Tell the American businessman in a hurry that Rome wasn't built in a day and he'll reply, 'That's because they didn't have an American foreman on the job.' " A European hunter who has led many Americans on safaris embellished this portrait with the remark, "The American is a fast, bang-bang-bang person. He expects to see and shoot the rarest gazelle in Africa within the first half-hour."

If in Europe the pace of business dealing seems maddeningly slow to the stateside businessman, in Japan it is excruciatingly stagnant. "It's the transition from the rat race to the turtle race," remarked one American businessman who finally made it by slowing down. It's an "in" joke among the Japanese that if Americans are kept waiting long enough, they will agree to do anything.

What's more, in Japan it is not unusual in the middle of a deal to have sudden periods of silence, sometimes lasting more than half an hour. To an American, brought up on a business culture of "the pitch and the sell," the lack of verbal communication can be unsettling indeed.

DIFFERING CONCEPTS OF TIME

Much of the rhythm of international trade is generated by the social circuit, and the American businessman is known the world over as a gracious, outgoing host. His wife, as hostess, is more the anxious type, for she must plan dinners without knowing who is going to show up when—if at all. If an American executive sets dinner for eight o'clock, his U.S. colleagues will arrive between five and fifteen minutes after the hour. They will find that the Norwegian guest is already there—most likely having ingratiated himself with his hostess by bringing her a small gift. The Latin American visitor will knock at about nine—apologizing for having arrived too early. An Ethiopian businessman might enter at about eleven, too polite to ask why everyone is already sipping after-dinner cordials. A Japanese, though he has accepted the invitation to avoid losing face by refusing, may not come at all.

Business appointments can be equally uncertain. Edward Hall, the anthropologist, calls "time" part of the "silent language".[5]

> Everywhere in the world, people use time to communicate with each other. In the United States, giving a person a deadline is a way of indicating the degree of urgency or relative importance of the work. But in the Middle East and in Latin America and Japan, the American runs into a cultural trap the minute he opens his mouth. 'Mr. Azuz will have to make up his mind in a hurry because my board of directors meets next week and I have to have an answer by then' is overly demanding and is exerting undue pressure. 'I'm going to Damascus tomorrow morning and I'll have to have my car tonight' is a sure way to get a mechanic to stop working, because to give another person a deadline in many parts of the world is to be rude, pushy and demanding.

An American suggesting a noon appointment with an Argentine businessman will often hear in response, "La hora latina? O la hora norteamericana?"—our time or your time?

STATUS SYMBOLS

In America, a man's office is a symbol of where he is and where he is going on the corporate ladder. His rug on the floor, his name on the door, whether it is private or shared—the office is a cultural index of his position in the pecking order. When assigned overseas, his status syndromes on this point begin to show. He frets at the fact that in France a high officer occupies a space half the size of a U.S. executive. But more disquieting is that the French manager is sharing his office with half-a-dozen assistants—the only sign of his authority being that his desk is in the middle of the room. Negotiations are conducted to a cacophony of noise, interruptions, and traffic. It's simply that the place where a man conducts his daily business affairs is not considered an important image-builder in the commercial mores of many countries.

But not in Germany. The compulsion for orderliness and formality is an ingredient of the German culture, and their offices reflect these national characteristics. For one thing, the Germans take their office doors very seriously. They are heavy, solid, soundproof. A German executive assigned to an office will, even before he inspects the interior, test the click of the latch just as Americans kick a tire or slam the door of a car to listen for a tinny rebound. American companies which have opened branch offices or subsidiaries in Germany have had to act as arbiters of clashes between U.S. executives and German managers over the issue of the "closed door vs. the open door." Americans keep their doors open; German, solidly shut. A whole generation of American businessmen has grown up in a tradition that the "open door" is a democratic virtue. To Germans, open doors are sloppy and disorderly and reflect an unbusinesslike air, where, to the Americans, the closed door conveys a conspiratorial atmosphere.

Chairs also create a culture chasm between Americans and German businessmen. Here the phrase "pull up a chair" is an invitation to informality. Among Germans, it is a violation of mores to change the distance between a chair and a desk. It is said that the great architect, Ludwig Mies van der Rohe, so rebelled against the American habit of moving chairs closer for conversation that he had his visitor's chair bolted to the floor and enjoyed watching the rupturous gymnastics of his American friends when they encountered the immovable seat.[5]

EMPLOYEE RELATIONS

The American executive runs into sweeping unorthodoxy (by U.S. standards) in employee and labor relations. It would not appear so at first. Men on an assembly line turn a bolt, weld a fender, inflate a tire in the same stance the world over. There is not a European or Asian way to run an American-made bulldozer or tractor. Textile production is so automated that workers are little more than standbys, and the ennui of policing the warps and woofs by sitting in a chair or pacing up and down an aisle equally afflicts those in developed and underdeveloped countries.

But surface standardization is deceiving. The newly assigned manager of a plant in Barcelona will soon discover that workers air their grievances in eerie fashion. When employees are unhappy over a managerial policy or decision, they gather in the courtyard of the plant and stare in silence into the window of the managing director.

"This silent treatment is right out of the Spanish Inquisition," an executive complained. "They just stand there and stare and stare for hours—or days. When you enter and leave the plant, you have a thousand eyes following you—and not a single word. It's damn effective, too. When a dispute comes up, I settle it right away even though I know that if I waited, I could negotiate a better deal."

In France and Italy, where many unions are Communist-dominated, the American manager is likely to find a red flag implanted in the center of the bargaining table, and he negotiates with a hammer and sickle fluttering in his face. The union's demands must sound strange indeed to a Detroit-trained manager brought up in the pragmatism of a Walter Reuther where the issues can be equated easily in terms of money.[6]

"Money is the least of our problems when we deal with French unions," an American vice president in Paris reflected. "On these demands we settle quickly. But tell me—what is a company supposed to do about ending the Viet-Nam war, breaking up the military industrial complex in the United States, or firing Mayor Daly?"

THE TEA BREAK

If the American in Paris thinks he has labor problems, he hasn't heard about the U.S.-owned company in England which was forced out of business because it tampered with the tea break. Back in 1965 a North Carolina company got the entrepreneurial bug to go international and bought up—at a bargain—a 150-year-old textile machinery company near Birmingham. Its hopes were to modernize the decrepit piece of property and to use its output as a springboard into the foreign market. The plant was made operational in 18 months, but efficiency lagged. What bothered and bewildered the management was the mountain of work rules that plague all of English industry.

"All that endless talk over whether a machinist can lift an oil can to lubricate a part or wait for a maintenance man to come around in his own sweet time to do it," lamented one of the production superintendents sent over by the States to "do something."

All the nitty-gritty stuff was gradually solved until one day the production head decided to "do something" about the big problem that was hampering output—the tea break. Among English workers this custom is a precious institution, and the American boss, a veteran of culture shocks on other assignments, approached the issue with due caution. In England tea breaks can take a half-hour per man, as each worker brews his own leaves to his particular taste and sips out of a large, pint-sized vessel with the indulgence of a wine-taster.

The rate of sipping is not constant, so that coordinated production does not return to its full rhythm until the slowest sipper has shuffled back to his job. The first meeting called by the management suggested to the union that perhaps it could use its good offices to speed up the "sipping time" to ten minutes a break. This is pretty much in line with the coffee-break time in America. The union agreed to try, but failed. Several employees were disciplined for overextending their tea breaks. They received one- or two-day suspensions, but after each decision, a wildcat strike ensued until the men were given back pay for their enforced layoffs. Then one Monday morning, the workers rioted. Windows were broken, epithets greeted the executives as they entered the plant and police had to be called to restore order. It seems the company went ahead and installed a tea-vending machine—just put a paper cup under a spigot and out pours a standard brew. The pint-sized container was replaced by a five-ounce cup imprinted—as they are in America—with morale-building messages imploring greater dedication to the job and loyalty to the company.

"Looking back, I could shoot myself for approving such an installation," the company president said.

The plant never did get back into production. Even after the tea-brewing machine was hauled out, workers boycotted the company and it finally closed down.

RECRUITING PROBLEMS

The problem of staffing—recruiting and selecting local personnel for the middle and the top of the hierarchy—is a walking-on-eggs experience for American businessmen. In almost every country he must be overly careful to skirt what foreigners consider to be the abrasive approaches of American hiring practices. Advertising for help—though coming into its own in some countries—draws only the dregs in the manpower market in other parts of the world. Job-changing is a culturally accepted road to promotion in America, and every management hopeful has a roving eye and a cocked ear for new opportunities. In Europe, this manner of career development is viewed as disloyal and unethical.[7] A special contempt is reserved for the American practice of submitting applicants to the intimacies of the personality test or the "depth interview"—a form of psychic undress which is criticized as an American vulgarism. One Englishman walked out on an interview when an American recruiter asked the seemingly harmless question, "What clubs do you belong to?" "None of your bloody business," was the indignant reply. The American practice of interviewing wives of prospective employees to determine whether they fit into the organization arouses the harshest reactions among foreigners. One marketing vice president, in considering an Italian for a sales manager's job, said: "I think you will do well in our organization, but before I make a final decision, I would like to see your wife." The man flushed angrily, stood up and rendered the American a salivary shower he didn't quickly forget.

When an American company ventures into Japan, the recruitment problem is doubly complex. A job is a commitment for life—to both the employee and the employer. Layoffs are unknown, discharges are rare, and job-hopping an occupational aberration.

All of these culture patterns faced one company when it decided to staff a subsidiary to produce and sell beds in Japan. The market was surely enticing—74 percent of the islanders sleep on floor pallets called futons. Here indeed was a potential bed of roses for a company which had successfully pierced difficult selling areas before. Finding a plant site and recruiting factory help was no problem. But putting together a sales force of bright, educated young men was something else again. Most Japanese firms recruit their marketing people from the colleges. University graduates are often reluctant to accept jobs with American firms because if they do not pan out, the employee cannot move into a Japanese company where progress is strictly by seniority. So, in this instance management felt that it would do better in smaller colleges and high schools outside the sophisticated Tokyo area, and its hunch was right. In six months it hired a small cadre of salesmen, filled their attaché cases with price lists and brochures, and sent them off to wholesalers and department stores to interest them in marketing American-type beds. When day after day the young men returned with blank order books, the company suspected a flaw in its sales program. And a flaw it found. When asked by prospective buyers about the product, the salesmen's answers had to be vague. None had ever slept in a bed before!

NOTES

1. Cleveland, Mangone, and Adams, *The Overseas Americans*, p. 26, McGraw-Hill, 1960.

2. R. Farmer, *International Management*, p. 37, Dickenson, 1968.

3. Arensberg and Niehoff, *Introducing Social Change*, pp. 59, 32, Aldine, 1964.

4. "American Technical Assistants Abroad," *Annals of the American Academy of Political and Social Science*, November 1966, pp. 40-49.

5. E. Hall, *The Silent Language*, pp. 247, 287, Doubleday, 1959.

6. S. Barkin, *International Labor*, p. 213, Harper & Row, 1970.

7. R. Lewis and R. Stewart, *The Managers*, p. 214, Mentor, 1969.

CREDITS AND PERMISSIONS

The authors wish to extend their thanks for reprint permission to •American Anthropological Association. "Body Ritual Among the Nacirema" by Horace M. Miner from THE AMERICAN ANTHROPOLOGIST, Vol. 58, No. 3, copyright 1956. By permission. •The Asia Society, Inc. Pp. 4-30 "Asia in American Text-books," 1976. By permission. •Dean C. Barnlund, author. *Public and Private Self in Japan and the United States*, pp. 66-90 and pp. 176-177 relating footnotes, copyright © 1975. By permission of the author and the publisher, The Simul Press, Inc. •Lurton Blassingame, author's agent. Pp. 131-148 from THE HIDDEN DIMENSION by Edward T. Hall. Copyright © 1966. By permission. •The Bobbs-Merrill Company, Inc. Pp. 147-167 from AN INTRODUCTION TO INTER-CULTURAL COMMUNICATION by John C. Condon and Fathi S. Yousef, copyright © 1976 by The Bobbs-Merrill Company, Inc. By permission. •Center for Global Perspectives. Pp. 8-12 "Cross-Cultural Awareness" from Robert G. Hanvey, AN ATTAINABLE GLOBAL PERSPECTIVE, copyright, 1976. By permission. •Doubleday & Company, Inc. Pp. 131-148. Excerpt from THE HIDDEN DIMENSION by Edward T. Hall. Copyright © 1966 by Edward T. Hall. By permission. •Exchange Magazine. "Culture Shock and the American Business-man Overseas," by Lawrence Stessin from INTERNATIONAL EDUCATIONAL AND CULTURAL EXCHANGE, 9, 1 (1973), pp. 23-35. By permission. •Harper & Row, Publishers, Inc. "An American Researcher in Paris: Interviewing Frenchmen" by Daniel Lerner from STUDYING PERSONALITY CROSS-CULTURALLY edited by Bert Kaplan. Copyright © 1961 by Harper & Row Publishers, Inc. By permission. •Meridian House International. Pp. 1-34 and pp. 125-126 relating footnotes, from *The Thai Way: A Study of Cultural Values*, by John P. Fieg. Copyright © 1976 by Meridian House International, Washington, D.C. By permission. •National Textbook Company. Pp. 97-114, line 22 from LIVING IN LATIN AMERICA by Raymond Gorden. Copyright © 1974 by National Textbook Company. By permission. •Melvin Schnapper, author. *Peace Corps: The Volunteer*, pp. 7-10, copyright June, 1969. By permission. •Society for Intercultural Education, Training and Research. "Culture Shock and the Problem of Adjustment to New Cultural Environments," by Kalvero Oberg in *Readings in Intercultural Communication*, Vol. II, copyright © 1972, David S. Hoopes, ed. By permission. •Edward C. Stewart, author. *American Cultural Patterns: A Cross-Cultural Perspective*, pp. 26-44. Copyright © 1972 by Edward C. Stewart. By permission. •Lorand B. Szalay and Glen H. Fisher, authors. "Communication Overseas," pp. 1-27. By permission.